KV-264-526

RELATIONSHIP-BASED
SOCIAL WORK
WITH ADULTS

Edited by Heidi Dix, Sue Hollinrake and Jennifer Meade

ACC. No: GCS O49 188

GOWER COLLEGE SWANSEA
LEARNING RESOURCE CENTRE

CLASS No: 361.32 DIX

**CRITICAL
SKILLS FOR
SOCIAL WORK**

First published in 2019 by Critical Publishing Ltd

All rights reserved. No part of this publication may be reproduced, stored in a retrieval system, or transmitted in any form or by any means, electronic, mechanical, photocopying, recording or otherwise, without prior permission in writing from the publisher.

Copyright © 2019 Heidi Dix, Sue Hollinrake and Jennifer Meade

British Library Cataloguing in Publication Data
A CIP record for this book is available from the British Library

ISBN: 978-1-912096-27-5

This book is also available in the following e-book formats:
MOBI ISBN: 978-1-912096-26-8
EPUB ISBN: 978-1-912096-99-2
Adobe e-book ISBN: 978-1-912096-98-5

The rights of Heidi Dix, Sue Hollinrake and Jennifer Meade to be identified as the Authors of this work have been asserted by them in accordance with the Copyright, Design and Patents Act 1988.

Cover design by Out of House Ltd
Text design by Greensplash Limited
Project Management by Newgen Publishing UK
Printed and bound in Great Britain by 4edge, Essex

Critical Publishing
3 Connaught Road
St Albans
AL3 5RX

www.criticalpublishing.com

Paper from responsible sources

Contents

RELATIONSHIP-BASED
SOCIAL WORK
WITH ADULTS

**CRITICAL
SKILLS FOR
SOCIAL WORK**

Gower College Swansea
Library
Coleg Gŵyr Abertawe
Llyrfgell

Other books you may be interested in:

Self-neglect: A Practical Approach to Risks and Strengths Assessment
By Shona Britten and Karen Whitby ISBN 978-1-912096-86-2

The Social Worker's Guide to the Care Act
By Pete Feldon ISBN 978-1-911106-68-5

Working with Family Carers
By Valerie Gant ISBN 978-1-912096-978

Titles are also available in a range of electronic formats. To order please go to our website www.criticalpublishing.com or contact our distributor NBN International, 10 Thornbury Road, Plymouth PL6 7PP, telephone 01752 202301 or email orders@nbninternational.com

Meet the **authors**

Kathryn Chard qualified as a social worker in 1998 and held roles both in the voluntary and statutory sectors as a hospital and community-based social worker. She also worked as a carers lead officer in a unitary authority in the North East of England, as well as undertaking a carers commissioning manager's role where she managed a multi-agency partnership and team of commissioning officers to deliver a carers strategy. More recently, Kathryn has worked in a consultancy role with Carers UK, and is a PhD student with the University of Essex where she is evaluating the effectiveness of the Care Act 2014 in supporting carers' participation and inclusion in economic and social life.

Simon Cobb is a social worker with experience of working within the field of child protection and is now specialising in working with families affected by addiction and domestic abuse. He is driven by social justice and abhors discrimination and intolerance. He has eight children, three cats and a small chilli sauce business. In his spare time he performs in heavy metal bands around the globe.

Mark Dimes has 35 years' experience working in the care sector and qualified as a social worker in 1991. He is currently a Learning and Development Advisor with Suffolk County Council and has worked in various roles as a Senior Practitioner, Team Manager, Professional Advisor, Commissioning Manager and Workforce Manager. He has a BA in social work, is a Practice Educator and enjoys supporting, mentoring and coaching staff. He commissions, co-ordinates and facilitates learning and development using a solution-focused approach and is working towards becoming an executive coach and mentor.

Heidi Dix has been a qualified social worker since 1997 and has experience of both adult and children's services. She holds a part-time management role within a Youth Justice Service where she supports research-informed and relationship-based practice. Heidi is also a lecturer in Social Work at the University of Suffolk where she teaches on a range of modules. As a practising social worker, Heidi is passionately committed to social justice and her interests include feminist social work, practice teaching and learning and co-production within the youth justice system.

Andy Fell is a professionally qualified Youth & Community worker, who has been involved in direct work and management of youth work, community and informal education and playwork practice for over 35 years. He has experience of working in both the statutory and voluntary sectors, including managing a borough-wide play service, leading on operational young people's participation and involvement within a local authority and managing an Early Help team. Andy manages a LGBTQIA youth charity he established with young LGBTQIA people 15 years ago; he also works for a community-based domestic abuse charity.

Sue Hollinrake is an Associate Professor who currently teaches on the BA (Hons) Social Work programme at the Univeristy of Suffolk. Sue worked as a social worker and then manager for many years in local authority social services departments. She began as a generic social worker working in Inner London boroughs, before developing a specialist role as a social worker in a special school for children with severe learning difficulties, and then became a service manager for Children with Disabilities. Sue later moved into professional education as a senior lecturer in social work and led the BA Social Work degree programme at the University of Suffolk. Her teaching and research interests are around professional values, informal carers, service user involvement, social work with adults and relationship-based practice.

Aisha Howells is a social worker, practice educator and lecturer at the University of Suffolk. Aisha's areas of interest include domestic abuse, the impact of trauma, social work research, practice education and student/practitioner well-being. Aisha has completed a Postgraduate Certificate in the Dynamics of Domestic Violence and is passionate about understanding how creative and relationship-based social work practice can support social justice.

Jennifer Meade is a Joint Head of a Youth Justice Service. Prior to this, she introduced the Drug Interventions Programme in Norfolk, worked as a senior probation officer in Nottinghamshire and probation officer in Derbyshire and as a volunteer manager at The Landmark, a centre for people living with HIV and AIDS. She has a long-standing interest in the role of case management within the context of relationships. She is also interested in how best to bridge the divide between policy, research and practice.

Dee Mustin has been a mental health social worker for many years and is currently a Senior Practitioner in a community team working with adults. She generally works with people experiencing psychosis and has an interest in exploring alternative models of intervention. Dee is also a Practice Educator and an Approved Mental Health Professional and is involved in supporting the AMHP Training Course in Suffolk.

Introduction

Heidi Dix and Sue Hollinrake

Relationships are at the heart of social work with people and carers; however, until recently most of the literature regarding relationship-based approaches has focused on describing and supporting work with children and their families. As editors, we have all either worked in or have connections with both children's and adult services and passionately felt that we wanted to contribute to the developing body of literature that is calling for a resurgence of relationship-based practice and in this instance on adult social care.

We feel that these are exciting times for the development of social work; pressure from advocacy groups and service user networks, together with the introduction of the Care Act 2014, has seen a move away from managerialist practice that had been a feature of adult social care since the 1990s with the introduction of the NHS and Community Care Act 1990. This piece of legislation brought the idea of 'Case Management', with social workers often described as 'Care Co-ordinators', or 'Named Assessors', and who acted as 'brokers' to commission and co-ordinate packages of care. Within this context, relationships were not considered an essential component of effective social work and those of us who were committed to this way of working found organisations did not provide the time and resources necessary to support this approach. With the current climate of deep austerity, many social workers and people and carers may feel that little has changed; eligibility and thresholds for services are high, resources are limited, and organisational structures often still do not support a way of being with people that is relationship-based.

However, it is often at times of crisis that creativity and innovation flourish and as this book illustrates, it is the relationships we develop with people who use services, with carers, and with other professionals which are instrumental in supporting and assisting change.

The book contains two parts; Part 1 provides a summary of a range of theoretical perspectives for relationship-based practice with adults as well as outlining the policy context for adult social care. The final chapter in Part 1 introduces us to the IDEAS Model: a useful framework to consider the various elements necessary for effective relationship-based work. Included in Part 2 of the book are eight chapters; the first four cover distinct areas of adult social care, while the next two focus on work with adult offenders and people who use substances. The decision to place the final two chapters at the end of the book, which discuss domestic abuse and highlight issues for people who identify as lesbian, gay, bisexual, transgender, queer, intersex or asexual, was purely for convenience. These chapters are different from the others in that the themes discussed within them are pertinent to all of the specialist areas of practice discussed in the preceding chapters. Also, there are some areas of practice not covered – in particular, people with physical and sensory impairments – but some of the issues discussed in the existing chapters will map across and be relevant to these areas.

The book is aimed at practitioners, managers, practice educators and students, including those who work in environments other than social work, eg health and probation settings. It can be used as a resource to dip into; you may wish to read a chapter that explores a specialism that you are interested in or currently working within, or you may wish to explore an element of the IDEAS framework across a number of practice areas by reading the 'Expertise' section for all the chapters included in Part 2, for example. Doing this supports the promotion of a shared understanding of work with adults and can help to avoid silo working.

A brief overview of the book contents

Part 1

A focus on strengths-based social work within adult services is emerging, with the Department of Health in 2017 publishing a report stating that *'Choice, control, citizenship and connectedness are common themes underpinning all strengths-based work'* (Department of Health, 2017, p 7). Building on this, the Department of Health and Social Care (2019) produced a practice framework to support strengths-based social work with adults. With this in mind, in **Chapter 1** of this book Sue Hollinrake outlines some of the strengths-based approaches that can be used by practitioners, as well as outlining other theoretical perspectives which have relationships as a key component. The case examples included in each of the chapters in Part 2 will help to illustrate how the theoretical perspectives summarised in this chapter can be utilised in practice.

Chapter 2 traces the policy developments that have shaped practice in social work with adults, looking at these in the wider context of political and ideological influences, and critiquing these from a relationship-based perspective. There is a particular focus on personalisation and co-production as major policy trajectories that have been gaining ground and are now firmly based in contemporary practice and can sit comfortably within a relationship-based approach and a supportive organisational context.

The ability to develop effective relationships within social work is often taken for granted; it is accepted as underpinning practice, but as the IDEAS model developed by Heidi Dix and Jennifer Meade and outlined in **Chapter 3** illustrates, adopting a relationship-based approach requires a combination of skills, knowledge and values. The IDEAS model was borne out of a curiosity from the authors to find out what contributes to effective practice and how best to support practitioners within a youth justice service to achieve this. Thus IDEAS was developed to support practitioners to think comprehensively about all aspects of their own individual practice as well as what they should expect from an organisation to support them to undertake their best work. The IDEAS model can also be a useful tool to aid supervision as it can be used to consider the conflicts, dilemmas and challenges that arise in working in a way that is relational and therefore identifies strategies, and the support required to overcome these to bring clarity to complex situations.

It quickly became apparent to us that the IDEAS framework is applicable to most, if not all, areas of social work practice and therefore the model underpins each chapter in Part 2 of this book, where different areas of social work are discussed in relation to the model.

Part 2

Chapter 4 in Part 2 looks at how the IDEAS model can be used by practitioners in their work with older people. Mark Dimes begins by discussing some of the perceptions of age and ageing and illustrates the importance of trust in developing a relationship that is able to challenge stereotypes to promote the well-being of older people.

Sue Hollinrake in **Chapter 5** highlights how relationships are at the heart of effective co-production at a strategic level by outlining how commissioners and service providers collaborated with people, families and their naturally connected networks to develop a Learning Disability Strategy in order to promote choice and control and achieve better outcomes for people. The chapter also focuses on how co-production and personalisation can occur at an individual level, that is, between the person and the practitioner.

Within **Chapter 6**, Kathryn Chard places an emphasis on the importance of practitioners needing to value and validate the experience of informal carers and through the use of case examples illustrates how some of the theoretical approaches outlined in Chapter 4 can support a relationship-based approach.

Chapter 7 discusses how the IDEAS model can provide a framework for practitioners working within mental health settings and Dee Mustin describes how utilising the knowledge gained from 'practice wisdom', from research and from listening to and responding to people's experiences are essential to the development of relationships to enable positive change to occur.

Jennifer Meade, in **Chapter 8**, argues that even though practitioners who work with adult offenders are no longer required to hold a social work qualification, the values required of practitioners working in a range of agencies and organisations that provide services to people in contact with the criminal justice system are similar to social work values and those that underpin relationship-based practice.

Chapter 9 uses the IDEAS model to illustrate how relationships are central to supporting people who have experiences of trauma, abuse and neglect and Simon Cobb emphasises how the application of therapeutic approaches are necessary to effectively work with people who misuse substances.

In **Chapter 10**, Aisha Howells argues that practitioners need to take a human rights perspective to working with people who experience domestic abuse and stresses the need to build trusting alliances with victims/survivors in order to support more effective interventions. Howells asserts how adopting a trauma-informed approach can enable organisations to provide safety for practitioners to undertake transformational social work.

We believe that relationships are at the interface between the personal and the political. Social work, by its very nature, is an inclusive profession and integral to the Professional Capabilities Framework is a commitment to promoting equality and diversity and the promotion of the fundamental principles of human rights, social justice and economic well-being (BASW, 2018). **Chapter 11**, with its focus on working with people who identify as lesbian, gay, bisexual, transgender, queer, intersex or asexual, offers practical examples to enable practitioners to utilise the power that is inherent within the social work role to identify, question and challenge inequality nationally and locally as well as providing information regarding the need to consider all aspects of a person's identity in order to support their well-being.

Several chapters in Part 2 of this book are written by practitioners and we are immensely grateful for their contributions; it is the content of these chapters that we believe makes this book a rich source of information. Two of the editors of this book are academics, one also works part-time as the practice and development manager within a local authority and the third editor is a Joint Head of a Youth Justice Service. Most of the practitioners who contributed to this book are working within a local authority that is involved in a Social Work Teaching Partnership, a government initiative to support the collaboration of HEIs and employers to recruit, train and retrain a high-quality social care workforce.

A key factor in the success of our Teaching Partnership is a shared understanding of the roles and responsibilities of all involved. The development of relationships based on empathy has created an environment where mutual respect and trust has helped to overcome differences in organisational cultures and values. In many ways this has mirrored the approach taken in the creation of this book, in that it is the trusting and respectful relationships that have been established between academics, practitioners, people who use services and carers which enabled this book to be written and we are all very proud of this achievement.

References

British Association of Social Workers (BASW) (2018) Professional Capabilities Framework for Social Workers in England. [online] Available at: www.basw.co.uk/system/files/resources/Detailed%20level%20descriptors%20for%20all%20domains%20wi%20digital%20aug8.pdf (accessed 28 February 2019).

Department of Health (2017) *Strengths-based Social Work Practice with Adults Roundtable Report.* [online] Available at: https://assets.publishing.service.gov.uk/government/uploads/system/uploads/attachment_data/file/652773/Strengths-based_social_work_practice_with_adults.pdf (accessed 5 June 2019).

Department of Health and Social Care (2019) Strengths-based Approach: Practice Framework and Practice Handbook. [online] Available at: https://assets.publishing.service.gov.uk/government/uploads/system/uploads/attachment_data/file/778134/stengths-based-approach-practice-framework-and-handbook.pdf (accessed 28 February 2019).

Part 1

Chapter 1 | Theoretical perspectives for relationship-based practice with adults

Sue Hollinrake

Introduction

This chapter will introduce the main theoretical perspectives that are important for understanding the dynamics of relationships within social care frameworks for practice, drawing on theories for understanding and making sense of relationships and theories for intervention in a social work practice context. This discussion is not intended to explore the theories in depth and detail as there is not the space here to do that and many books have been written on each of the theoretical perspectives included below. Each of the following sections offers an overview and the chapter forms the basis for the later chapters in Part 2 of this book, where links between theory and practice will be furthered in specific areas of practice through case examples which will illuminate the theories and methods applied.

Relationship-based practice has seen a revival in recent years (eg see Wilson et al, 2011), though this may seem curious at first glance as social work has always been about the individual in their social context and hence with an emphasis on relationship, as stated by many a social work writer (eg Seden, 2005; Payne, 2011; Parker and Doel, 2013). David Howe expressed this succinctly in his Foreword to another insightful textbook on relationship-based practice in 2015:

If you really render social work to its basics then there isn't much left other than the relationship between worker and client, practitioner and service user. Of course, social workers have statutory duties and powers, can access and organise resources, and do employ a variety of theoretically based techniques and interventions. But each of these only takes place in the medium of the worker-client relationship. The quality and character of the relationship therefore matters; it matters a great deal.

(Howe, cited in Megele, 2015, p vii)

The influence of Freud and post Freudians such as Bowlby (2005) and Winnicott (1964) has been significant within the developing theory base of the profession in acknowledging relationship as an important resource for practice. While Radical Social Work in the 1970s criticised the psycho-analytic influences within social work, even radical social workers had to form relationships to work alongside their service users. However, in the 1980s and 1990s, social work became subject to wider political and policy shifts as neo-liberal influences took hold, introducing the market into social care, and this changed the nature of the relationship between social worker and service user, particularly in the statutory sector (Phung, 2014, p 231).

For social work with adults, it was the implementation, in 1993, of the NHS and Community Care Act 1990, strongly influenced by neo-liberal ideology, that changed relationships within the delivery of welfare. Social workers became care managers who commissioned packages of care, which brought to the fore a rational-technical approach to practice, incorporating IT developments. This impacted on the recording of practice and promoted a more predictable risk management approach which was *procedure-driven and formulistic* (Megele, 2015, p 4), with increased auditing and measurement of activity and outcomes. In the face of an approach to social work with adults that emphasised assessment and management of need through a market-based social care sector, with increasing emphasis on the service user as consumer, the concept and use of relationship-based practice receded.

Dominelli and Hoogvelt (1996) criticised the fragmentation and routinisation of assessment under Care Management, which meant that relationships with people who use services became short and focused on task management, eliminating more complex aspects of professional engagement in assessment. However, as this risk-averse, managerialist approach became more established, accompanied by the introduction of a business culture into social work (Harris, 2003), some social work academics (eg Cooper, 2014; Howe, 1998; Ruch, 2005 and 2010; Trevithick, 2003) began to revive interest in the significance of relationship and the need for it to return to a central position in practice, in recognition that real change in the lives of people under stress requires more than risk management and surveillance or a 'tick box' approach in a target-driven organisational culture. This return to relationship in social work practice was also suggested by work undertaken with people who use services by Beresford, Croft and Adshead (2008). Service user movements themselves have had an influence on policy and professional practice through redressing the imbalance of power in traditional approaches (Duffy, 2010), and have emphasised the use of personal relationships to identify need and seek solutions *with* rather than for people. More recently, Chief Social Worker Lyn Romeo has emphasised the importance of social workers with adults working therapeutically, and in the community (Principal Social Workers Adults Network 3.7.14), and the Care Act 2014 recognises the significance of relationship in promoting change, in particular in the context of a strengths-based approach, supported by a recently published framework and handbook to support social workers and social care professionals in applying a strengths-based approach to their work with adults (Department of Health, 2019), which follows a report in 2017 on the same subject (Department of Health, 2017).

A relationship-based approach is key to social work because many service users have experienced distress, damage, trauma and loss. These result in feelings arising from emotional pain which may be difficult to manage and which are present within interactions with social workers. In the course of their work, individual social workers may well identify in some way with the issues emerging within the relationship that relate to need, a sense of injustice, experiences of loss, difference, abuse, deprivation – all part of the human condition. Practitioners need to be aware of where the boundaries are between themselves and their own experiences and those of the adults they are working with – where it is useful to identify but to also know how to avoid over-identification (see below in relation to the effective 'use of self'). Human behaviour is complex and multi-faceted and people are not simply rational beings but have affective dimensions that complicate (and enrich) interactions with others. In social work practice, therefore, this involves acknowledging an individual's emotional life as well as working together to provide practical solutions. As Hennessey (2011, p 8) says:

We are all affected profoundly by our experiences of relationships and this is why the relationship between a social worker and her client can alter the practice outcome.

Ruch et al (2010) clearly and convincingly present a case for relationship-based social work founded on a psycho-dynamic approach and object-relations theory. They define relationship-based practice as an approach that:

builds on psychosocial approaches to practice and the psycho-dynamically informed casework tradition (Hollis 1964). The central characteristic of relationship-based practice is the emphasis it places on the professional relationship as the medium through which the practitioner can engage with and intervene in the complexity of an individual's internal and external worlds.

(Wilson et al, 2011, p 9)

The approach in this book, however, is to widen the scope to encompass not just psycho-dynamic insights and understandings for relationships, but also theoretical insights drawn from a range of other approaches – humanistic, person-centred theory and practice; strengths-based approaches; solution-focused practice; and motivational interviewing – as more appropriate for adult social care based around the policies and practices of personalisation, which has become increasingly significant in the last decade or so (Lymbery, 2012), and co-production, both of which are embedded within the Care Act 2014, as will be explored in the next chapter.

Psychoanalytic and psychodynamic theory and practice

Contemporary psychoanalytic theory is based on Freud's ideas about the role of the unconscious in influencing behaviour through the pre-conscious and unconscious mind. The theory is only briefly sketched here. Freud presented a dynamic developmental framework for the mind from birth to adulthood, providing a theory of human personality, showing how the adult character develops. He suggested that childhood experiences affect emotional development, through the psychosexual stages, and determine adult personality (Freud, 1905). Unpleasant experiences in childhood, when unresolved, are buried or repressed by the conscious mind in the unconscious, but, through processes that Freud termed 'fixation' or 'regression' (ie where the individual is 'stuck' at a developmental stage or their behaviour is reminiscent of an earlier stage), they continue to affect how individuals develop, see the world around themselves and respond to the world through their perceptions, interpretations, emotional responses and behaviours. Freud also presented a model of the mind (Phillips, 2006) – id (basic instincts), ego (engages with reality and 'manages' the id) and superego (an inner authority internalised through socialisation with parents and other forms of authority which disciplines the id and is also 'managed' by the ego). The interaction between these three elements affects the emotional development of the individual and the formation of personality, through the conflict and the striving for equilibrium between them. This takes place across the five stages of sexual development (oral, anal, phallic, latency and genital stages), which are all important for the development of emotions and personality. Disruptions across these stages, and the interactions of the id, ego and superego within them, can have a significant impact on personality in adult life and by understanding the impact on a service user of their early emotional development, light can be shone on the origins of contemporary behaviour, which is particularly useful where the behaviour is destructive, harmful to self or others or even anti-social.

If one accepts the existence of an unconscious, then there are useful concepts and 'tools' that can be employed to reveal unconscious processes that affect behaviour. These may be useful for social work practice as a means of opening up discussion with a service user about negative feelings and behaviours that are affecting their relationships with the social worker and with others in an unhelpful way, and to thereby help people to process difficult and disturbing feelings that the experiences of loss and change evoke when people who use services face difficulties in their lives. Repression is a means of burying unpleasant feelings and memories. According to Freud (Phillips, 2006), this can be managed through specific defence mechanisms, which function to protect the ego from the threat of too much anxiety, blocking or distorting impulses to make them more acceptable. To some degree, these defence mechanisms are healthy, but if over-active, they can become damaging.

Repression – this is the fundamental defence mechanism that highlights the process by which disturbing thoughts and feelings that threaten to overwhelm the individual are repressed or pushed out of consciousness to prevent discomfort and retain some psychic equilibrium.

Denial – again this is fundamental to the process of defending oneself from a distressing reality by denying that reality in order to avoid the pain of recognition. This is the result of repression and involves the active distortion of the truth. The opportunity for healthy and useful adaptation to the real situation is lost when denial occurs and helpful opportunities and supportive relationships may be missed. Those who try to re-orientate the individual (or group) may have the negative feelings that lie underneath the denial 'projected' onto them and they may be seen in a negative light while the individual (or group) that is in denial may retain all the positive perceptions (known as 'splitting').

Projection – this refers to the ascribing of feelings to others that an individual has difficulty owning and dealing with themselves.

Reaction-formation – this occurs when an individual suppresses feelings that are too difficult for them to express to another by behaving towards them in a manner directly opposed to the 'real' feeling – eg when someone is angry and irritated by the demands of another but behaves in a 'super' sweet way towards them instead.

Displacement – this refers to the 'redirection' of feelings that are difficult to deal with where they belong onto someone/something else that is less threatening (eg getting angry with one's partner at home following an unresolved issue at work).

Sublimation – this occurs when the energy created through destructive feelings and angry impulses is changed into something more socially acceptable, such as channelling anger about an oppressive work situation into trade union involvement, or redirecting negative feelings about injustices in one's own life into voluntary work for a charity.

Rationalisation – this occurs when someone provides a reason for their behaviour or their feelings that is not accurate but is more comfortable to acknowledge than the 'real' feeling or behaviour – eg someone arrives late for a meeting and says the traffic was bad when they were really anxious about attending but did not want to admit this.

Social workers can use these concepts as a way of understanding present adult behaviour and emotional responses to social situations based on an appreciation that present behaviour is influenced by responses to past experiences that have become patterns of avoidance. They can appreciate how they have achieved equilibrium in the psyche through the use of defence mechanisms, which, when rigidified over time, lead to inappropriate and maladaptive behaviours and create difficulties in the present. A social worker who is emotionally intelligent (ie sensitive to and aware of their own, as well as others' feelings [Howe, 2008]) will be able to offer containment for negative feelings through recognition that these may arise because of past hurts that have gone unrecognised and unprocessed. This containment promotes insight for the person using services and powerful emotions can be 'worked through' (Freud, 1914) and managed so that reality is not distorted through the power of the associated memories that may have been buried in the unconscious. Social workers working in an anti-discriminatory way, using a social model rather than an 'expert' medical model, and a strengths-based approach rather than a deficit one, would not wish to take a powerfully expert position in relation to the person using services, but could still use the theoretical knowledge that this approach offers as a shared resource for increased understanding and behaviour change, as it makes sense to the individual.

Attachment theory

Being cared for and cared about is fundamental to human survival not only in infancy, but throughout life, in varying degrees at different times in the life cycle. Care in early life can be loving and containing but it can also be inconsistent and damaging if the needs of the carer conflict with the needs of the infant in this crucial phase of development and the conflict cannot be contained. The attachment system develops during the first five years of life between the child and their significant caregiver(s) and as we develop, it affects how we regulate our moods and arousal and how we relate to people when we are needy or distressed.

Attachment theory (Bowlby, 2005), as a theory of personality development which is based within psychoanalysis, has significance, too, for relationship-based social work with adults, because understandings gained from observations of infants and young children about significant relationships in early childhood provide insights to assess 'here and now' relationships for attachment-informed practice, through recognising and working with the psychological defences and behavioural strategies that individuals have established to manage the pain of early childhood rejection and loss, neglect and abuse. The theory draws on evolutionary biology and object relations theory in psychoanalysis and suggests that human beings are programmed to develop physically and emotionally within a close relationship that features physical proximity and a close emotional bond between the baby and a primary caregiver who is a constant figure in the early years. From the age of about six months to approximately two years, proximity seeking for the infant or young child is at its height, and separation from the attachment figure results in anxiety and anger which, if it lasts too long, will provoke sadness, despair or hopelessness in the child. This is not necessarily linked to the frequency of separations because a responsive attachment figure can mitigate separation anxiety by 'tuning in' to the infant to help to contain its distress.

Conversely, the behaviour of an inattentive or unresponsive primary carer will provoke an anxious response in the infant which can feel overwhelming and unmanageable over time. These repeated experiences, as time passes, form a pattern in the child's mind that is referred to as an 'internal working model' which is a pattern on which the child models other significant social relationships throughout its life. The expectations about relationships, the feelings and thoughts, and related behaviours that this significant first relationship engenders, form a 'blueprint' that tends to be transferred to subsequent relationships, though this can be modified by significant others. If the attachment with the primary caregiver is positive and 'good enough', then there is a 'secure base' from which the child can grow in confidence to explore the wider world with a strong internal working model to rely on so that, internally, and externally, they can experience security and support in their development. Prolonged physical or emotional absence from the primary carer will cause anxious attachment behaviour to develop, and the insecurity which the child feels during this significant early period will become established as its internal working model and be repeated in later life as distress and insecurity within other significant relationships. Ainsworth (1989) and Main (1995) have developed theories from research on attachment through observation (Ainsworth) to the development of adult attachment styles (Main). Adult attachment styles offer useful insight to practitioners to understand how their own, and those of people using services, may be triggered in interpersonal contexts. A caring and understanding response from a practitioner can ameliorate a particular attachment style triggered within an anxious, fearful or angry individual under stress internally from adverse life situations and events.

Humanistic, person-centred theory and practice

Carl Rogers introduced person-centred counselling (Rogers, 1961), which has had a significant impact on social work through its value base and through the skills in interpersonal relationships that have since been developed (Egan, 2009). Humanistic, person-centred practice in social work promotes a therapeutic climate of support for individuals to engage in, in their own capacity, to understand and manage their own lives. Linked to Maslow's hierarchy of needs (Maslow, 1943), it is based on the idea that human agency and the individual's capacity for growth and change can be harnessed to empower individuals to achieve their own identified goals – Rogers referred to this as the 'actualising principle', which is akin to Maslow's self-actualising principle. Rogers' core conditions – congruence, unconditional positive regard and empathic understanding (Rogers, 1957) – underpin the therapeutic alliance from the 'helper's' position and are useful in humanistic person-centred social work practice for forming the basic 'container' for relationship-building, establishing trust (without which people using services will not feel secure enough to explore their difficulties and work towards change) and respect and providing a platform for change.

Payne (2011, p 136) defines humanistic social work as being:

About connection with others because it is an interpersonal practice to work with people's own experiences of their self and their situation.

Person-centred practice was incorporated into social work in the 1970s and 1980s and continues to have relevance, particularly because social work with adults has embraced, in recent years, policies underpinned by personalisation and co-production (see Chapter 2), both of which draw on a person-centred approach to interventions in practice, and in the statutory sector, the emphasis on prevention and building on service users' strengths and promoting resilience is important. The core conditions represent 'use of self' in which the practitioner is mindful of how she presents to the person using services, uses her 'emotional intelligence' to 'tune in' (Taylor and Devine, 1993) to the situation that has brought them together, and its meaning for the individual. Egan (2009) provides the foundational introduction and the practice skills required but many social work textbooks cover the essential skills.

Strengths-based approaches

Strengths-based approaches seek to adopt a positive and optimistic approach to situations that require change in order to promote a 'can do' mindset through the positive acknowledgement of the skills, abilities and capabilities of the person using services and those within their surrounding community that can be drawn on. A strengths-based approach in social work practice derives from the work of Saleeby (2009) and recognises that everyone has strengths, capabilities and resources, which practitioners need to emphasise to promote a hopeful attitude that positive change is possible and achievable, increasing self-esteem and self-efficacy. It emphasises that service users have agency and the capacity to determine good outcomes, within a collaborative partnership, which focuses primarily on assets.

This asset-based approach utilises insights from the work of the Disability Movement (see Oliver et al, 2012), which has emphasised a 'rights-based approach' with professionals able and confident to share power and accept service users' expertise to co-produce solutions, with the role of the professional moving away from *fixers who focus on problems to becoming catalysts who focus on abilities'* (Needham and Carr, 2009, p 4). The strengths-based approach to practice emphasises the need to move away from deficit-led assessments and refocus service users' needs and difficulties into learning opportunities and learning from these difficulties (Maclean and Harrison, 2015). There are also clear links with the 'exchange model' of assessment which utilises a relational approach to interaction between people using services and professionals (Smale and Tuson, with Biehal and Marsh, 1993), highlighting the *exchange of expertise* and power-sharing required between the individual, the informal carer and the practitioner. This has been a model for individual social care practice for some time, following the implementation of the NHS and Community Care Act 1990, though overshadowed in recent years by a more technical-rational approach which emphasises the use of an objective body of knowledge from research that can be applied and replicated across similar scenarios. A strengths-based approach to assessment should be an empowering, collaborative venture, which does not pathologise the person using services, and is mindful of language to avoid unhelpful and negative labelling which can lead to stereotyping and an essentialist positioning. Context and environmental issues that contribute to the difficulties experienced by the individual need to be acknowledged and considered (Saleeby, 2009), so that a person-in-context balance is achieved and issues beyond the control of the immediate relationship can be acknowledged. This links to a social constructionist approach, as discussed by Parton (2003) who emphasises the importance of relationship-building to achieve a mutually understood and co-produced assessment of what is going on and what needs to change in order to move forward, within often complex and uncertain situations in practice. Practitioners must avoid the 'power of first impressions', as Munro warned (1995), and be aware that there is a range of possible ways of interpreting a situation, and the assessment process should provide a means, through relationship, of exploring and negotiating these. Person-centred skills (Egan, 2009) and reflection and mindfulness (Hennessey, 2011, pp 96–105) are important aspects of this approach.

Connected to the strengths-based approach discussed above, narrative approaches rely on person-centred skills to establish a good rapport with the service user, based around trust, empathy, a collaborative engagement and commitment to change. Active listening is also crucial as the social worker must be able to hear and communicate that they have heard the individual's story fully, while being aware of the dominant discourses that it contains.

Narrative approaches are based on the premise that people have stories about themselves and their lives that can become 'problem-saturated' and do not help them in situations where change is required to function better. They will have a 'dominant plot' (Morgan, 2000) which gets in the way of them seeing their way through to changing aspects of their lives for the better. This approach draws on social constructionism (Berger and Luckman, 1966), which posits that all reality is negotiated between people in an inter-subjective manner, but it can become 'fixed' and perceived as 'common sense' and immutable in people's minds. This can include socially constructed social roles and expectations – such as gender roles or stereo-typical expectations of 'old age'. These narratives that people form about themselves can become part of their identity through which they interpret the world and others around them. As the Roundtable Report on strengths-based practice with adults (Department of Health, 2017, p 4) states, *'Problems are separate from people and the relationships between people and their problems can change'.* Problems, however, can trap and limit people's choices in life and undermine agency. The narrative approach suggests that we make our own meanings, which means we can re-make them, or 're-story' them when they no longer work well for us (White and Epston, 1990). Using a narrative approach and through critical questioning, a social worker can help the people they work with to understand the limitations of their 'dominant plot' and work to construct a different story, or see the contradictions in their 'dominant plot' that frees them from the all-consuming problem and enables them to see a different 'reality' which is more helpful and hopeful.

Miller and Rollnick (2002) drew on cognitive psychology, and person-centred approaches, linked with theory about self-efficacy and models for achieving change to develop motiv-ational interviewing. They have defined this as:

a client-centred, directive method of enhancing intrinsic motivation to change by exploring and resolving ambivalence.

(Miller and Rollnick, 2002, p 25)

Within a collaborative relationship, established using other tools referred to earlier (such as the core conditions from person-centred approaches), the social worker supports the service user to establish a specific goal for change – identifying where they would like to be at the end of the work they do together. The individual's ideas about the change they want to achieve are explored within an empathic and trusting relationship, and strengths and current achievements and abilities are drawn on in a positive way, emphasising their capabilities and focusing on and building their confidence and motivation for change. This can work effectively with people using services who may be feeling stuck, and the power and momentum of the relationship can sweep them up in a positive way and harness their motivation, building on their desire to change, even if it feels very difficult to achieve. Scales of 0–10 are used to rate their determination to change and they are required to articulate the detail of the steps to their goal and how they will achieve these. Acceptance and empathy are important qualities and skills within which to ground the motivation for change, as is some confrontation around any discrepancies that arise along the way between actual behaviours that fall short of the desired changes. Ambivalences have to be clarified and thought about within a non-judgemental and trusting relationship. An understanding of defences (see above) is required, and how these can be overcome, not by judging the person using services, but by reflecting back in a neutral way what the social worker observes, ie mirroring so that the person can see their own difficulties and remain engaged with the pro-cess. At the same time, the social worker will need to hold the hope for change and the belief in the self-efficacy of the person using services when obstacles seem insurmountable, so that 'change talk' remains on the agenda. The support of the worker helps the individual to retain their motivation and strength to make the changes they desire. Care and empathy are important elements on the part of the social worker to hold and contain the process through difficult patches.

A solution-focused approach, at its simplest, is based on the premise that talking about the history of the problem and the difficulties that people are experiencing is not necessary or indeed helpful to assist people to find solutions. It has its roots in Eastern philosophy and in the idea that nothing is static, and that change is constantly happening around us and is part of everyday life (de Shazer et al, 2007). At its foundation, solution-focused practice has a questioning-based approach and the version developed by George et al (2018) has three core themes which are:

1. Contracting – to get to where a person wants to be, they need to know where they want to go. Asking at the very beginning of a session what a person's best hopes are for their time with you invites them to think about the outcome they desire and enables a person-centred, non-directive approach to be taken (Berg and Szabo, 2005).

2. A focus on a preferred future – facilitating a person to identify a goal, ie their 'best hopes', helps to begin a conversation that enables people to consider and explore what a future would look like without the problem or difficulty being part of it, with as much behavioural detail as possible, to assist a person to identify and think through a day that does not have the problem in it, thereby encouraging it to happen (George et al, 2018). Obtaining a detailed picture of a problem-free day seeks to provide a focus and to show that life without the difficulty can be possible, which is sometimes enough to promote spontaneous movement and for change to take place (Winbolt, 2011).

3. Identifying current and previous strengths and resources – because in almost every problem we encounter there are also times when it does not exist. Encouraging an individual to explore and amplify those times, together with supporting people to notice exceptions and days when things are different (de Shazer and Dolan, 2007), works to build a sense of self-efficacy. Using specific questions which stimulate people to consider the skills and resources they have used or are currently using, supports the idea of self-determination and aspires to develop self-confidence and a belief that things can be different. Other types of questions such as relationship questions, eg asking what somebody's friend/child/partner/teacher would notice, can also help build a vivid picture and reinforce individual strengths. The use of scales is an important tool used within this approach and these are used flexibly in a variety of ways to connect somebody's preferred future with the present (Shennan, 2019).

As with a strengths-based approach, underpinning a solution-focused approach is the belief that people have the necessary skills and resources to equip them with whatever it is they want to achieve. Self-perception theory suggests we are more likely to believe what we hear ourselves say (Bem, 1972), and therefore a core element of a solution-focused approach is to explore the skills and resources a person has and enable them to appreciate these.

Similarly, an Appreciative Inquiry approach involves focusing on what has gone well, rather than what is going wrong, and the model follows a four-stage process of:

1. looking at what is going well;
2. envisioning what could be improved in the future;
3. planning how to achieve such a vision;
4. considering how to deliver this change.

This approach has a clear strengths-based quality, which encourages creativity and can inject hope and reduce stress in practitioners when motivating people to change, which they can then communicate back to the individual using services to re-invigorate their motivation and create a more positive outlook. It sits well with a caring approach in supervision linked to Kittay's notion of nested obligations discussed subsequently, and moves away from a deficit model within supervision, so that the hope instilled in practitioners can be passed on through the work with the person using services to inspire their motivation and agency.

Feminism and a feminist 'ethic of care'

Key aspects that the above approaches to practice have in common derive from the way in which the social worker relates to the person using services and the values informing this. Care is an important component – even when working with people who the social worker may find it difficult to like because of behaviours that have brought them to the attention of the agency/organisation. It is nonetheless important to ensure that they receive a fair and proper service.

A particular school of thought and philosophical approach which is part of the ethical framework underpinning professional social work, and which connects well with a relationship-based approach to social work with adults using services, is that of a feminist 'ethic of care'. This is a practical moral approach which grounds moral behaviour within caring relationships and the feelings and emotions which care evokes (though not excluding thinking and reasoning).

A feminist ethic of care's emphasis on interdependence – connection and mutuality – and the power of the relationship based on empathy, respect and responsiveness, shares much in common with a relationship-based approach to practice. Both reject the notion of the autonomous, independent human being and stress interdependence, with the elements of attentiveness, responsibility, competence, responsiveness and trust (Tronto, 2013). Seeking to promote resilience through the empowering and transformational potential of the two-way dynamic of the relationship, the feminist 'ethic of care' derives from Gilligan's (1993) work on the gendered differences she found in her studies of male and female views of caring. It emphasises personal connectedness arising from the relationship between the carer and the cared-for person, rather than stemming from a more abstract moral principle about social responsibility based on rights and duties (as derived from Enlightenment thinking – eg Kantian philosophy). It is based on the premise that care is basic to human life and crucial – it is not an optional extra, though its relevance, traditionally, has been confined to the private sphere of the home and to women's work. An ethic of care emphasises that interdependence and reciprocity underpin all human relationships and challenges the *'dominant masculinist values such as autonomy, independence, conflict and power'* (Cloyes, 2002, p 203). It proposes a more collective vision that contradicts the illusion that individuals are separate beings and that the unknown 'other' need not concern us. As a practical ethic, emphasising what happens within a caring relationship between two people, the feminist 'ethic of care' does not fall into the category of virtue ethics, as it is more the actions between those in the caring relationship, as much as the qualities of the carer, that are important.

So, in practice, an ethic of care stresses the importance of acting on the concrete needs of individuals within caring relationships (Engster, 2004). As a practical ethic, it demands a personal, mental 'engrossment' in a particular, concrete situation (Noddings, 1984, p 90). Discussions mainly focus on the nature of the relationship involving the one-caring (who can be a formal carer [social worker or social care worker] or an informal carer) and the cared-for (service user). In this 'caring relationship', the one-caring is attentive to the needs of the cared-for and their actions determined by an understanding of these needs (Tronto, 1993; Noddings, 2010). Both carer and cared-for benefit from the relationship and the role of empathy is also highly significant within the caring relationship (Hollway, 2006; Slote, 2007). Another important feature of the 'ethic of care' that differentiates it from a Kantian duty to care is that, rather than concerning itself with impartial action, an ethic of care approach recognises that there are situations in which partiality is morally neutral (ie it is not 'wrong') and indeed is understandable, desirable and serves to motivate action (Holm, 2011; Nortvedt et al, 2011), because it leads to greater attentiveness to the cared-for person and insight into their individual needs (Nordhaug and Nortvedt, 2011), making the care outcomes much more likely to be effective. Feminist writers such as Noddings (2010) suggest that an ethic of care is a prerequisite for an ethic of justice, since the act of caring at a one-to-one level can lead to a wider concern for tackling injustice and inequality, and in this sense, sits well with social work's emancipatory value base (Thompson, 2015, pp 137–45). Key characteristics of an 'ethic of care' are that it is reciprocal, interdependent, equal and joint, which make it compatible with relationships-based practice, and also importantly link it with strengths-based approaches as discussed earlier.

Kindness

Linked to the foregoing is the value of kindness within a caring relationship. This takes us back into the realm of values, and now specifically of Aristotelian virtue ethics (see Hugman, 2014, pp 166–9), in which the individual with good characteristics is seen as contributing to both the well-being of others and of society more generally, through the qualities they draw on to achieve good outcomes in practice. Acts of kindness, or benevolence, often refer to actions that are delivered by one person to another in a helpful and generous manner, meant to convey sympathy and some relief to the other's suffering, or to make them feel better in some way. The quality which informs the behaviour or act derives, in meaning, from an Old English noun 'cynd', which meant family or kin (Ballatt and Campling, 2011) and links to the word 'kinship' or sameness which found expression in the Christian concept of 'caritas' (neighbourly love) in which people recognise themselves in the other (Phillips and Taylor, 2009). It suffered from being marginalised as a way of being and doing during the Enlightenment period, and it became feminised in Victorian times, as a sentimental trait of someone seeking moral approval and also *a virtue of losers* in people who were not com-petitive and self-seeking (Phillips and Taylor, 2009, p 7) – winners being those who succeed through self-interest. As a consequence, in present-day society we have an ambivalent atti-tude to kindness (see Ballatt and Campling [2011, pp 12–17] for a good discussion of this, and the consequent perceived risks to individuals and societies more concerned with co-operative and kind acts. While neo-liberal thinking continues to cast a cloak of suspicion over the motivation for kind acts, kindness is at the heart of relationships and utilises the skills of attentiveness to build connection through compassion and understanding. Being kind to others strengthens solidarity and connection.

Emotions and emotional labour

Much of what has already been discussed in this chapter will involve the management of emotions within a caring relationship, which is significant in social work because many people using services are seeking support, or are required to accept social work intervention because they are under stress or feeling threatened and uncertain due to problems in their lives, or because others consider them to have problems that require change. Stress generates emo-tional distress and the first steps in promoting change in people's lives are taken through the recognition of the emotional distress that they are experiencing. The role that social workers play in supporting individuals to recognise and manage feelings and emotions is significant in establishing an empathic and trusting relationship and involves emotion work (Howe, 2014, pp 82–4). The use of emotions that the social worker feels and uses to create a con-tainer and a working relationship to promote change is part of the labour required of the social worker. This has some connection with the concept of emotional labour. Theodosius (2013, p 179), drawing on the work of American sociologist Arlie Hochschild (1983), defines emotional labour as *'the induction or suppression of feeling in order to sustain an outward appearance of feeling that produces an emotion in others ... it draws on a deep sense of self that is integral to the individual.'* Social workers are taught skills in relationship work and emotion work and are then accountable to their employing organisation for this work. However, when organisations expect a quick turnover of work, with social workers managing high caseloads with the changes to practice seen under new public management (Lymbery and Postle, 2015), then there can be issues. As research shows within the field of nursing, where similar changes have taken place (Mann, 2005; Erickson, 2009), risk of stress and burnout and job dissatisfaction have a direct link to the impact of emotional labour, pointing particularly to the significance of professionals developing emotional resilience (Grant and Kinman, 2014).

It is therefore very important that organisations provide ongoing training and supportive supervision for professionals involved in relationship-based practice and that emotion work is given high priority, because, as Kittay describes, when we are involved in caring relationships, which are based in connectedness and the demands this connectedness brings for us, we need to claim support for ourselves to maintain our well-being:

Such claims are entitlements first to a relationship in which one can be cared for if and when appropriate, and second to a socially supported situation in which one can give care without the care-giving becoming a liability to one's own well-being.

Kittay (1993, p 66)

Kittay refers to this as a set of 'nested obligations' or 'nested dependencies' (Kittay, 1993, p 67) which are not based on immediate reciprocal exchange but which are based within *'a relationship that sustains her as she sustains her charge'* (p 68).

This relates well to the supervision setting in which the whole person of the supervisee, thinking and feeling, should be 'in the room' and not just the technical-rational, procedurally driven practitioner who has to bury his or her feelings as there is no time to consider their significance and importance. Feelings have to be explored in supervision in order to contain them. This leads to safer practice as the social worker will gain deeper insight into their practice and be able to control the emotions arising from their interactions, by understanding what belongs to them, and how their own feelings (or avoidance of certain feelings) may be influencing their practice, and thereby regulated, and what belongs to the person using services and may be influencing what is going on between them.

Relating across difference

Much has been written in social work literature about the importance of anti-discriminatory and anti-oppressive practice. These concepts recognise the structural forces that create oppression at the same time as working with individuals in ways that mitigate its impact and promote social justice. Power has to be recognised and Ryde (2009, p 148) states that:

a constructive relationship can develop when issues of power and culture have been well identified and acknowledged, then you can get busy with another way of relating.

Cultural competence and sensitivity refer to various skills and knowledge of techniques that can be used to practice competently with diverse groups of adults using services. Papadopoulos (2006) states that cultural competence is defined as an ability to maximise sensitivity and minimise insensitivity from practitioners and services towards culturally diverse communities. Giuntoli and Cattan (2012) talk about the importance of social workers having awareness of their own cultures, and, crucially, social work education and training needs to ensure that students and practitioners continue to reflect critically on their cultural backgrounds and how their own socialisation and absorption of cultural values might impact on their practice to the detriment of the person(s) they are working with (see eg Crofts, 2013).

Significantly, an important part of social work practice is the recognition of difference and diversity as positive, contributing to the richness of the lived experience rather than a deficit to be feared, denigrated and rejected. Effective anti-discriminatory social work practice must use the attentiveness identified by Tronto (1993), as one of the core elements of an ethic of care, to ensure that there is a positive openness to difference in the service user and in the social worker. It requires a gentle curiosity and empathy for the other and through the identification of human-kindness, to recognise the suffering of others, though over-identification due to a situation resonating closely with one of one's own, which may not even be conscious, needs guarding against through sensitive use of self and reflective supervision.

Use of self, self-awareness and critical self-reflection

Social workers have the potential to act as the container for distressed individuals by tolerating and understanding their distress and expressing confidence in their ability to learn to manage their own distress (Ruch et al, 2016). While social workers act as a container for people who use services, it is important that social workers also have this for themselves through the use of management and supervision, and also work discussion groups (Hingley-Jones and Ruch, 2016). Ruch (2007) described a model for supervision that is holistic and 'contains' the supervisee on three levels – emotional (being), epistemological (knowing) and organisational (doing) – all to have equal focus to be worthwhile in protecting the social worker, the service user and the organisation. Hingley-Jones and Ruch (2016, p 245) contend that in austere times, the focus tends to be on the organisational (the doing):

tending to take over from time spent thinking and informing practice. And it almost suffocates the possibility of 'being' in practice, the capacity to reflect and to feel one's way into and through professional encounters.

This offers a very useful model for supervisors to follow to ensure that safe spaces are created and that the organisation does not promote and collude through a current tendency to function on a technical-rational level, ticking the boxes in a procedural manner and avoiding the uncomfortable but crucially informative aspects of relationships in practice.

When social workers enter helping relationships, they enter with their own biases and prejudices, which can affect how they listen to people's problems and then how they intervene to address the issues and problems presented. Supervision carries the potential for enabling social workers to develop their self-awareness and critical self-reflection to ensure that their use of self in practice works for the good of the people using services who they work with.

Conclusion

As can be appreciated from the preceding sections in this chapter, relationship-based practice for social work with adults who use services offers a rich palette of theories, methods and approaches to meet one of the overriding requirements from the Care Act 2014 to ensure that practitioners work in a strengths-based way, to minimise power differences between themselves and the people they work with, separate the person from the problem and avoid a deficit approach that risks undermining change and creativity that can instead promote positive outcomes. Language and the way the person's experiences are framed is important, so that strengths are emphasised and lead to a solution. It is person-centred not prescriptive and permeates all interventions:

A strengths-based approach in social care spans a variety of interventions and supporting process. It is integral to the assessment process, the review, the support and/or care planning process, within safeguarding activities and should be used in all settings. Other activities like provision of information and advice or supervision should also have a strengths-based approach to ensure consistency in all activities.

(Department of Health and Social Care, 2019, p 42)

This is the current direction of travel and the range of theories and underpinning values discussed in this chapter can all, in one way or another, fit into this pathway for change. The following chapter will look at policy developments to trace how we have travelled to this particular place and will offer a critique of the influences along the way. The chapters in Part 2 will then look at the application of these theories within contemporary practice.

Further reading

Hammond, S A (2013) *The Thin Book of Appreciative Inquiry* (3rd edn). Bend, OR: Thin Book Publishing Company.

Hennessey, R (2011) *Relationship Skills in Social Work*. London: Sage.

Shennan, G (2019) *Solution-focused Practice: Effective Communication* (2nd edn). London: Macmillan IHE.

References

Ainsworth, M (1989) Attachments beyond Infancy. *American Psychologist*, 44: 706–16.

Ballatt, J and Campling, P (2011) *Intelligent Kindness: Reforming the Culture of Healthcare*. London: Royal College of Psychiatrists.

Bem, D J (1972) Self-perception Theory. In Berowitz, L (ed), *Advances in Experimental Social Psychology* (vol 6, pp 1–62). New York: Academic Press.

Beresford, P, Croft, S and Adshead, L (2008) 'We don't see her as a social worker': A Service User Case Study of the Importance of the Social Worker's Relationship and Humanity. *British Journal of Social Work,* 38: 1388–407.

Berg, I K and Szabo, P (2005) *Brief Coaching for Lasting Solutions.* New York: Norton.

Berger, P L and Luckman, T (1966) *The Social Construction of Reality: A Treatise in the Sociology of Knowledge.* New York: Doubleday & Company.

Bowlby, J (2005) *A Secure Base. Clinical Applications of Attachment Theory.* London: Taylor and Francis.

Cloyes, K G (2002) Agonising Care: Care Ethics, Agonistic Feminism and a Political Theory of Care. *Nursing Inquiry,* 9: 203–14.

Cooper, A (2014) Making Space: Relationship Based Practice in Turbulent Times. [online] Available at: http:cfswp. org/education/paper.php?s=making-space-relationship-based-practice-in-turbulent-times (accessed 2 March 2019).

Crofts, P (2013) Critical Race Theory and Exploring 'Whiteness'. In Bartoli, A (ed) *Anti-racism in Social Work Practice* (pp 103–24). St Albans: Critical Publishing.

de Shazer, S and Dolan, Y with Korman, H, Trepper, T, McCollum, E and Berg, I K (2007) *More than Miracles: The State of the Art of Solution-focused Brief Therapy.* New York: Routledge.

Department of Health (2017) *Strengths-based Social Work Practice with Adults. Roundtable Report.* London: Department of Health. [online] Available at: https://assets.publishing.service.gov.uk/government/ uploads/system/uploads/attachment_data/file/652773/Strengths-based_social_work_practice_with_adults.pdf (accessed 25 April 2019).

Department of Health and Social Care (2019) *Strengths-based Approach. Practice Framework and Practice Handbook.* London: Department of Health and Social Care. [online] Available at: https://assets.publishing.service. gov.uk/government/uploads/system/uploads/attachment_data/file/778134/stengths-based-approach-practice-framework-and-handbook.pdf (accessed 6 March 2019).

Dominelli, L and Hoogvelt, A (1996) Globalisation and the Technocratisation for Social Work. *Journal of Critical Social Policy*, 16(47): 45–62.

Duffy, S (2010) The Citizenship Theory of Social Justice: Exploring the Meaning of Personalization for Social Workers. *Social Work Practice,* 24(3): 253–65.

Egan, G (2009) *The Skilled Helper* (9th edn). London: Cengage Learning.

Engster, D (2004) Care Ethics and Natural Law Theory: Toward an Institutional Political Theory of Caring. *The Journal of Politics*, 66: 113–35.

Erikson, R (2009) The Emotional Demands of Nursing. In Dickson, G and Flynn, L (eds) *Nursing Policy Research: Turning Evidence Based Research into Health Policy* (pp 155–78). New York: Springer.

Freud, S (1988) *Three Essays on the Theory of Sexuality.* London: Basic Books (original printed in 1905).

Freud, S and Freud, A (ed) (2005) *The Essentials of Psychoanalysis.* London: Vintage Books.

George, E, Iveson, C and Ratner, H (2018) *BRIEFER: A Solution Focused Practice Manual.* London: Brief.

Giuntoli, G and Cattan, M (2012) The Experiences and Expectations of Care and Support Among Older Migrants in the UK. *European Journal of Social Work*, 15(1): 131–47.

Grant, L and Kinman, G (2014) *Developing Resilience for Social Work Practice.* London: Palgrave Macmillan.

Harris, J (2003) *The Social Work Business.* Abingdon: Routledge.

Hennessey, R (2011) *Relationship Skills in Social Work.* London: Sage.

Hingley-Jones, H and Ruch, G (2016) 'Stumbling through'? Relationship-based Social Work Practice in Austere Times. *Journal of Social Work Practice*, 30(3): 235–48.

Hochschild, A (1983) *The Managed Heart.* Berkeley: University of California Press.

Hollway, W (2006) *The Capacity to Care: Gender and Ethical Subjectivity.* Hove: Routledge.

Holm, S (2011) Can 'Giving Preference to My Patients' be Explained as a Role Related Duty in Public Health Care Systems? *Health Care Analysis*, 19: 89–97.

Howe, D (1998) Relationship-based Thinking and Practice in Social Work. *Journal of Social Work Practice*, 12(1): 45–56.

Howe, D (2008) *The Emotionally Intelligent Social Worker.* Basingstoke: Palgrave.

Howe, D (2014) *The Compleat Social Worker.* London: Palgrave Macmillan.

Hugman, R (2014) *A-Z of Professional Ethics.* Basingstoke: Palgrave Macmillan.

Kittay, E F (1999) *Love's Labor: Essays of Women, Equality and Dependency.* New York: Routledge.

Lymbery, M (2012) Social Work and Personalisation. *British Journal of Social Work*, 42: 782–93.

Lymbery, M and Postle, K (2015) *Social Work and the Transformation of Adult Social Care: Perpetuating a Distorted Vision?* Bristol: Policy Press.

Maclean, S and Harrison, R (2015) *Theory and Practice: A Straightforward Guide for Social Work Students* (3rd edn). Lichfield: Kirwin Maclean Associates Ltd.

Magele, C (2015) *Psychosocial and Relationship-based Practice.* Northwich: Critical Publishing.

Main, M (1995) Interview based Adult Attachment Classifications: Related to Infant- Mother and Infant-Father Attachment. *Developmental Psychology*, 19: 227–39.

Mann, S (2005) A Health-care Model of Emotional Labour: An Evaluation of the Literature and Development of a Model. *Journal of Health Organization and Management*, 19(4/5): 304–17.

Maslow, A H (1943) A Theory of Human Motivation. *Psychological Review*, 50(4): 370–96.

McLaughlin, K (2010) Control and Social Work: A Reflection on Some Twenty-First Century Developments. *Practice: Social Work in Action*, 22(3): 143–54.

Miller, W R and Rollnick, S (2002) *Motivational Interviewing: Preparing People for Change* (2nd edn). New York: Guilford Press.

Munro, E (1995) The Power of First Impressions. *Practice: Social Work in Action,* 7(3): 59–65.

Needham, C and Carr, S (2009) *Co-production: An Emerging Evidence Base for Adult Social Care Transformation.* Social Care Institute for Excellence, Research Briefing 31. London: SCIE.

Noddings, N (1984) *Caring: A Feminine Approach to Ethics and Moral Education.* Berkeley: University of California Press.

Noddings, N (2010) Moral Education in an Age of Globalisation. *Educational Philosophy and Theory*, 42(4): 390–6.

Nordhaud, M and Nortvedt, P (2011) Justice and Proximity: Problems for an Ethics of Care. *Health Care Analysis*, 19: 3–14.

Nortvedt, P, Marit, H H and Skirbekk, H (2011) The Ethics of Care: Role Obligations and Moderate Partiality in Health Care. *Nursing Ethics*, 18(2): 192–200.

Oliver, M, Sapey, B and Thomas, P (2012) *Social Work with Disabled People* (4th edn). Basingstoke: Palgrave Macmillan.

Papadopoulos, I (ed) (2006) *Transcultural Health and Social Care: Development of Culturally Competent Practitioners.* London: Churchill Livingstone.

Parker, J and Doel, M (eds) (2013) *Professional Social Work.* London: Sage/Learning Matters.

Payne, M (2011) *Humanistic Social Work: Core Principles in Practice.* Basingstoke: Palgrave Macmillan.

Perlman, H H (1957) *Social Casework: A Problem-Solving Process.* Chicago: University of Chicago Press.

Phillips, A (ed) (2006) *The Penguin Freud Reader.* London: Penguin Random House.

Phillips, A and Taylor, B (2009) *On Kindness.* London: Penguin.

Phung, T (2014) Relationship-based Social Work. In Lishman, J, Yuill, C, Branham, J and Gibson, A (eds) *Social Work: An Introduction* (pp 268–79). London: Sage.

Rogers, C (1957) The Necessary and Sufficient Conditions of Therapeutic Personality Change. *Journal of Consulting Psychology*, 21 : 95–103.

Rogers, C (1961) *On Becoming a Person.* Boston: Houghton Mifflin Company.

Ruch, G (2005) Relationship-based Practice and Reflective Practice: Holistic Approaches to Contemporary Child Care Social Work. *Child and Family Social Work*, 10(2): 111–23.

Ruch, G (2007) Reflective Practice in Contemporary Child-care Social Work: The Role of Containment. *British Journal of Social Work*, 37: 659–80.

Ruch, G, Turney, D and Ward, A (2010) *Relationship-based Social Work: Getting to the Heart of Practice.* London: Jessica Kingsley.

Ryde, J (2009) *Being White in the Helping Professions: Developing Effective Intercultural Awareness.* London; Philadelphia, PA: Jessica Kingsley Publishers.

Saleeby, D (2009) *Strengths Perspective in Social Work* (5th edn). Boston: Pearson.

Seden, J (2005) *Counselling Skills for Social Work Practice* (2nd edn). Buckingham: Open University Press.

Shennan, G (2019) *Solution-focused Practice: Effective Communication to Facilitate Change* (2nd edn). London: Palgrave.

Slote, M (2007) *The Ethics of Care and Empathy.* Abingdon: Routledge.

Taylor, B and Devine, T (1993) *Assessing Needs and Planning Care in Social Work.* London: Routledge.

ter Meulen, R (2008) The Lost Voice: How Libertarianism and Consumerism Obliterate the Need for a Relational Ethics in the National Health Care Service. *Christian Bioethics: Non-ecumenical Studies in Medical Morality*, 14(1): 79–94.

Theodosius, C (2013) Emotional Labour. In Gabe, J and Monaghan, L F (eds) *Key Concepts in Medical Sociology* (2nd edn) (pp 179–83). London: Sage.

Thompson, N (2015) *Understanding Social Work: Preparing for Practice* (4th edn). London: Palgrave.

Trevithick, P (2003) Effective Relationship-based Practice: A Theoretical Exploration. *Journal of Social Work Practice*, 17(2): 163–76.

Tronto, J (1993) *Moral Boundaries: A Political Argument for an Ethic of Care.* New York: Routledge.

Tronto, J (2013) *Caring Democracy, Markets, Equality and Justice.* New York: New York University Press.

White, M and Epston, D (1990) *Narrative Means to Therapeutic Ends*. New York: Norton.

Wilson, K, Ruch, G, Lymberry, M and Cooper, A (eds) (2011) *Social Work: An Introduction to Contemporary Practice* (2nd edn). Harlow: Pearson.

Winbolt, B (2011) *Solution Focused Therapy for the Helping Professions.* London: Jessica Kingsley Publications.

Winnicott, D (2000) *The Child, The Family and the Outside World.* London: Penguin.

Introduction

Adult social care covers potentially all adults who may have eligible social care needs over the age of 18 years, but services are usually organised in relation to specific groups: people of working age with disabilities – ie people with a learning difficulty; a physical disability; a sensory disability; or an enduring mental health problem; and older people, including adults 'at risk of harm' within these groups. This chapter provides an overview of the current policy context as background for the chapters in Part 2 of the book which frame the practice applications with different groups of people using services articulated through the IDEAS model. The chapter will trace important policy developments that shape the current delivery of social care and structure the practice setting for a relationship-based approach with the groups of people using services as discussed in Part 2 of this book. The chapter will briefly note relevant legislation for current practice, eg the major change in adult social care law with the passing of the Care Act in 2014 which now forms the main backdrop for statutory social work with adults following its implementation in 2015. It is not, however, the intention of this chapter to examine the legislation in any detail as this is done very well elsewhere (see, for example, Brammer and Boylan, 2017; Feldon, 2017; Johns, 2017).

Briefly, the Care Act replaces the assessment function under the NHS and Community Care Act 1990 and provisions under previous Acts relating to services for adults. Further, a regulatory framework adds to this legislative framework with interpretations of the law under High Court adjudications, various directions, regulations and local authority circulars and national service frameworks such as those for Older People, Mental Health and Learning Disability. Other significant legislation that interacts with the Care Act 2014 includes the Mental Capacity Act 2005, the Human Rights Act 1998, and the Equality Act 2010.

The Care Act 2014 delivered a fundamental reform in its own right, to simplify and clarify over 60 years of legislation, following the recommendations of a three-year review by the Law Commission (2011). It delivers many of the commitments in the *Caring for Our Future* White Paper (Department of Health, 2011) but following several reports, including the Dilnot Report on the funding of adult social care costs (Dilnot, 2011) which recommended a new capped-costs system for funding care and support, governments have continued to delay thinking about and implementation of change to cap care costs.

The Act also retains much of the philosophy of its predecessor, the NHS and Community Care Act 1990, in which social workers in their statutory organisations became assessors rather than providers of services. Significantly, the NHS and Community Care Act 1990, as a major piece of neo-liberal legislation, introduced what has been termed the Purchaser/Provider split, in which local authority social services departments were to act as co-ordinators and purchasers rather than providers of care, as previously. Social workers became care managers, working in partnership with people using services, with an emphasis on service user participation in assessment and decision making but with the local authority still in control in relation to decision making and budgets. The marketisation of care was facilitated through the creation of markets in public services (a defining feature of neo-liberalism), which introduced competition between providers of services (as a result of the Act, 85 per cent of financing for community care had to be spent in the independent sector).

This foundation for the management of care needs within the community has continued through into the Care Act 2014, but the Care Act 2014 brings into sharper focus the need to develop strengths-based relationships in assessments. The statutory guidance does not say much about what is required in using a strengths-based approach (Feldon, 2017, p 306), but there is no shortage of guides from elsewhere. The Social Care Institute for Excellence (SCIE) produced a guide in 2015 (SCIE 2015), Think Local Act Personal (TLAP) produced one in 2016 (TLAP 2016) and the Department of Health and Social Care has produced a Practice Framework and Handbook in early 2019 (Department of Health and Social Care, 2019).

The Care Act works with other legislation such as the Mental Capacity Act 2005 and the Mental Health Acts 1983 and 2007 and related guidance and policy, as well as the Equality Act 2010 and the Human Rights Act 1998. However, the focus of the discussion here, as stated earlier, will be more on significant policy developments. So, the first part of the chapter will trace various historical pathways in social policy developments impacting on the main groups of adults using social care and social work services – ie people with disabilities – in particular, people with learning difficulties; older people and people with mental health difficulties. Following this, the focus will move to current policy themes that have developed to promote inclusion and individual agency and which apply to all adults using services, and which provide the policy context for a relationship-based approach to social work practice.

Histories of policy developments

The move towards inclusion

In the United Kingdom, people with physical, learning and mental health difficulties have historically been 'outsiders', often segregated from mainstream society. Changing work arrangements during the Industrial Revolution of the eighteenth and nineteenth centuries rendered them unemployable and unprofitable as the demands on the workforce moved to skilled labour, and those who were not able to adapt were viewed as financial burdens on their community. The Poor Law Amendment Act 1834 introduced workhouses and thereby segregation from the community for sections of the population.

As a group, people with disabilities were stigmatised, along with other marginalised groups, and came to be seen as responsible for social ills and this further justified their separation from ordinary living in the community. The segregation of people who were broadly 'not fit' for work was based on ideas of scientific rationalism which justified the creation of institutions as a means of social control. This was part of the agenda of 'liberalism', also supported by Social Darwinism (Johns, 2011, pp 25–6), which viewed some people as 'lesser human beings', justified through a classification system that marked out stages of human life and the subdividing of people in the population in terms of their ability/disability and perceived risk to society. While the 'eugenics movement' reached its zenith under the Nazi regime in Germany during the 1930s and 1940s, it also thrived in this country during the late nineteenth and early to mid-twentieth centuries, and represented a set of beliefs that held that some groups of people, including people with learning difficulties and mental ill-health, represented an *'inherent social menace'* (Wolfensberger, 1969, p 103) and a degenerative threat to the population if allowed to reproduce. Large programmes of sterilisation were introduced in some European countries, while in the UK the preferred policy was that of institutionalisation and segregation (Mencap, 2008). A custodial form of care developed in the large institutions of Victorian times. By the early twentieth century these were referred to as 'colonies' or 'asylums'– ie self-sufficient communities, which later were termed hospitals under the National Health Service Act 1946, making them the responsibility of regional hospital boards rather than of local councils. The medicalisation of care for people with learning difficulties developed, confused with and alongside that of people with mental illnesses.

During the 1950s and 1960s, there was a number of events that challenged the institutionalisation of people – namely: escalating costs of maintaining these large hospitals; the 'scandals' that emerged from the discovery of abuse, neglect and dehumanising treatment in some of them (eg the Committee of Enquiry into Ely Hospital [Department of Health and Social Security, 1969]); the publication of sociological studies that highlighted the detrimental effects of institutional living (eg Goffman, 1968, then Oswin, 1971 and 1978); the pharmacological developments in the 1950s which opened up the possibility of medical treatments for mentally ill people in the community; and the emergence of human rights perspectives (Council of Europe, 1950). The prevailing power of the medical profession at the time, and of the 'medical model' (Oliver, 1990), constructed these adults as 'sick' and hospitalisation and segregation were deemed the logical response, as eugenicist ideas retreated (Stainton, 2000). Policy makers were especially persuaded by economic arguments that community-based options would be cheaper to implement than the continuing upkeep of large institutions from the Victorian era, and at the same time, the politicisation of disability from the 1960s onwards (more noticeably in the 1980s in the UK), the emergence of the anti-psychiatry movement in the 1970s with psychiatric system survivor pressure groups and the agenda for change that the social model of disability provoked (a model that sees disability as a social construct [Oliver, 1990]), grounded the struggle for social justice and recognition for people with disabilities and psychiatric system survivors within a human rights context. From the late 1970s onwards, the service user movements' pressure for social justice found an unlikely bedfellow in the neo-liberal ideologies which were finding expression in social policies under several Conservative administrations through to 1997, and then to some degree continued by New Labour (1997–2010). These emphasised freedom of the individual and the choice and control that autonomous individuals should be exercising within a free market context, so the two agendas from different ideological bases found common cause, which has continued through to the present time, as seen in the Care Act 2014, which embraces the policy concepts of personalisation and co-production (see below).

In the face of these developments, for people with learning difficulties, supported by the emergence of the highly influential concept of Normalisation (Nirje, 1969; Wolfensberger, 1972), a more enlightened professional approach was developed to mitigate the crippling effects of institutionalisation on residents. Normalisation later evolved through Social Role Valorisation (Wolfensberger, 1983), Ordinary Life Principles (Kings Fund Centre, 1983) and John O'Brien's Five Accomplishments (O'Brien and Tyne, 1981; O'Brien, 1986) and became firmly embedded in approaches to service organisation and delivery (community presence, choice, competence, respect and participation), which many agencies then named as values that underpinned their services. These developments had a major influence on the progress of linked policies of de-institutionalisation, the resettlement programme (which managed the closure of long-stay hospitals), and community care. Community integration for people with learning difficulties progressed, while the White Paper (Department of Health, 1989), leading to the NHS and Community Care Act 1990, introduced the idea of choice and service provision in the community for all adult service users, better linked to individual need. This was the first significant legal expression of the ideas of choice and autonomy for people who use services.

Disability through the lens of people with learning difficulties

These changing values influenced the philosophy behind the development of community care for people with learning difficulties, significantly affected too by the force for change generated by the Self-Advocacy Movement (notably People First), which had its philosophical roots in the Civil Rights Movement of the 1960s and 70s, and which sought, and continues to seek, to support individuals with learning difficulties to achieve more agency and control in their lives. At the same time, the emergence of the Independent Living Movement, with the establishment of the Independent Living Fund in 1988, replaced the idea of care with support, and promoted a rights-based philosophy premised on the achievement of full human and civil rights for people with disabilities (Beresford et al, 2011, p 5). These encompass the interrelated rights to protection from the abuse of power and the right to freedoms enjoyed by the rest of society achieved through inclusion, choice, independence and a normal life. The right to a normal life, with inclusion, as full citizens, in mainstream services and facilities has become the demand of people with learning difficulties. The impact on government policy of the Social Model of Disability (Oliver, 1990 and 2009) alongside the Twelve Pillars of Independent Living (Disability Rights UK, 2014), which state clearly what needs to be changed in society for people with disabilities to be full and active members of their community, represents a shift in power from professionals to individual citizens and people who use services. However, despite these positive changes, the reality of life for some adults with disabilities can still be challenging. Young people with autism and challenging behaviours can still find themselves hospitalised in specialist institutions at great distance from their families (Birrell, 2018) and hate crime is a phenomenon that can destroy the lives of those living in the community (Scope, 2008; Amnesty International UK, 2017).

At government level, the White Paper *Valuing People* (Department of Health, 2001a), influenced by the Service User Advisory Group, which published its own supporting report (Department of Health, 2001b) and the subsequent work of the Learning Disability Task Force, were all expected to drive change at a strategic level, founded on the principles of self-determination and social inclusion. At a local level, Partnership Boards were set up to promote stronger local partnerships (members include people with learning difficulties, their families and carers, senior leaders in local authorities, health and other local services, as well as third sector organisations). These developments have done much to make the demands for inclusion more of a reality.

Valuing People (Department of Health, 2001a) promoted a vision of better lives for people with learning difficulties with an emphasis on human rights, citizenship and personalisation. This was built on in 2009 with *Valuing People Now: A New Three-year Strategy for People with Learning Disabilities* (Department of Health, 2009a), which continued this policy direction, stressing that people with learning difficulties should lead ordinary lives and use mainstream services wherever possible with an emphasis on housing, employment and health. It sought to strengthen policy developments in this area, to bring health and social care closer together and promote social inclusion, person-centred planning and equal rights (Department of Health, 2005; Department of Health, 2006; Department of Health, 2007; Department of Health, 2008; Department of Health, 2010; Department of Health, 2011). The Direct Payments Act 1996 and personalised budget schemes have made a significant difference to the levels of control for service users with a learning difficulty, and in terms of recent legislation, the Care Act 2014 introduced a new focus on preventing and delaying the need for care and support, with a duty to provide information and advice on meeting and preventing need for people not eligible for local authority support, as well as building on strengths in the community with an emphasis on personalisation, which strongly links to co-production (Needham and Carr, 2009) (as discussed later).

However, old attitudes in relation to people with learning difficulties sadly linger in the community. A Mencap report (Mencap, 2015) highlighted the need for more positive images of people with learning difficulties in the media, more contact in the general population between learning disabled and non-learning disabled people, and especially among children and young people through more inclusive activities, education at an early age in schools on learning disabilities and active and high-profile campaigning for equal rights for people with learning disabilities in education, employment social and leisure activities. The more the general population experience people with learning difficulties through everyday contact then the more prevailing myths, misrepresentations and misunderstandings will be dispelled.

Nonetheless, the accumulative policy shifts and changes discussed earlier, when taken together, represent a major ongoing trajectory towards the desired full community inclusion for people with disabilities as citizens with rights, alongside closer partnership working and involvement in the design, planning and delivery of services that they may choose to use. Disability rights, Independent Living, inclusion and co-production have all played their part in a continuum of change – a slow evolution that has been magnifying the voice of people who use services from the second half of the twentieth century onwards.

Mental health

Some of the early history of how the growing state managed people experiencing mental distress has been outlined earlier in relation to other groups of people who were seen as 'social problems' and as such, requiring segregation from their local community. The Mental Health Act 1959 represented the beginning of a more structured and more community-orientated policy position towards people with mental health problems. The following paragraphs provide an overview of more recent developments in mental health services in England, in order to provide a context for the way services are currently delivered.

After the establishment of the large generic social services departments, under the Local Authorities Act 1970, there was a move away from generic social work in the 1980s towards the development of specialist areas of practice. The Care Programme Approach (CPA) was introduced in 1991 as a form of case management for people with severe mental health problems. With it came a greater focus on the importance of closer working between health and social services. There followed the development of Community Mental Health Teams (CMHTs), where Care Management and CPA care planning processes were eventually combined to produce a single care plan and risk management process for people using mental health services. The introduction of the National Service Framework for Mental Health in 1999 promoted greater integration of services as well as effective partnership arrangements with primary health care, social services, housing and other agencies, with multidisciplinary mental health teams enabling better joint working between social workers, mental health nurses, psychiatrists, psychologists and other allied health professionals. The different roles of nurses and social workers within these teams gradually became better integrated and the 'care co-ordinator', whether nurse or social worker, would focus on the needs of the whole person, including medical, social, physical, occupational, financial needs etc, utilising the support and expertise of other team members as necessary. Section 75 Partnership Agreements (National Health Service Act, 2006) led to arrangements for the pooling of financial resources and the delegation of certain NHS and local authority health-related functions to other partners. This led to better integration of services and service provision within CMHTs, and care processes were put in place to enable all care co-ordinators to obtain funding to meet the social care needs of people using services.

Until 2007, when the Mental Health Act (1983) was amended, only social workers could be approved by the local authority (following specific training) to become Approved Social Workers (ASWs), and thereby to carry out Mental Health Act assessments and make other specific legal decisions. The Mental Health Act amendments allowed certain other mental health professionals to train to undertake this role, and the qualification and role title therefore changed to Approved Mental Health Professional (AMHP). AMHPs are more likely to be social workers, however. In Scotland they have the title Mental Health Officers.

From the development of integrated mental health services to the present day there have been further stages of development and change. There has been a focus on a greater degree of specialism with separate pathways within CMHTs and within secondary care services generally. As well as separate Adult and Child and Adolescent Mental Health Services (CAMHS), teams in a particular area often include Later Life; Neuro-Development; Assertive Outreach; Forensic and Early Intervention in Psychosis. There are also likely to be Crisis and/or Home Treatment services, Psychiatric Liaison (in general hospital), and others. There are, however, differences emerging in the way services are configured in different parts of the country and these configurations are changing with increased budgetary pressures and increased demand on services. This has, in part, led to the dissolving of Section 75 Partnership Agreements in some English counties. An understanding of the multidisciplinary nature of mental health service provision is important in order to consider the particular opportunities and challenges for social workers using a relationship-based approach in their work with people using mental health services.

Challenges for social workers in this field of practice are characterised by the continuing stigmatisation of people with mental health difficulties, particularly the commonly held fears of perceived unpredictability and aggression which can be perpetuated by the media. Policy has, however, moved towards trying to raise the perception of mental health services alongside those of physical health (Department of Health, 2012). Numerous policy documents have highlighted the discrimination and inequality that people with mental health difficulties have to face (eg Department of Health, 1999; Department of Health, 2006; Department of Health, 2012). Nonetheless, the danger remains, especially in times of 'austerity' and scarce resources, that contemporary mental health practice may resort to excessively cautious risk assessment procedures (and increasingly, the more positivist and scientific/binary risk assessment tools are coming in for heavy criticism in terms of unreliability), and reactive case management. In contrast, relationship-based practice styles offer an opportunity to engage more productively with people using services, their carers and other key participants in the processes of assessment and intervention, to work to reduce the need for restrictive intervention. An understanding and application of relationship-based practice can facilitate and maintain better community-based care and treatment options and reduce the social and economic impact of interventions associated with mental disorder and ill-health. A major strength of relationship-based practice is the ongoing positive and restorative impact the approach can promote throughout the later stages of stabilisation and recovery. When a period of personal instability has been overcome and outcomes appear more positive, the personal subjective interpretation of previous destabilising events can provoke less positive outcomes in interpersonal and family relationships, but the uncertainty and possible fear expressed by those personally involved can be addressed and overcome more effectively with professionals supporting family systems using a relationship-based practice approach. For younger people, however, the notion of 'relationship' is changing. Forming relationships can be undertaken easily now in a digital world without face-to-face contact. Something akin to a moral panic is emerging where the internet is portrayed as a demonic negative force. Currently, professionals lack understanding around how people in distress or experiencing mental disorder interact with online services. Also, online first contact services disregard the importance of human relationships and do not provide the more nuanced interactions required when the professional and the person using the service engage in the initial relationship building stage. This is essential given the emotional and mental vulnerability evidenced in people who become mentally unstable. This is clearly an area where more research is indicated.

Old age

Older people have for a long time been a focus for social policy, and within an ageing society like the UK, the prevailing concerns of predominantly centre-right and right-wing governments in recent decades have been about limiting the costs of state care by promoting social inclusion and independence. Political attitudes have shifted significantly since the introduction of the Welfare State post 1945, particularly in relation to welfare costs, partly due to economic recessions (eg in the early 1970s when the rising cost of oil from Middle East producers impacted on the economies of Western nations like the UK). The global economy forced advanced capitalist countries in the West like the UK to aim to sustain economic growth while incurring low social costs, and, in this respect, the soaring residential care costs for older people during the1980s (Audit Commission, 1986) contributed to the drive for care in the community (or as some feminist writers would label it, low-cost care by the community and by women in particular [Dalley, 1996]). As the 'core business' of statutory agencies narrowed with the expansion of the private, voluntary and independent sector, so rationing replaced universalism in providing support in the community, to the detriment of individual service users and the freedom and professional autonomy of individual practitioners.

As discussed in the previous section, the shift away from professional dominance in services occurred alongside the moves towards community care, which had begun in the 1960s and affected all groups of adults using services. For older people, maintaining independence and autonomy was seen as crucial to retaining active citizenship (Lloyd, 2006). To achieve this, the link between social support, access to social networks and health and well-being was viewed as significant. This was reviewed by McMunn et al (2006), drawing on a range of studies to demonstrate reduced risks of physical and psychological ill health and indeed health benefits from access to social support in old age, through increased confidence, self-esteem and practical and financial resources arising from emotional, practical and informational support. These benefits were also summarised in the government document *Mental Capital and Wellbeing* (Government Office for Science, 2008) and this broad aim was fundamental to the Coalition Government's Vision for Adult Social Care (Department of Health, 2010), which looked to a transformation within adult social care, from the state to local communities to benefit individuals through diverse service provision, community involvement and community development and closer working between the NHS and local services including social care, early intervention and prevention to reduce isolation and improve health and well-being.

Social care has a comprehensive role to play in promoting the psychological and physical well-being of older people from 'lower level' preventative input to more 'acute' provision through intermediate care which facilitates an older person's transition back into the community following a hospital admission, or into longer-term care when living in the community is no longer viable for an individual. The organisation and delivery of Adult Care Services in England which include services for older people have, since the 1980s, gradually moved from a service-led, through to a needs-led and care managed form of delivering care, and then towards a personalised approach involving direct payments, individual self-assessment and individual budgets (see section on Personalisation below). The changes were first introduced in the NHS and Community Care Act 1990 (implemented in 1993), which was a neo-liberal piece of legislation introduced by the Conservative Government of Margaret Thatcher, imbuing public services with the principles and practice of the private sector, introducing private providers and a mixed economy of care which would significantly reduce the heavy reliance on local authority provided and managed services, with the marketplace improving quality through the three 'Es' (economy, efficiency and effectiveness) alongside the market discipline created by consumer choice. The modernising agenda of the Labour Government in the late 1990s (Department of Health, 1998) did not significantly challenge this policy trend and developed policies and legislation aimed at giving adults in need of formal support services more control over how their care needs should be met, with, in addition, increasing acknowledgement by government (Department of Health, 1999, 2008 and 2010) of the crucial support offered by informal carers within the welfare mix. *Modernising Social Services: Promoting Independence, Improving Protection, Raising Standards* (Department of Health, 1998) was supported by three other White Papers – *The New NHS: Modern, Dependable* (Department of Health, 1997), *Modern Local Government: In Touch with the People* (Deputy Prime Minister, 1998) and *Modernising Government* (Cabinet Office, 1999). There were key themes common to all these papers that emerged from the underlying political philosophy and policy prioritisation contained within them all, which impacted on the organisation and delivery of social services to older people in this country in the years that followed their publication. Relevant to the present discussion are the themes of:

» developing prevention strategies and services, promotion of well-being, and support for increasing independence;

» a partnership approach across the health and social care sector and more widely, to include participation of service users and the wider community.

From the year 2000 onwards, under 'New Labour', which sought to find a 'Third Way' between the extremes of neo-liberalism and state domination of health and welfare from a more collectivist approach, there was a slow shift from care management to models based more on 'responsibilisation' of individuals and communities, and social inclusion, with a focus on social capital and the collective value of social networks; personal choice and control with continuing emphasis on the service user as 'consumer', while the NHS and local authorities were involved in managing eligibility and funding inequalities; the development of personalisation; the expectation of the integration of health and social care; and managing the costs of care and the increase in the populations (in particular of older people with increasingly complex needs) needing services. In its policy document *Modernising Social Services* (Department of Health, 1998), which included a focus on social work and services for older people, New Labour wanted to ensure quality of provision through mechanisms such as 'Best Value' and performance targets. In pursuance of this, The National Service Framework for Older People (Department of Health, 2001c) introduced a set of standards to promote consistency and clear expectations about what older people and their carers could expect when in need of a service, particularly in terms of who was responsible for doing what, and in making expectations more consistent across different local authorities (and lessening the so-called 'postcode lottery').

Of relevance to the experiences of older people with health and social care needs, the breaking down of the barriers between health and social care has been a preoccupation of government policy makers for some years, as has the emphasis on service user and carer involvement through recognising their valuable knowledge and expertise (see previous section on disability). A significant theme of New Labour's policy approach, the promotion of partnerships, was not without tensions (Lymbery, 2006; Hatton, 2008). Policy documents (Department of Health 2005, 2006, 2007) acknowledged the need to modernise delivery of services in relation to the changing demography, with an increasingly ageing population who are living longer with long-term medical conditions, and 'changing family structures' (Department of Health, 2007). They proposed to do this through partnerships with people using services, their carers and a range of agencies, embracing multi-agency working across the private and voluntary sector with the need for joint planning and commissioning relating to all aspects of adult care, including housing, transport, leisure, health and social care. The National Service Framework for Older People (Department of Health, 2001c) was reviewed in 2006 by the Commission for Healthcare Audit and Inspection, the Commission for Social Care Inspection and the Audit Commission, and the conclusion was reached that to advance the positive experiences of public services for older people, then key areas such as addressing diversity and tackling discrimination, and ensuring partnership and collaboration between services, were essential priorities. This was then further emphasised by the Coalition Government's Vision for Adult Social Care, in which closer co-operation was to be developed between the NHS and local government with the latter taking on new responsibilities, including health improvement responsibilities and the lead role in drawing up joint strategic needs assessments (JSNAs) (Department of Health, 2010, p 14).

The main policy themes discussed earlier, from the late 1990s onwards have, more recently, also found expression in the Care Act 2014. The Act now incorporates Safeguarding (previously carried out through the No Secrets policy and guidelines) and the Act and its accompanying statutory guidance requires local authorities to set up their Safeguarding Adults Board and develop their own policies and procedures based on developing knowledge and research (see Feldon, 2017, pp 197–246). Efforts had already been made to bring in choice and control where possible, through a personalised approach to safeguarding following the No Secrets Review (Department of Health, 2009b), emphasising the importance of empowerment and decisions, where possible, being taken by the individual concerned. The Care Act 2014 also requires local authorities to promote integration and partnership with a wide range of organisations including housing, health and leisure services, in order to ensure they carry out their care and support responsibilities. These range from the provision of residential and nursing care, for rehabilitation/reablement or for long-term care, to care in the home where financial assessments may be required where an older adult must contribute to the costs of their care (see Feldon, 2017, pp 105–20). Communities remain important and autonomy and choice remain central to the provision of support through the personalisation agenda and the well-being principle which is central to the Act, through the promotion of universal services, person-centred care and support planning and the use of personal budgets (see Feldon, 2017, pp 134–5). Preventative work and early intervention are emphasised in order to keep people out of specialist services which enables them to access universal services and retain their independence for as long as possible. Encouraging people to find their own support in their own networks, including the availability of information, is emphasised along with self-assessment of care and support needs and self-direction of the care plan. This can work well with more active and IT-literate older people, but there may be difficulties for older people with complex health and care needs, where energy and motivation are lacking or where mental capacity is an issue. Here the role of informal carers may be very relevant, and will be discussed next.

Carers

Informal care is an unpaid social relational activity and carers are people who look after family or friends who, because of illness, disability or frailty, cannot manage without help and support.

Informal care has a legal definition: under the Care Act (2014) a carer is *'an adult who provides or intends to provide care for another adult (an "adult needing care")'* (Department of Health Care Act Guidance 2014, paragraph 6.16). There is now a large body of literature about carers and caring, much written through feminist analysis of its social construction as a normal and natural activity for women (though men now increasingly take on the role of caregiving to partners in old age). Hollinrake (2013, p 184) discusses in some detail the development of informal care as a policy concept, drawing on feminist critiques, and how Western neo-liberal governments have viewed informal carers as an important resource for the state. The circumstances of carers' lives, such as combining employment and care-giving with other responsibilities, often mean it is more likely they will experience problems with their own well-being and health. The indirect costs of caring, such as lost careers and pension contributions, savings and family breakdown, receive much less attention in the literature compared to the physical, emotional and psychological effects (Arber and Ginn, 1992; Glendinning, 2008; Buckner and Yeandle, 2011; Clements, 2013). As populations age and the demand for care grows, the need for care (and care by families) is growing also. It has been suggested that by 2020 the number of people requiring care will outstrip the number of family and friends available to provide care (Carers UK, 2014). It is against this backdrop that policy and legislative reform over the last 15 years has seen a steady increase in recognition of the need to support carers through increased rights to assessment of need, culminating in the strong focus on carers in the recent Care Act 2014.

The Care Act places an increasing emphasis on carers as 'rights-holders'. It builds upon earlier carers legislation by increasing rights to assessment, based upon appearance of need and rights to public funds via personal budgets for eligible carers giving them parity of esteem alongside the adult with care and support needs. Never before have carers been given access to public funds based upon a national eligibility criterion. Care Act Guidance recognises the benefit of taking a strengths-based approach to assessment, exploring what is working well rather than only what is not, within a caring relationship (Department of Health, 2014). This is an important element of practice because it recognises that caring can be rewarding and people can gain a lot from the role, rather than perceiving it as a burden, which it may become without support. Support planning is the process used in the Care Act 2014 to determine how unmet eligible needs can be met through a personal budget. This follows a decision about eligibility, based upon eligible needs that have a *'significant impact upon well-being'* (see Department of Health, Care Act Guidance 2014, paragraph 6.117). Necessary care is also legally defined as *'If the carer is providing care and support for needs which the adult is capable of meeting themselves, the carer may not be providing necessary support'* (paragraph 6.119). In other words, if a carer is doing something for someone that they are more than capable of doing for themselves, for example, preparing meals or support with personal care, then this may not constitute *necessary* care. The Guidance (paragraphs 6.125, 6.126) suggests that *significant* must be understood to have its 'everyday meaning'. Local authorities have to consider whether the carer's needs and their inability to achieve the outcomes will have an important, consequential effect on their daily lives, their independence and their own well-being. In making this judgement, local authorities should look to understand the carers' needs in the context of what is important to them. The impact of needs may affect different carers in different ways, because what is important to one individual's well-being may not be the same in all cases.

Despite these changes, informal care remains undervalued in welfare systems and the Care Act with its focus on carers as 'rights-holders' represents a government attempt to manage the tension between a policy need to draw on informal care and support while recognising this otherwise hidden and private aspect of the economy that has become more exposed as a result of economic challenges and demographic changes. Clements' (2013) paper *Does Your Carer Take Sugar?* suggests that the gendered nature of caring must be viewed in the context of a neo-liberal framework. It is the hostility to dependency inherent in the neo-liberal approach to welfare that leads to the social exclusion that carers experience.

Personalisation

The promotion of the independence of the individual 'consumer' of social care is a narrative that is integral to the marketisation of the social care system. Neo-liberal ideology emphasises the ability of the individual to pursue their own self-interest independent of state intervention – based on the liberal values of liberty and autonomy (Rogowski, 2010, p 29). This has been translated into the system through the policy of personalisation (Leadbetter et al, 2008) emerging from the New Labour think-tank, 'Demos', and representing the adherence of the New Labour (1997–2010) administration to the market economy, through continuing to use practices, or investment, from the private sector, in continuation of previous Conservative administrations' reforms (Rogowski, 2010, p 104).

New Labour's agenda of modernisation and transformation of social services (Department of Health, 1998) proposed more user-centred services and the promotion of independence. Personalisation represented a new and different approach to working with people who use services, away from the more traditional, dependency-inducing form of care and service delivery – moving instead towards a more equal relationship in the planning and receiving of support. Power differences have to be considered within the relationship between the social worker and their organisation and how power is experienced by the adult in receipt of support. Personalisation would seem a logical step to further inclusion for marginalised groups, with its emphasis on choice and control, where possible using universal resources in the community. As a strategy to shift the balance of power away from the professional to the person using a service, it should enable the person to have complete control over how their needs are defined, how their rights are recognised and how interventions to address these are delivered. Personalisation was officially introduced through the Ministerial Concordat, 'Putting People First: A Shared Vision and Commitment to the Transformation of Adult Social Care' (Department of Health, 2007), which aimed to reform the way in which individuals eligible for services are positioned within the system. Instead of organisations being at the centre of the service, fitting people in to what they are offering, it proposed to turn this around completely and ensure that the person receiving the service is at the centre, with the organisation working around them. However, this policy direction was not without tension and contradiction. LeGrand et al commented that, in some cases:

consumers of health and social care may not possess the usual attributes of sound judgement and rationality that consumers are usually assumed to possess.

(LeGrand et al, 2008, p 55)

Provision is there through the Mental Capacity Act 2005 for those without capacity to have someone who can act in their best interest (though this may bring soul searching and moral questioning for those taking on this role). However, in particular in the period of austerity that has followed the banking crash in 2008, financial restrictions on spending have led to much more targeted provision and, arguably, a less 'provision-laden counter' from which the 'consumer' can exercise choice and control. Ferguson (2007) has contended that personalisation involves the de-professionalisation of social work and a tacit acceptance of its marketisation. In this sense, it can be seen to be prompted more by a modernisation strategy which set out to manage demographic and financial pressures within a continuing diminishment of the state for ideological purposes. However, at the level of practice, and from the perspective of managing finances, the way personal budgets are managed offers a more transparent process in which outcomes for the individual are tightly tied in to budgets and spending.

So, personalisation is a complex and multilayered concept, which, while it should carry a social justice message and motive (Duffy, 2006) with the importance it places on the person using services as a citizen (Duffy, 2010), also responds to wider financial pressures within the economy and a political agenda wedded to a neo-liberal view of the role of the state. From the perspective of the individual seeking or using a service, it should provide an experience that is person-centred and relationship-based. Personal budgets can, however, prove stressful and there is evidence to show that their impact is mixed. In the Think Local Act Personal (TLAP) Survey (2017), around three-quarters of people reported that the support they get was good or very good in terms of amount of support received, the quality and dignity involved, and choice and control, but people were less positive about the impact of support on everyday activity like relationships and taking part in the community. However, personal budgets are just one aspect of personalisation, and as the Care Act 2014 confirms, other important aspects are market and provider development, information and advice and co-production, which will be discussed next.

Co-production

Co-production has come into prominence in policy developments in recent years and is rooted within the personalisation agenda, viewing individuals and communities in their own unique context as agents for change. It starts with the belief that people have the capacity and resources within, whether that be knowledge, skills or experience, to support themselves in managing life events. Where help is needed, it is provided on the basis that people develop expertise by experience, through informal and subjective routes. Co-production features in several parts of the Guidance for the Care Act 2014, including at a 'one-to-one' level, when an individual using services influences the support and services received, or when groups of people get together to influence the way that services are designed, commissioned and delivered. A definition of co-production is included in the Care Act 2014, as follows:

Local authorities should, where possible, actively promote participation in providing interventions that are co-produced with individuals, families, friends, carers and the community. 'Co-production' is when an individual influences the support and services received, or when groups of people get together to influence the way that services are designed and delivered.

As a means of ensuring that the overall aims of the Care Act 2014 are achieved, co-production should be considered in the implementation of all aspects of the Act from information provision, prevention, the promotion of well-being and the achievement of positive outcomes for people using services.

At a policy level, co-production was first referred to in the White Paper 'Putting People First' (Department of Health, 2007), and has played a significant part more recently in the trajectory of increasing inclusion for people with learning difficulties, physical disabilities and those with mental ill health.

Nesta, a charity which aims to support the development of innovative and more efficient public services, produced a definition (Boyle and Harris, 2009, p 11) based on principles of reciprocity and mutuality, which states that:

Co-production means delivering public services in an equal and reciprocal relationship between professionals, people using services, their families and their neighbours. Where activities are co-produced in this way, both services and neighbourhoods become far more effective agents for change.

This definition makes it clear that co-production is wider than the Care Act definition of the involvement of people using services with local government, encompassing other members of the community or the public more widely, and seeking change. Indeed, Cahn held that:

By creating parity for individuals and communities in their relationships with professional helpers, it gave promise of effecting systemic change.

(Cahn, 2004, p 23)

Cahn also highlighted four core characteristics that identify co-production – individuals' assets and expertise (which professionals had traditionally overlooked); a revaluing of work to encompass activity in the non-market economy such as informal caring; reciprocity, (which emphasises the human impulse for giving back after receiving), and inter-dependency; and the importance of social capital, and social infrastructure which is built through trust, reciprocity and civic engagement (Cahn, 2004, p 24). Cahn is clear that professionals have to change in the way they work with individuals and communities through a process of sharing power and control that eschews professional exploitation and gain (in esteem, approval and salary through taking the credit for effecting change for those using services) and profes-sional domination of problem definition and solution. This has to be replaced by the drive for social justice.

Allied to the above notion of the realignment of professional and lay relationships is the work of Dzur (2008) in his book *Democratic Professionalism, Citizen Participation and the Reconstruction of Professional Ethics, Identity and Practice*. Dzur critiques the work of radical thinkers on the role of 'technocratic' professionalism (in the service of a state elite and their dominant policy paradigm) in contemporary western societies, and finds signifi-cance in their views of the professions as buffers between the state and the lay community, which serve to disempower and immobilise the latter and undermine democracy, through their status and authority, decision-making power, specialist knowledge and 'task mon-opoly' (Dzur, 2008, p 92). Dzur suggests that dismissing professionals in order to empower marginalised groups, as some radical critics propose, misses the opportunity to utilise enlightened professionals, working together with lay people, to develop civic participation and serve a broader democracy through 'democratic professionalism'– ie professionals *'as facilitators in a more active and engaged democracy'* (p 105) based within citizen par-ticipation and citizen action. This approach characterises a 'social justice' approach to relationship-based practice which will be explored in more detail and illustrated in a var-iety of ways in discussion and in practice examples, using the IDEAS model, in the chapters that follow in Part 2.

In practice, co-production points to important shifts in organisational culture that char-acterise people who use services/citizens as active asset-holders rather than passive con-sumers; the relationships between people using services and professionals as collaborative and not paternalistic; and a focus on not just changing service agendas but on outcomes for people, a feature emphasised in the Care Act Guidance (2015). Service users' expertise is invaluable and can help to improve services, but this requires a shift in culture within organisations to be successful. Professionals have to be prepared to share power, and ser-vice users have to be prepared to take decisions – sometimes difficult ones – to ensure that power and responsibility is fully shared within a relationship. An example which illustrates the complexities of this shift in practice is provided in Part 2, in the chapter on relationship-based work with people with learning disabilities (see pp 81–3).

The Care Act's preventative emphasis on harnessing the power of communities to respond to need, looking more to people's natural networks for support and considering ways that communities can be more welcoming of diversity ripples through the guidance. This is important to consider because a duty is placed upon local authorities to consider how a prevention offer may help to reduce or delay the onset of, for example, a carer's needs. The expertise element will reflect on the complementary tension that neo-liberal frameworks pose when prevention considers natural networks (ie families) as the first responders to need at the same time as advocating the rights of carers to self-determination.

Conclusion

In broad terms, the changes outlined across a range of services and supports for adults represent, for professionals and for adults who use services, a transition from the 'charity', or 'professional gift' model (where the individual accessing the service is at the bottom of a chain controlled by the state with professionals as experts and controllers of service delivery), to an 'empowerment' or 'citizenship' model, with individuals and their carers as central to the process (Duffy, 2006).

The following are core principles and issues that find expression in the current legal and policy frameworks common to working with adults:

» The promotion of well-being.

» The promotion and supporting of independence, capacity and personal agency.

» The pursuit of equality and social justice through practice that is anti-racist, anti-oppressive and anti-discriminatory, and adheres to the principles of human rights, to challenge the impact on people using services who are vulnerable to the effects of being pathologised, demonised, infantilised and marginalised.

» The drive for integration of health and social care: policy and guidance, including the Care Act 2014, stresses that Health and Social Care teams should be integrated where this will deliver better outcomes for people.

Taken together, these core principles offer a context for an appreciative and strengths-based approach to social work with adults. The positive impacts of viewing people who use services and their carers as having strengths and resources can support a positive framing for the normalisation and humanisation of need, vulnerability, disability and disadvantage. These can be alleviated or ameliorated through the promotion of personal agency, personalisation (and personal budgets), the provision of advocacy and representation through collective organisation (service user groups) in co-production, and working in a person-centred and relationship-based way to promote social justice can achieve positive outcomes for people using services. Locating and utilising the strengths and power available to people using services, including methods of self-actualisation and group empowerment, can be key to determining how service users and carers can establish and maintain their own safety and well-being. These concepts, however, can be problematic and their application over-simplified, as this chapter suggests.

The delivery of the personalisation and co-production agendas reveals tensions and contradictions, as outlined earlier. Their ability to construct a fully participative approach has been questioned in relation to the tension between 'value for public money', diminishing services in a period of austerity, and a 'rights-based' approach consistent with professional values (Galpin, 2009, pp 101–5), so that practitioners (and people using services) may feel compromised and demoralised in practice. However, it is a belief within this book that political awareness of the impact of structural issues and a relationship-based approach that promotes honesty, trust and openness can together support practitioners in providing opportunities for change and improvement for individuals in the pursuance of social justice. From a human rights perspective, Ife (2008, p 210) states that:

social work is constantly being redefined ... it is important for human rights-based social workers to become part of that redefinition and actively engage in the processes of re-structuring, so that structures more conducive to the realization of human rights can be facilitated.

The reader is now invited to explore the final chapter in Part 1, which introduces the IDEAS model as a framework for exploring the key elements of practice in a relationship-based approach to working with adults.

Further reading

Brammer, A and Pritchard-Jones, L (2019) *Safeguarding Adults* (2nd edn). Basingstoke: Palgrave Macmillan.

Feldon, P (2017) *The Social Worker's Guide to the Care Act 2014*. St Albans: Critical Publishing.

Johns, R (2014) *Capacity and Autonomy*. Basingstoke: Palgrave Macmillan.

Johns, R (2017) *Using the Law in Social Work*. London: Learning Matters.

References

Amnesty International UK (2017) Tackling Hate Crime in the UK: A Background Briefing Paper from Amnesty International UK. [online] Available at: www.amnesty.org.uk/files/Against-Hate-Briefing-2.pdf (accessed 29 January 2019).

Arber, S and Ginn, J (1992) Class and Caring: A Forgotten Dimension. *Sociology* 26(4): 619–34. Available through Albert Sloman Library (accessed 25 June 2018).

Audit Commission (1986) *Making A Reality of Community Care*. London: Audit Commission.

Bache, I, Reardon, L and Anand, P (2014) *Happiness, Well-Being and the Role of Government: The Case of the UK*. Paper presented at Well-being 2013 conference, 24–25 July.

Beresford, P, Fleming, J, Glynn, M, Bewley, C, Croft, S, Branfield, and Postle, K (2011) *Supporting People: Towards a Person-centred approach*. Bristol: Policy Press and Joseph Rowntree Foundation.

Birrell, I (2018) A Teen with Autism Is Locked in Solitary Confinement and Being Fed through a Hatch: Have We Really Moved on from Bedlam? *iNews, The Essential Daily Briefing* 7 October 2018. [online] Available at: https://inews.co.uk/opinion/nhs-treatment-learning-difficulties-bedlam (accessed 29 January 2019).

Boyle, D and Harris, M (2009) *The Challenge of Co-production*. London: NESTA.

Brammer, A and Boylan, J (2017) *Critical Issues in Social Work Law*. London: Palgrave Macmillan.

Buckner, L and Yeandle, S (2011) Valuing Carers. [online] Available at: http://circle.leeds.ac.uk/files/2012/08/110512-circle-carers-uk-valuing-carers.pdf (accessed 31 May 2019).

Cabinet Office (1999) *Modernising Government*. London: The Stationary Office. [online] Available at: https://webarchive.nationalarchives.gov.uk/20131205110329/http://www.archive.official-documents.co.uk/document/cm43/4310/4310-00.htm (accessed 6 March 2019).

Cahn, E S (2004) *No More Throw Away People: The Co-production Imperative*. Washington, DC: Essential Books.

Carers UK (2014) *The Cost of Caring – Impact Report*. [online] Available at: www.carersuk.org/for-professionals/policy/policy-library/caring-family-finances-inquiry (accessed 31 May 2019).

Carers UK (2016) *Annual State of Caring Survey.* [online] Available at: www.carersuk.org/for-professionals/policy/policy-library/state-of-caring-2014 (accessed 31 May 2019).

Clements, L (2013) 'Does Your Carer Take Sugar?'– Carers and Human Rights. *Washington & Lee Journal of Civil Rights & Social Justice*, 19(1): 397–434. [online] Available at: www.lukeclements.co.uk/does-your-carer-take-sugar-carers-and-human-rights (accessed 25 April 2019).

Council of Europe (1950) *European Convention on Human Rights.* Rome, Italy: Council of Europe.

Dalley, G (1996) *Ideologies of Caring: Rethinking Community and Collectivism.* London: Macmillan.

Department of Health (1989) *Caring for People: Community Care in the Next Decade and Beyond.* White Paper Cmnd. 849, London: HMSO.

Department of Health (1991) *Care Management and Assessment: Summary of Practice Guidance.* London: Department of Health.

Department of Health (1997) *The New NHS: Modern, Dependable.* London: HMSO.

Department of Health (1998) *Modernising Social Services.* London: HMSO.

Department of Health (1999) *The National Service Framework for Mental Health: Modern Standards and Service Models.* London: The Stationery Office.

Department of Health (2001a) *Valuing People: A New Strategy for Learning Disability for the 21st Century*. London: Department of Health.

Department of Health (2001b) *Nothing About Us, Without Us.* London: Department of Health.

Department of Health (2001c) *The National Service Framework for Older People.* London: HMSO.

Department of Health (2005) *Independence, Well-being and Choice: Our Vision for the Future of Social Care for Adults in England* (Green Paper). London: Department of Health.

Department of Health (2006) *Our Health, Our Care, Our Say.* London: Department of Health.

Department of Health (2007) *Putting People First: A Shared Vision and Commitment to the Transformation of Adult Social Care.* London: Department of Health.

Department of Health (2008) *Transforming Adult Social Care.* London: Department of Health.

Department of Health (2009a) *Valuing People Now: A New Three Year Strategy for People with Learning Disabilities. Making It Happen for Everyone.* London: Department of Health. [online] Available at: http://webarchive.nationalarchives.gov.uk/20130107105354/http:/www.dh.gov.uk/prod_consum_dh/groups/dh_digitalassets/documents/digitalasset/dh_093375.pdf (accessed 25 April 2019).

Department of Health (2009b) *Report for Consultation: The Review of No Secrets Guidance.* London: Department of Health.

Department of Health (2010) *A Vision for Adult Social Care: Capable Communities and Active Citizens.* London: Department of Health.

Department of Health (2011) *Caring for Our Future: Shared Ambitions for Care and Support.* London: Department of Health.

Department of Health (2012) *No Health Without Mental Health: Implementation Framework.* London: HM Government.

Department of Health and Social Care (2019) *Strengths-based Approach: Practice Framework and Practice Handbook.* London: Department of Health and Social Care. [online] Available at: https://assets.publishing.service.gov.uk/government/uploads/system/uploads/attachment_data/file/778134/stengths-based-approach-practice-framework-and-handbook.pdf (accessed 6 March 2019).

Department of Health and Social Security (1969) *Report of the Committee of Enquiry into Allegations of Ill Treatment of Patients and Other Irregularities at the Ely Hospital, Cardiff* (Howe Report) Cmnd 3785. London: Her Majesty's Stationery Office.

Deputy Prime Minister (1998) *Modern Local Government: In Touch with the People.* [online] Available at: www. politicsresources.net/docs/DETR1998.pdf (accessed 6 March 2019).

Dilnot, A (2011) *Fairer Care Funding Report: The Report of the Commission on Funding of Care and Support (Dilnot Report).* [online] Available at: http://webarchive.nationalarchives.gov.uk/20130221121529/https://www.wp.dh. gov.uk/carecommission/files/2011/07/Fairer-Care-Funding-Report.pdf (accessed 25 April 2019).

Disability Rights UK (2014) *Independent Living: Disability Rights UK Factsheet F38.* [online] Available at: www. disabilityrightsuk.org/independent-living-0 (accessed 25 April 2019).

Duffy, S (2006) *Keys to Citizenship: A Guide to Getting Good Support for People with Learning Disabilities* (2nd edn). Birkenhead: Paradigm.

Duffy, S (2010) The Citizenship Theory of Social Justice: Exploring the Meaning of Personalization for Social Workers. *Social Work Practice*, 24(3): 253–65.

Dzur, A W (2008) *Democratic Professionalism: Citizen Participation and the Reconstruction of Professional Ethics, Identity and Practice.* University Park: Pennsylvania State University Press.

Feldon, P (2017) *The Social Worker's Guide to the Care Act 2014.* St Albans: Critical Publishing.

Ferguson, I (2007) Increasing User Choice or Privatising Risk? The Antinomies of Personalisation. *British Journal of Social Work*, 37(3): 387–403.

Galpin, D (2009) Personalisation: From Consumer Rights to Human Rights. In Galpin, D and Bates, N (eds) *Social Work Practice with Adults* (pp 1–15). Exeter: Learning Matters.

Goffman, E (1968) *Asylums – Essays on the Social Situation of Mental Patients and Other Inmates.* Harmondsworth: Penguin.

Government Office for Science (2008) *Mental Capital and Wellbeing: Making the Most of Ourselves in the 21st Century.* London: Government Office for Science. [online] Available at: https://assets.publishing.service.gov. uk/government/uploads/system/uploads/attachment_data/file/292450/mental-capital-wellbeing-report.pdf (accessed 25 April 2019).

Hatton, K (2008) *New Directions in Social Work Practice.* Exeter: Learning Matters.

HM Government (2007) *Putting People First: A Shared Vision and Commitment to the Transformation of Adult Social Care.* London: Home Office.

Hollinrake, S (2013) Informal Care. In Gabe, J and Monaghan, L F (eds) *Key Concepts in Medical Sociology* (pp 183–8). London: Sage.

Ife, J (2008) *Human Rights and Social Work: Towards Rights-based Practice.* Melbourne: Cambridge University Press.

Johns, R (2017) *Using the Law in Social Work.* London: Sage/Learning Matters.

Law Commission (2011) *4.6 UK Law Commission Review of Adult Social Care.* London: Law Commission. [online] Available at: www.proceduresonline.com/jersey/adults/chapters/plawcommission.html (accessed 6 March 2019).

LeGrand, J, Popper, C and Smith, S (2008) *The Economics of Social Problems* (4th edn). Basingstoke: Palgrave Macmillan.

Leadbetter, C, Bartlett, B and Gallagher, N (2008) *Making It Personal.* London: Demos.

Lloyd, L (2006) A Caring Profession? The Ethics of Care and Social Work with Older People. *British Journal of Social Work*, 36: 1171–85.

Lymbery, M (2006) United We Stand? Partnership Working in Health and Social Care and the Role of Social Work in Services for Older People. *British Journal of Social Work*, 36(7): 1119–34.

McMunn, A, Breeze, E, Goodman, A, Nazroo, J and Oldfield, Z (2006) Social Determinants of Health in Old Age. In Marmot, M and Wilkinson, R (eds) *Social Determinants of Health* (2nd edn). Oxford: Oxford University Press.

Mencap (2008) *Changing Attitudes.* London: Mencap.

Mencap (2015) *Changing Attitudes to Learning Disability: A Review of the Evidence.* London: Mencap.

National Health Service Act (2006) [online] Available at: www.legislation.gov.uk/ukpga/2006/41/contents (accessed 10 March 2019).

Needham, C and Carr, S (2009) *Co-production: An Emerging Evidence Base for Adult Social Care Transformation.* Social Care Institute for Excellence, Research 19 Briefing 31. London: SCIE.

NHS (1999) *The National Service Framework for Mental Health Modern Standards and Service Models.* [online] Available at: www.gov.uk/government/publications/quality-standards-for-mental-health-services (accessed 10 March 2019).

Nirje, B (1969) The Normalisation Principle and Its Human Management Implications. In Kugel, R and Wolfensberger, W (eds) *Changing Patterns for Residential Services for the Mentally Retarded* (pp 179–95). Washington, DC: President's Committee on Mental Retardation.

O'Brien, J (1986) A Guide to Personal Futures Planning. In Bellamy, G and Wilcox, B (eds) *The Activities Catalog: A Community Programming Guide for Youth and Adults with Severe Disabilities* (pp 171–90). Baltimore: Paul H. Brookes Publishing Company.

O'Brien, J and Tyne, A (1981) *The Principle of Normalisation: A Foundation for Effective Services.* London: Campaign for Mentally Handicapped People.

Oliver, M (1990) *The Politics of Disablement.* Basingstoke: Macmillan.

Oliver, M (2009) *Understanding Disability: From Theory to Practice* (2nd edn). Basingstoke: Palgrave Macmillan.

Oswin, M (1971) *The Empty Hours: A Study of the Weekend Life of Handicapped Children in Institutions.* Harmondsworth: Penguin.

Oswin, M (1978) *Children Living in Long-Stay Hospitals.* Spastics International Medical Publications Research Monograph No. 5. London: Heinmann Medical.

Rogowski, S (2010) *Social Work: The Rise and Fall of a Profession?* Bristol: Policy Press.

Scope (2008) *Getting Away with Murder. Disabled People's Experiences of Hate Crime in the UK.* [online] Available at: www.scope.org.uk/scope/media/images/publication%20directory/getting-away-with-murder.pdf (accessed 20 January 2019).

Stainton, T (2000) Equal Citizens? The Discourse of Liberty and Rights in the History of Learning Disabilities. In Brigham, L, Atkinson, D, Jackson, M, Rolph, S and Walmsley, J (eds) *Crossing Boundaries. Change and Community in the History of Learning Disability* (pp 87–101). Kidderminster: Bild.

Think Local Act Personal (TLAP) (2016) *Developing a Well-being and Strengths-based Approach to Social Work Practice: Changing Culture.* [online] Available at: www.thinklocalactpersonal.org.uk/Latest/Developing-a-Wellbeing-and-Strengths-based-Approach-to-Social-Work-Practice-Changing-Culture (accessed 6 March 2019).

Think Local Act Personal Act (TLAP) (2017) *Personal Outcomes Evaluation Tool (POET) for Adults in Receipt of Social Care Support – 2017 Report.* [online] Available at: www.thinklocalactpersonal.org.uk/Latest/Personal-Outcomes-Evaluation-Tool-POET-for-adults-in-receipt-of-social-care-support-2017 (accessed 5 June 2019).

Wolfensberger, W (1969) The Origin and Nature of Our Institutional Models. In Kugel, R and Wolfensberger, W (eds) *Changing Patterns in Residential Services for the Mentally Retarded* (pp 59–171). Washington, DC: President's Committee on Mental Retardation.

Wolfensberger, W (1972) *The Principle of Normalisation in Human Services.* Toronto: National Institute of Mental Retardation.

Wolfensberger, W (1983) Social Role Valorisation: A Proposed New Term for the Principle of Normalisation. *Mental Retardation,* 21(6): 234–9.

Yeandle, S and Buckner, L (2011) *Valuing Carers 2011.* London: Carers UK.

Heidi Dix and Jennifer Meade

Introduction

Having looked, in the preceding two chapters, at the main theoretical perspectives and concepts pertinent to relationship-based practice, and at the current legislative and policy context, this chapter will introduce the IDEAS framework for Part 2 of this book. This conceptual framework incorporates the key elements that support effective practice and will enable social work students and practitioners to use this as a benchmark to evaluate their individual practice. Managers may also find this framework useful as a quality assurance tool. The framework should encourage the reader to think critically about practice through the application of each of the elements of the IDEAS framework which draw attention to key aspects of contemporary practice that a relationship-based approach is lodged within, and to ensure appropriate consideration of the way in which external influences such as policy, legislation and organisational contexts impact on the internal dynamics of the professional relationship between social worker and people, and how these can be managed to promote the development of a meaningful relationship through which positive change can be achieved – for example, through the use of legitimate authority within a relationship-based approach in the context of statutory social work. The reader will be encouraged in Part 2 of the book to use this framework critically, to understand the barriers and challenges as well as the opportunities that this approach offers.

The Model

IDEAS stands for Influence, Delivery, Expertise, Alliance, and Support. The IDEAS model utilises a framework as an attempt to explain, as simply as possible, a set of interconnected knowledge, skills, attitudes and personal qualities, which research evidence suggests are all part of what it takes to be an effective practitioner in the human services. The framework came from work to develop an 'Effective Intervention Strategy' in a youth justice setting (Dix and Meade, 2013), and the fields of mental health and probation were areas of practice that we drew on very heavily in the creation of this. Although we made the interventions strategy as user friendly as possible, we nevertheless found that there was a tendency to focus on one part of the content (eg recommended interventions) at the expense of another (eg relationship skills). The extent that this occurred varied, with the focus being dictated by the individual interests, past experience and, to some extent, the professional background of the person concerned (Smith and Haaker, 2014). IDEAS was developed to try and counter

Figure 3.1 The IDEAS framework

this and to describe the totality of what it takes for an individual to be an effective worker in a social care setting, or indeed in any of the 'people's professions' (Thompson, 2012) where relationship is the foundation for change.

We originally chose to use the human body as a way of illustrating the concept, as although each part of IDEAS is described separately, they are all vital and have to work together to make up a functioning and organic whole. However, in order to describe the totality of IDEAS, the elements that make it up have been separated out in order to define and distinguish them in a way which is obviously artificial and does not reflect what actually happens in practice. In reality, there are clear areas of overlap between the different elements; however, in terms of the description of the framework we have minimised these in order to give as clear and unambiguous an account as possible.

The introduction and development of practice based on research and the best evidence available is a rapidly developing field and very much a work in progress. We hope that the IDEAS framework offers a useful way to conceptualise and understand the different elements that go to make up 'ideal' practice.

Influence

Influence is the first element of the IDEAS framework. The ability to have and to use influence is essentially about the conscious and positive use of role and personal authority. On first examination it is an idea which may not sit easily with practitioners whose professional education, training and natural style have emphasised the ability to work collaboratively with people. However, this does in fact underpin collaboration with people because it promotes honesty and trust, allowing the worker to be authentic and so appear congruent within the relationship.

To achieve influence requires practitioners to work effectively within the boundaries that statutory or other obligations place round them, and be able to explain what is and is not negotiable clearly to people in ways that make sense to them and still allow space for a working alliance to develop. It requires clarity about the rules, regulations and professional boundaries that are a part of many interactions between workers and people who use services particularly in non-voluntary settings. It is therefore important for *'social workers to be clear, honest and upfront about what elements of the service the clients are being offered choice about, and also what elements are not negotiable'* (Social Work and the Centre for Research on Families and Relationships, 2010, p 2).

As Influence is about the conscious use of authority, an essential component is a recognition of the power differentials that exist not just between people, but between different parts of society. Although there may be some commonalities that workers may share such as experiences of racism, or sexism for example, a working relationship that does not acknowledge that practitioners and people who use services are in different situations, often on both an individual and societal level, is not likely to be effective as it will not achieve trust and will not be based on honesty. Centrally, influence involves an understanding of anti-discriminatory practice and anti-oppressive practice.

Influence is also about recognising the role authority that the worker has and offers an opportunity to bring about change. Exercising influence requires practitioners who will consistently act in ways that mean they are positive role models. The concept of pro-social modelling underpins this aspect of the IDEAS model. Trotter (2010) breaks pro-social modelling down into modelling pro-social values (eg punctuality); identifying and reinforcing pro-social comments or actions and challenging comments or actions which are anti-social. Trotter (2010, p 133) concludes that *'while worker relationship skills are important, they may only be valuable if they are combined with other effective practice skills such as pro-social modelling and problem-solving'.*

As mentioned earlier, we have used the human body as a way of illustrating the interconnected nature of the IDEAS framework. Influence, therefore, is the blood supply which connects all the other elements and is essential to their functioning, but works in the background behind the scenes.

Delivery

The next element of the model, Delivery, refers to the professional tools and systems that support practice and the ability to use them with skill. Perhaps one of the simplest ways to describe this element is that is refers to doing the things that your organisation and/or profession requires you to do within any timescales that have been set and using any tools or processes that have been specified. It includes following the assessment, planning and intervention processes relevant to a particular area of practice and practising within agency policy and procedures. This helps to ensure safe working practices for practitioners and assists in keeping vulnerable people safe. If the human body is used to help explain the concept, delivery would be compared to the skeleton which is the support structure which contains and protects everything else.

There are differing opinions on the purpose of assessment. For example, is it to determine need (Taylor and Devine, 1993), assess risk (Kemshall, 1998), does it provide a 'snap-shot in time', or is it a more fluid process which contains an element of intervention (Turnell, 1999)? However, one common thread that links these differing perspectives is the idea that assessment needs to be undertaken in partnership, with everybody involved understanding the *'purpose, nature and extent of professional involvement'* (Wilson et al, 2011, p 273). Therefore in order to undertake an effective assessment, practitioners need to have a clear understanding of the role and nature of the assessment process that takes place within the organisation in which they are working.

The nature of public services means that these are influenced and shaped by a number of different factors and stakeholders, which include political ideology, government (local and national) and service user movements and as such, organisations are constantly evolving. Depending on the practice specialism, practitioners need to be aware of the regulatory or inspection body pertinent to their specific area of practice so they can ensure they are complying with expected standards, eg practitioners working in residential or community settings will need to be familiar with expectations of the Care Quality Commission.

The extent of focus on process, including prescribed timescales for the completion of assessments and plans, has been criticised in recent times (Munro, 2010; Community Care, 2014). The increase in bureaucratic and managerialist processes can be linked to the rise in 'new public management' (Clarke and Newman, 1997) which suggests that business methods used in the private sector can be applied within public sector services. This view was adopted by New Labour in an attempt to reform public services to make them more effective, efficient and economical. However, critics of this approach (Ferguson and Woodward, 2009; Turbett, 2014) have suggested that this has led to practitioners feeling constrained and disempowered by bureaucratic and managerialist practices. Criticism of this approach has also come from within the business sector itself. For example, the reader is advised to *'reject the idea – well-intentioned but dead wrong – that the primary path to greatness in the social sectors is to become more like a business'* (Collin, 2006, p 1). Delivery is about adherence to organisational processes but it does have to be balanced by the other parts of IDEAS in order to be a useful part of the framework. In common with all the other elements of the IDEAS framework, the concept of 'Delivery' in isolation and overemphasised at the cost of the other part of the framework may be counterproductive and will not on its own achieve good outcomes for people. This element is described as the skeleton as it provides the framework for practice.

Expertise

Expertise refers to knowledge of research and theory in relation to a specific field, and how to translate this into practice, acknowledging the importance of 'practice wisdom', ie knowledge acquired through professional practice and people's lived experiences. Mathews and Crawford (2011) break down knowledge into different types. Expertise draws largely on what they describe as research knowledge – generated by academic inquiry or 'field' research but it also includes practitioner knowledge, 'practice wisdom' gained through reflective practice and draws on the idea that people become 'experts by experience' in relation to their individual circumstances.

Above all others, Expertise is the element that has to be present to allow creativity to flourish since it ensures that innovation is grounded in a solid bedrock of research and expert knowledge. To demonstrate expertise, an individual worker will need to: know what is effective in their area of practice and other closely related fields and know how to apply their knowledge; understand the importance of keeping up to date with new developments; use reflection as a learning tool and be open to feedback and make use of it. They will also require the critical thinking skills to enable them to assess the applicability of a particular approach at a given time and in a given setting (Pollio, 2006). The ability to develop expertise over time is closely related to the support that the organisation gives to continued staff development and its attitudes to learning, but it is also related to individual practitioner attitudes. The practitioner who remains open to learning and continues to be interested and curious about their field of practice is also likely to want to remain up to date and to take care to do so.

It is important that both managers and practitioners understand that what constitutes evidence-informed practice in social work is a contested area. For example, the statement that there is no evidence of the effectiveness of a particular approach is not the same thing as an approach being definitely ineffective, although it is not uncommon to hear the two statements confused. It is important that practitioners know enough to understand that there may not be existing evidence of the effectiveness of a particular intervention simply because research has not been done in that area, or if it has been done it is simply not robust enough to prove things one way or another.

Expertise implies a sophisticated ability to understand that what constitutes evidence-based practice (EBP) is not straightforward and what gets included and left out of definitions of it may be significant in themselves. Smith (2004) points out that while the roots of EBP lie in medicine, a commonly used definition from that field included reference to the *'skills which allow the doctor to evaluate both personal experience and external evidence'* (Sackett et al, 1997, p 71, cited in Smith, 2004, p 8). By the time this definition had been adapted to social work practice by Sheldon and Chilvers (2002, cited in Smith, 2004), all mention of the skills of the practitioner had been left out and the focus was on the use of evidence alone in decision making. Smith (2004) concludes that it is difficult to understand why widely used definitions of evidence-based social work would leave out practitioner skills when clearly a combination of practice wisdom needs to be combined with external evidence.

The question of what counts as evidence, and who decides this, is also discussed by Smith (2004) and he poses challenges to a narrow version of EBP which places emphasis on 'methodological rigour' at the expense of all other ways of gaining knowledge about whether a particular approach is effective or not. Smith (2004, p 13) also points out that *'the reflective social worker uses evidence ... but she also treats her own experience as a source of evidence'*. This process of *'disciplined reflection on practice'* (Smith, 2004, p 14) is not easily measured within a rigid scientific approach but that does not mean it is not helpful and useful in practice. We describe this element of the framework as the mind.

Alliance

This element refers to the use of relationship as a mechanism for change – both with the people who use services and in working with other professionals. The importance of relationships being at the heart of any intervention has been well documented in recent times (Lishman, 1994; Ruch et al, 2010; Trevithick, 2012; Megele, 2015) and is the motivating factor for this book. How a person experiences an intervention about planned work is important; and their involvement and input into decisions and their plan is crucial for its effectiveness.

The social worker needs to be able to demonstrate traditional social work values and qualities such as empathy, respect, warmth and integrity should be the conduits that demonstrate the belief that people have the capacity to change should they wish to do so. Being persistent and hopeful can help people develop a belief in a possible and positive future and this can lead to change taking place (Miller and Rollnick, 2013).

Skills in active listening and mentalisation are important here too. Practitioners need to be able to tune in to both themselves and the lived experiences of others. The tuning in process supports the building of trust and empathy – social workers need to tune in to the individual needs of people, be it their social circumstances or where they are physically, socially and psychologically. Workers also need to tune in to themselves and to consider their own feelings about the relationship to identify any blocks that may be getting in the way – eg through the examination of possible transference and counter-transference issues. Considering personal values and identifying any conflicts or tensions that may exist, together with developing emotional intelligence, can assist the development of relationships. Mayer, DiPaulo and Salovey (1990) describe emotionally intelligent people as those who are able to understand their own emotional responses and those of others, and are also able to regulate their own emotional and physical responses accordingly. Social workers are often working with people at times of crisis, when emotions are raw and heightened. Being able to self-regulate and help to regulate the emotions of others can assist the development of relationships, as well as helping practitioners to remain resilient.

Developing positive relationships with other professionals to ensure that intervention is joined up is also necessary. Shifts in contemporary policy and practice mean that different services such as health and social care are now often co-located and operating from the same premises. In theory, this should mean that effective relationships between providers of services exist. However, an analysis of Serious Case Reviews over a ten-year period (2003–2013) highlighted failures in communication and effective joined-up working between agencies (Hull Safeguarding Adults Partnership Board, 2014). Therefore, traditional social work values highlighted earlier, ie empathy and respect, also need to be adopted when working with other practitioners from disciplines other than social work, particularly when professional values may differ. Being aware of other organisational cultures, ethos and priorities can help to build mutually trusting relationships to benefit people who use services.

Continuing the analogy of the human body, this element would be the heart, clearly linked to the blood, which pumps round the body and therefore enables influence to occur.

Support

Social work is an immensely important profession and one that brings enormous amounts of satisfaction for practitioners, but it can also provide a number of challenges. The need for resilience within practice is increasingly being recognised and there are a number of factors that encourage and support resilience in social workers. These include emotional intelligence, reflective thinking skills, empathy and social skills (Grant and Kinman, 2014). However, organisations also have crucial a role to play in developing resilient practitioners and indeed they have statutory responsibilities to ensure the well-being of employees and volunteers and are increasingly recognising the importance of a work–life balance.

In order for all of the above elements to exist, organisational support needs to be provided at all levels of management. It is important that social workers feel able to take risks, to be creative and to learn from situations if they do not go as planned, without feeling that they will be dealt with punitively. A particularly useful way of thinking about this was described in the first chapter of this part – Eva Kittay's concept of 'nested dependencies' (Kittay, 1999, p 68). This suggests that in order for practitioners to display traditional and emancipatory social work values within their practice, the organisation in which they are operating also needs to be demonstrating these. Frontline and senior managers should model the behaviour they expect staff to model. Support should be provided for staff who take decisions that are reasonable and defensible, whatever the outcome, and thereby contain anxiety.

Investment in supervision is crucial for professional expertise to be developed. Workers should be able to expect regular, high-quality supervision that provides a space for reflection, learning and opportunities to develop professional practice (Morrison, 2005; Wonnacott, 2012). Such supervision also needs to reflect the values expected within practice. Other learning opportunities such as access to quality training and protected time to consolidate learning needs to be provided for staff. Less formal learning can also take place in practice development sessions, reflective circles and, with the increase and access to technology, through web-based learning such as databases and webinars.

Gower College Swansea
Library
Coleg Gŵyr Abertawe
Llyrfgell

Positive relationships need to be developed across all levels of the organisation, which are non-defensive and where giving and receiving constructive feedback is part of the culture. In order to be effective, practitioners need to feel that they are truly working within a learning organisation (Senge, 1990) which takes a whole service approach that reflects the values that lay at the heart of social work. Therefore, we suggest that this element of the model is the muscles that hold everything together. The more they are used, the better the body is able to function and the stronger it becomes.

Conclusion

In summary, a practitioner working in the human services needs to have an understanding of power and authority and use this legitimately, demonstrate a commitment to anti-discriminatory and anti-oppressive practice and apply their knowledge of theoretical modules and concepts while adhering to policies and processes at the same time as drawing on their emotional intelligence to work in partnership with people. The IDEAS model outlined in this chapter provides a useful guide to support practitioners to reflect upon their own knowledge, skills and values, as well as providing a model for organisations to consider whether they are supporting the development of effective practice. Part 2 of the book will now apply the framework to a range of practice settings, which will be used to demonstrate the challenges and opportunities for practitioners working within a relationship-based approach.

References

Clarke, J and Newman, J (1997) *The Managerial State: Power, Politics and Ideology in the Remaking of Social Welfare.* London: Sage.

Collin, J (2006) *Good to Great and the Social Sectors: A Monograph to Accompany Good to Great.* London: Random House.

Community Care (2014) Safeguarding Timescales Should Be Revised to Enable Person-centred Social Work, Report Councils. [online] Available at: www.communitycare.co.uk/2014/04/07/safeguarding-timescales-revised-enable-person-centred-social-work-report-councils (accessed 25 April 2019).

Dix, H and Meade, J (2013) In Practice: Translating Research into Reality. In Stephenson, M and Allen, R, *Youth Justice: Challenges for Practice* (pp 111–34). London: Unitas.

Ferguson, I and Woodward, R (2009) *Radical Social Work in Practice: Making a Difference.* Social Work in Practice series. Bristol: Policy Press.

Grant, L and Kinman, G (2014) *Developing Resilience for Social Work Practice.* London: Palgrave.

Hull Safeguarding Adults Partnership Board (2014) A Decade of Serious Case Reviews. [online] Available at: www.adass.org.uk/media/4654/a-decade-of-serious-case-reviews-august-2014.pdf (accessed 25 April 2019).

Kemshall, H (1998) *Risk in Probation Practice.* Aldershot: Ashgate.

Kittay, E F (1999) *Love's Labor: Essays on Women, Equality and Dependency.* London: Routledge.

Lishman, J (1994) *Communication in Social Work.* Basingstoke: Palgrave.

Mathews, I and Crawford, K (2011) *Evidence-based Practice in Social Work.* Exeter: Learning Matters.

Mayer, J D, DiPaulo, M and Salovey, P (1990) Perceiving Affective Content in Ambiguous Visual Stimuli: A Component of Emotional Intelligence. *Journal of Personality Assessment*, 54: 772–81.

McNeill, F, Raynor, P and Trotter, C (2010) *Offender Supervision: New Directions in Theory, Research and Practice.* Oxford: Willan Publishing.

Megele, C (2015) *Psychosocial and Relationship-based Practice*. Northwich: Critical Publishing.

Merrington, S and Stanley, S (2004) 'What Works?': Revisiting the Evidence in England and Wales. *The Probation Journal*, 51(1): 7–20.

Miller, W R and Rollnick, S (2013) *Motivational Interviewing, Helping People Change* (3rd edn). New York: Guildford Press.

Morrison, T (2005) *Staff Supervision in Social Care (revised edition)*. Brighton: Pavilion.

Munro (2011) *The Munro Review of Child Protection: Final Report. A Child-centred System*. London: The Stationery Office.

Pollio, D E (2006) The Art of Evidence-Based Practice. *Research on Social Work Practice*, 16(2): 224–32.

Ruch G, Turney, D and Ward A (2010) *Relationship-based Social Work: Getting to the Heart of Practice*. London: Jessica Kingsley.

Senge, P M (1990) *The Fifth Discipline: The Art and Practice of the Learning Organisation*. London: Random House.

Smith, D (ed) (2004) *Social Work and Evidence-Based Practice*. Research Highlights in Social Work. London: Jessica Kingsley Publishing.

Smith, N and Haaker, M (2014) *Scoping Effective Intervention*. University of Suffolk. (Unpublished).

Social Work and the Centre for Research on Families and Relationships (CRFR) (2010) *Engaging with Involuntary Service Users in Social Work: Key Themes from Research*. University of Edinburgh.

Taylor, B and Devine, T (1993) *Assessing Needs and Planning Care in Social Work*. Farnham: Ashgate.

Thompson, N (2012) *The People Solutions Sourcebook*. Houndsmills: Palgrave Macmillan.

Trevithick, P (2012) *Social Work Skills: A Practice Handbook*. Buckingham: Open University Press.

Trotter, C and Evans, P (2010) *Offender Supervision: New Directions in Theory, Research and Practice*. Cullompton: Willan.

Turbett, C (2014) *Doing Radical Social Work*. Reshaping Social Work. Houndsmills: Palgrave Macmillan.

Turnell, A and Edwards, S (1999) *Signs of Safety: A Safety and Solution Orientated Approach to Child Protection Casework*. New York: W W Norton.

Wilson, K, Ruch, G, Lymbery, M and Cooper, A (2011) *Social Work: An Introduction to Contemporary Practice* (2nd edn). Harlow: Pearson Education.

Wonnacott, J (2012) *Mastering Social Work Supervision*. London: Jessica Kingsley Publishers.

Part 2

Chapter 4

Relationship-based social work with older people

Mark Dimes

Introduction

This chapter will look at relationship-based practice in the context of social workers working with older people and, through the IDEAS model, we will explore how the landscape of social work in this area of practice has developed over the last few decades and is further establishing itself as a respectful and meaningful platform for interventions.

Generally, when we refer to 'older people', it brings with it a set of assumptions and interpretations, some of which can be construed as stigmatising, wrapped up in centuries of stories and beliefs about ageing. There is variance in how different societies perceive older people, with some perhaps viewing them with greater reverence than our own and other Western-style societies (Alibhai-Brown, 1998). In the UK, it is commonplace to refer to older people as being 'older and wiser', or 'silver surfers', or people of a 'third-age generation'. These terms help to construct positive images of older people who are deemed active and independent. Indeed, only a small percentage of the population ever encounters or requires support from the 'social services' (Gilleard and Higgs, 2007), though this may change. People in older age are often more active nowadays for longer into old age; they have more time available, and in many instances are better off financially than they were 50 years ago. And, they are more likely to question and challenge the medical profession and expectations of quality and standards of care are higher than ever before (see, for example, The Kings Fund, 2013).

However, recent reports (Age UK, 2018, 2019) identify time and again that for those in need of services, expectations of the availability of social care for older people regularly exceed what is actually on offer. The Age UK Report (2017) highlighted that 1.2 million older people with a social care need in England were not receiving the help they needed, with numbers rising as the state-funded system continues to retreat. This poses significant challenges for social workers who are aware of the existence of need every day and not always able to respond in the way they would like. To develop connections and enhance well-being, we need strong relationships, and these are born out of shared beliefs and a shared cultural system, making us intelligible to one another. Yet, it can be argued that this has been undermined over the last decade by the impact of austerity policies so that every day, social workers are dealing with the effects of oppression on the people they work with – eg from the structural impact of poverty, while also, for some time, they themselves have experienced organisational oppression from being audited and performance managed (Lymbery, 2004; Stepney, 2006; Rogowski, 2013).

Social work continues to be procedurally driven, with seemingly ever-increasing amounts of documentation to complete, electronic data to input and understand, and the addition of processes previously carried out by administrators which are now the responsibility and function of social workers. And so, with social workers struggling to find the time to develop the much-needed relationships, the evidence is that they are spending increasingly more time in the office, locked into processes, paperwork and recording systems. How, then, do they influence change and develop effective working relationships within these constraints? Using the IDEAS model, this chapter will explore this question and some of the other issues and challenges facing social workers working within a relationship-based approach with older people. For the purpose of this chapter, the term 'older people' will refer to people over the age of 65, which is now the average state pension age and is going to increase to 66 for both men and women by 2020 (Age UK, 2019).

Influence

Older people often have rich experiences and accumulated wisdom: a life of making and, hopefully, learning from their mistakes, along with observing other people's behaviours and their respective errors and misjudgements. They may be parents and grandparents, and have most likely experienced feelings of love, grief, guilt and regret. They will have well-formed, and sometimes fixed, views and opinions about politics, race and religion. And, most likely, they will have anchored ideas about what it is to be polite and respectful, what it means to be socially acceptable and what they define as appropriate norms and behaviours.

In many cases, older people want to work with the social worker, and with this assumption, we can assert that there is likely to be synergy, especially once shared outcomes have been established. And yet, where these outcomes are not being achieved, other factors could be at play, such as resistance to change and a 'risk averse' approach from the individual concerned, their family or the social worker. A relevant question to ask might be: as a society, have we created a 'culture of dependency' – with the expectation that the state will provide and resolve? Perhaps the answer can be traced back to the creation of the 'Welfare State' and the early thinking and planning behind the establishment of the National Health Service in 1947. Certainly, the gradual withdrawal of state involvement in welfare in the last few decades has largely reduced statutory responsibility to the management of risk and pro-vision of services proportionate to how high this risk is perceived (Bamford, 1990, cited in Rogowski, 2010).

Social workers are therefore influenced and challenged to allow for 'assessed risk' and 'unwise decisions', as directed under the Mental Capacity Act 2005, while families and others may pressurise social workers to provide services/residential care placements as, histor-ically, this was often the solution to managing risk with this group of people, particularly from pre-community care days when social security funding was used to support residential care placements based on financial, rather than care needs, assessments (Bamford, 2015, p 58). This may result in professional collusion through a feeling of responsibility to 'rescue' people. Even though meeting individual care and support needs from 'cradle to grave' has altered in meaning; in practice, expectations can vary significantly. Those people born into the early years of the Welfare State are the very people who are now in old age or fast approaching old age, and for some, there can be an expectation that their problems will be addressed and resolved for them, while others may have an attitude of fierce independence and self-sufficiency, resisting state interference, having digested war-time mottos such as 'make do and mend'. Then, there are others who resist engagement due to the assumed stigma of being involved with social services. This may be because many people see the (often negative) media portrayal of social care, undermining independence and autonomy, and many people have little idea of the nature and context of social work with adults until, through disability or illness, they need help themselves or for someone close to them.

The introduction and development of personalisation, with self-directed solution-finding (eg through a strengths-based approach advocated by the Care Act 2014), has assisted social workers to be more enabling and it promotes resilience and self-determination. It is individually motivational and should not distance social workers from feeling valued and validated in their role. The development of personalisation has been tracked and critiqued in Chapter 2. It requires knowledgeable people (policy, legislation and best practice) who understand risk assessment and risk management, who focus more on what people can do and what they aspire to, and accepts that people make choices and have personal responsibility for their own decision making.

The social worker is therefore a catalyst for change, with a basket full of tools that include: professionalism, openness, honesty, an anti-discriminatory stance, and an active listening approach (utilising appropriate body language, ie eye contact and facial expressions). With an awareness that the pace of the conversation may need adjusting, and in some instances (eg when speaking to someone with dementia) the content kept clear and straightforward, they ask pertinent questions, and are supported by a wide knowledge base to help inform and advise. These skills and expertise frame the democratic use of 'influence' through asking open and sometimes difficult questions, exploring individual preferences, and examining wants and needs. What often sets social workers apart in this setting is their 'chameleon-like' demeanour, adapting to the personality and environment of the person or family they are working with, with an ability to blend in and build rapport. These may be vital qualities that cannot be simply taught, and it is their training that furnishes developing practitioners with the resources to tap into and develop those attributes further, through critical reflection, knowledge of interventions, models and theories, emotional intelligence and self-awareness. Social workers should be mindful of the vulnerability of some individuals, recognising the ease with which trust can be gained with some people and ensuring that they raise awareness with the person, their family, and carers in relation to this vulnerability. Effective use of 'influence' is important in developing positive and effective relationships which should shift the conversation away from discussing deficits to focusing more on capabilities and this, it is anticipated, will result in self-determination, with more likely to be achieved positive outcomes.

'Give a man a fish and you feed him for a day. Teach a man to fish and you feed him for life' (Chinese Proverb). The ethos of giving people the tools to be able to help themselves to live self-sufficiently is empowering. And teaching and supporting people to develop the skills they need for life, so that they can stand on their own two feet without depending too heavily on others, can provide freedom through independence, and interdependence. Some may see social work with older people as 'arranging residential or day care placements' but clearly it is so much more than that, with the enabling of people often overlooked or not understood. Social work is about building relationships and using skills to build trust and engagement. The work is rich and challenging, sometimes conflicting, and often complex. Social workers have a strong value base (see, for example, Beckett et al, 2017) with a sense of fairness and justice, equality, and the promotion of self-actualisation (Maslow, 1943). They often drive along this road with an innate desire to work with people, but with no prior understanding of what that could mean in each individual circumstance, as each person they engage with has lived a life unique. They have to skilfully listen to people, using their influence to give the disadvantaged a voice and in doing so, they may need to challenge the individual, society at large and the state in promoting human rights and protecting vulnerable people.

Case Example

Sue, a White British social worker, had known Brian, also White British, for about three months and this followed on from a referral from Brian's daughter who was concerned about how her father was coping. Brian, who was 69, had recently been diagnosed with motor neurone disease (MND). His daughter wanted her father to go into a residential care home where she believed he would be safe and looked after. He had fallen at home and banged his head recently and was struggling with his mobility and had also been prescribed with anti-depressant medication. Brian was initially reluctant to engage with Sue, telling her that she was wasting her time, that he was a lost cause and that 'the only way I'm leaving here is in a box'. Undeterred, Sue visited Brian a couple of times and phoned him on more than one occasion. Despite the organisational pressure on Sue to close his case file, she persuaded her manager to allow her one more visit. It was on this third visit that Brian 'opened up' to her and told her how worried and how alone he felt. He had lived alone for several years and did not want that to change even though he knew that it was worrying his daughter. After further discussion, Sue established that Brian had a wide range of interests and a good network of friends and family but had lost hope since his diagnosis. With Brian's permission, Sue was then able to support Brian's wish to remain at home by advocating on his behalf, connecting him with a couple of old friends and by discussing the situation with Brian's general practitioner (GP), occupational therapist, and daughter. Brian proactively developed a care and support plan with Sue's help and that helped him regain a sense of control and his daughter was reassured and supportive of the plan. Sue carried the hope and motivation for change for a while, but gradually Brian built up a more resilient approach.

The social worker went through a process and understood that she needed to use her influence, through relationship-building, to gain Brian's trust and form a relationship with him before she could help effect some positive change. When meeting with Brian, she used non-verbal proxemics and kinesics and active listening skills (mirroring, paraphrasing, summarising, probing), solution-focused questions (exploring Brian's best hopes, focusing on his preferred future, and establishing expectations and instances of success) (de Shazer et al, 2007) and she 'tuned in' to Brian's situation, as well as acknowledging the inclusivity and different perspectives of others, such as his daughter. In this way, she made clear what the limits and possibilities of her role were, and used her personal and professional influence to develop trust between herself and Brian, unlock his defensiveness which was based on a fear of being made to do something by more powerful others (like social workers), and revive his hope. This enabled them to together explore other options that were realistic and acceptable to Brian to improve his well-being and quality of life.

However, for various reasons, the outcome may not have been so successful. For example, the manager may have refused Sue another visit (but Sue's assertiveness and use of her personal and professional authority here avoided this outcome); Brian could have continued to refuse support (but her relationship-building skills enabled her to engage with him and gently, but assertively, confront his initial opposition); and, increasingly prevalent, is the pressure to conduct assessment and information-gathering tasks by telephone (which would have lost the benefits of face-to-face communication and possibly undermined Sue's ability to pick up on emotional issues and 'melt' his defensiveness as a means of retaining control). If Brian had continued to refuse support, the social worker may have been left with negative feelings, unable to find a solution and now worried about his perceived vulnerability because of his refusal to accept intervention. Supervision (formal and informal), recording practice, good communication with involved parties, critical reflection, resilience and emotional intelligence are all key to how the social worker manages these feelings and situations, within a value base that encourages individual involvement and influence, in an anti-discriminatory way, to achieve a positive outcome and to effectively find solutions, which is the goal of 'influence'.

Delivery

The role of social work is to *'promote social change and development, social cohesion, and the empowerment and liberation of people'* (International Federation of Social Workers,

2014). By doing this, it is hoped that social workers can help to support the conditions that will lead to a more socially just society. In the 1970s, social work was overtly politicised through the radical social work movement and its preoccupation with class oppression (Bailey and Brake, 1975), which was carried through into other areas of oppression in the following decade, such as race, gender and sexuality (Langham, 1998). However, as discussed earlier, the focus on managerialism and the control of resources through a *'micropolitical regulatory approach, substituting as it does, a focus on interpersonal rather than on social or structural politics'* (McLaughlin, 2008, p 140) shifted the balance. *The Guardian*, in a piece entitled 'A Guide to Radical Social Work', captures opposing views of social work, stating that *'social workers' legitimacy stems from their identity as creatures of the state and a more radical approach would suggest that social work has earned its recognition through an ability to grasp and utilise the transformative political power of the people they work with'* (*The Guardian*, 2016). The reconciling of the different roles ascribed to social work, depending on the political perspective adopted, has to come from its value base which has developed, as described by Jones et al, to *'coalesce and organise around a shared vision of what a genuinely anti-oppressive social work might be'* (Jones et al, 2004, p 4). This requires a relationship-based approach that promotes openness and partnership, and actively listens to older people using services and their carers, to hear what life is really like for them; works alongside them collaboratively to promote positive change, while being open and honest about what the limits of their role and influence are, within the boundaries and constraints of their organisation, notwithstanding the need to challenge these where possible, using their influence, through the use of professional authority with self-awareness and emotional intelligence (see above).

The legal and procedural tools for intervention are to be found in the Care Act 2014 as outlined in Chapter 3. Responsibilities and duties are detailed and interpreted locally and then translated into frameworks and forms for completion before being transferred to agency recording systems. Models of intervention are numerous, with trends varying from the recovery model, to cognitive behavioural therapy, and strength-based approaches. Within these differing approaches, the Care Act 2014 states that the assessment process should be designed around the person's communication needs (Department of Health, Care and Support Statutory Guidance 6.37, 2016). How you communicate with someone needing care and support will likely determine the relationship you form with them. If you can establish good rapport, it will undoubtedly improve the flow of valuable information and insights that help to establish individual strengths and skills that will inform desired outcomes and promote improved independence and well-being. It will also help in the continuing relationship with this person during care planning and reviews. As part of the delivery, social workers build relationships with people, carers, families and communities, so they do much more than just assess, and complete care and support plans and reviews. They help to build confidence, confirm strengths, and re-ignite hope and positivity. The skill is to do both at the same time: simultaneously assessing while building a trusting relationship. The relationship and the skills that the social worker uses in forming and sustaining it are part of the delivery of the service within the system that supports the practice. When working with older people with dementia, then communicating in ways that do not just involve words may be necessary (Woodcock Ross, 2016, pp 232–3).

The Care Act 2014 refers to the assessment and planning process as a 'genuine conversation' and, in doing so, it promotes a shift in the relationship between social worker and the person referred, to something perhaps less rigid and formal in nature. A visit to somebody's home should not really be planned without the social worker conducting research on aspects of the referral and reading, before leaving the office, any previous recording of contact. This is to ensure that the social worker is aware of the person's cultural heritage, preferred lifestyle and specific living circumstances. Relationship building is, therefore, fundamentally important because it helps to determine the constituent parts of the assessment but must be done within the confines of the agency's purpose and remit, so that the person supported has a clear understanding of the reasons why the agency has become involved, the possibilities for support and change, and the limits and boundaries of that involvement. Developing rapport builds trust and openness in a relationship (Covey, 2006) and enables the sharing of concerns and the exploration of risk. Therefore, social workers should make the creation of trust an explicit objective and with this, the barriers to effective communication will be more likely to subside. Minimising formal procedural assessment processes and promoting a 'genuine conversation' can encourage a more collaborative and empowering environment that is more productive and respectful to individuals. Smale and Tuson's 'exchange model' (Smale and Tuson, with Biehal and Marsh, 1993) remains an important model in this respect, not withstanding, at times, the need to use a more questioning or procedural approach, depending on the specifics of the assessment.

'Genuine' and open conversations may require some careful and considered pre-planning to ensure doors are not closed to discussion of important areas for care planning for some service users who identify as LGBTQIA. Heteronormative assumptions in assessments from health and social care professionals using a 'one-size-fits-all' approach may result in older LGBTQIA people receiving poorer outcomes for assessment and service delivery because, even with a personalised approach, they are not provided with sensitively offered opportunities to talk about important relationships. Some people may feel confident to be open about their sexual orientation but others, based on past experiences, may find this difficult. Open, clear and confident questions, with clear reasons for asking but without pressure, presented in a positive way will help to reassure people of the importance of addressing those issues that have a bearing on their health and well-being (see Hafford-Letchfield, 2014). For a more detailed discussion of these issues, then please see Chapter 11.

Social workers do not build and develop relationships solely through communicating with people effectively. It is wider than that and is also based on the subjective view of the person being assessed; how they feel on the day; their expectations of what the worker will deliver and discuss; their own unique human prejudices and experiences; the way the worker presents themselves (ie time-keeping, eye contact, appearance, body language etc) and possible influences from family, carers and/or other people in attendance. The delivery of a 'service' is dependent on the principles of a good assessment and sound judgement, and these will help inform and support the social worker through this process. These are outlined in Section 9 of the Care Act with specific reference to advocacy, timescales, carer needs, strength-based approaches, proportionality and appropriateness. Of note, under timescales is the need to conduct assessments in an '*appropriate and reasonable time scale*', with local authorities being asked to '*inform individuals of an indicative timetable over which their assessment will be conducted and keep the person informed throughout the assessment process*' (Care Act 2014 S9, 6.29). This, more implied, collaborative approach promotes good communication and relies in part on the busy social worker's organisational skills.

Case Example

Social worker Adam was struggling to manage his throughput of work, partly due to the complexities of his caseload and because of the demands placed upon him and the team. Adam designed a spreadsheet that assisted him to plot a process timeline for each service user, enabling him to capture outstanding actions and data and thereby he was more confidently able to 'keep on top of things' bureaucratically. He recognised quite clearly that this functional monitoring missed out the very important process of rapport and, while the spreadsheet identified work to be done, it did not show that people live life at different speeds, with unique lifestyles and personal experiences, and individual perceptions, prejudices and beliefs. And how was risk to be managed and minimised via his spreadsheet?

So, the managerial aspects of the social work role need to be balanced with the person-centred nature of the desired intervention and outcome for the person they are working with.

The Care Act 2014 states that duties under the legislation should be carried out by an appropriately trained assessor (Care Act Support Statutory Guidance 2018, 6.7). So, for local authority social workers, the council policies support the essential role of training and all workers should complete relevant learning and development in relation to the core issues, eg the well-being principle, eligibility decisions, care and support planning, safeguarding, strength-based questions, mental capacity, deprivation of liberty etc. Social workers, predominantly through supervision, personal reflection and training, learn how to overcome challenges and, as they become more competent and confident, they can achieve better outcomes, eg working with people to establish individual strengths, networks, and helping people to consider what is working well and can be built on further. Support through training and supervision is crucial to enable social workers to effectively deliver practice in a way that encourages:

» advocating for individual human rights, supporting people to communicate in a way which works for them (eg utilising appropriate tools; visual, use of interpreter, consideration of cultural norms and values etc);

» an exploration of power dynamics, anti-discriminatory and non-judgemental behaviour;

» the development of self-awareness through critical reflection, coaching, mentoring and feedback;

» evidence-based research and analysis;

» meeting the person's goals/aspirations and thereby avoiding prescribed outcomes.

Expertise

As social workers receive and obtain relevant skills and knowledge, supervision should promote self-awareness and critical reflection. Intra-personal skills will improve accordingly and this development will be crucial to their personal and professional relationships. Crucially, with this development of expertise, it is likely that those social workers who take the time to listen, self-reflect and engage in learning, will be the ones more able to nurture trusting and open relationships with people. For example, as noted in the last section, the Care Act 2014 supports the notion of rapport building with the people we work with through the description of a 'genuine conversation'. But to create effective connections, social workers need to understand and reflect on their own patterns, behaviours and attachments and knowing oneself is key to forming effective relationships. The social work challenge is to individualise the principle of well-being and help maintain the view that individuals are experts and the best judges of what they need for their own well-being. In this sense, both parties bring their expertise to the table to promote the required change – the professional expertise and knowledge (including self-knowledge) of the social worker and the personal expertise and experience of the person being supported.

Case Example

Harold is a 79 year-old White male who has lived alone since his wife died two years ago. He is a wheelchair user and receives support to carry out most of his daily activities, such as washing and dressing. He feels socially isolated and this has led him to feel depressed, with low self-esteem. Harold's daughter wants him to move into more supportive accommodation, but Harold would like to stay at home where he has lived for the past 50 years. With the daughter's agreement, the social worker, Solma, of Bangladeshi origin, works with Harold at his pace, using skills in communication, knowledge about relationship issues (eg attachment theory and loss – of his wife, of his own mobility and independence, and social contacts) and about resources and support services. Together they explore the options and Harold establishes a preferred future that enables him to leave home occasionally and socialise with friends, which helps to boost his confidence and feelings of self-worth. After several weeks, Harold's mood and general well-being have noticeably improved and his daughter is delighted with his progress.

Of course, the concept of well-being differs for each of us, and for one person being able to eat a good balanced diet and to have a daily shower may be essential but for someone else, a strip wash and a micro meal may suffice, and the ability to engage in recreational activities, eg to attend a church, mosque or synangogue or meet with friends, may be a priority for others. And yet another may base most importance on contributing something to society – eg being supported to be a befriender or doing a volunteer job. Listening to and understanding the person is therefore paramount to this conversation. In the foregoing example of Harold, it was the relationship that determined a positive outcome. The social worker, Solma, used her skills and expertise in relationship-building as a platform and made no judgements, gave no opinions, worked at Harold's pace, offered a bridge (hope) towards a different future which Harold could use to create his own and liaised with his family to develop a person-centred care and support plan.

So how do social workers recognise the fake positive smiles? How do they 'get under the skin' of what is being presented to them by the person they are working with? Language, tone, body position, facial expression ... social workers act as behaviour detectives, noticing small incongruent behaviours, picking up signs of conflict and tension because establishing emotions and tuning in to what the person is really thinking and feeling is key to empathy. Howe describes this as a 'visceral' experience (Howe, 2013, p 124) and the quality of the relationship is at the heart of that discovery. And this is not about making assumptions or ascribing value judgements. This is about observation skills, communication skills, collaboration and working with all parties involved, establishing the facts, using incisive questioning, critically reflecting on their own feelings and thoughts and checking things out with people, eg when reflecting back what they have heard from them, or later reflecting with colleagues, reading and evaluating written records and utilising constructive discussions in supervision.

The formation of this insightful and collaborative relationship helps to conceptualise the social worker's role with people, and to facilitate the planning of a normative strategy. Meaningful conversations informed by the social worker's theoretical skills and knowledge (eg see Chapter 2 on attachment theory, hope and strengths-based practice) can help people to understand the root of their thinking and behaviour and only then will they be able to consider lasting change. And fixating on the presenting problem should not be the starting point for any new relationship as everything will not be clear straight away and the development of the relationship will reveal more. Listening attentively with empathy, emotional intelligence (Ingram, 2015, pp 22–3) and respectful acceptance of the person's goals is at the core of this relationship development and drives the agenda for change (see O'Connell, 2012, pp 44–5). The capacity for change is not the same for everyone, and so proceeding at the pace of the person being worked with will help them to realise and decide their own direction and strategy.

Case Example

Lenny, who is a Black African Caribbean man in his 70s, experienced physical frailty and memory loss and had recently moved into a residential care home with the assistance of his social worker, Ben, a White male in his thirties. As Lenny was estranged from his immediate family, Ben commenced conversations with Lenny about the sale of his property and management of his financial affairs. It was clear that Lenny would benefit from some external expertise to resolve this situation, but he was reluctant to engage with this idea and the situation appeared to be stuck. Ben met with Lenny and talked to him using solution-focused questions, as it had already been determined that he had capacity to make informed decisions. At no point did Ben make suggestions or lead Lenny to a preferred outcome or agenda. Ben's role here was to 'tune in' and actively listen to Lenny's wants, hopes, fears and wishes, to ask clarifying questions and then reflect back to Lenny his understanding of what had been said. Establishing the detail became critical to this conversation and within the hour Lenny had reached his own conclusion that he was satisfied with and a course of action was planned and agreed.

This relationship promoted a good attachment and relied on consistent and predictable behaviours that promoted a move away from paternalistic interventions and care management. Understanding someone's life story, and how an individual best makes decisions, helps practitioners to work with people so that they can start to appreciate and empower themselves more and get in touch with their own thoughts and feelings. Utilising the Signs of Safety Practice Framework (Turnell and Murphy, 2017), developing questioning skills in ways that are strengths-based and solution-focused (de Shazer et al, 2007) and using expert knowledge from research and evidence-informed practice (eg on hoarding, dementia, alcohol and substance misuse in older people) will all significantly assist social workers positively in their day to day practice. And social workers need to regularly update their practice in order to be at their best. For example, financial abuse and 'scams' have been well publicised in the last few years (see, as an example, the Association of Directors of Adult Social Services Guidance on Financial Abuse and Scams, 2017) and social workers need this knowledge so that they have insight and know what to do and where to turn for advice, guidance and support.

The loss of a significant relationship can be quite devastating. Indeed, loneliness and isolation can lead people to form inappropriate relationships because it occupies their time, gives them something gainful to do, and perhaps gives some people hope and expectation of what might be. When conducting an assessment, rapport development can be hindered if someone feels embarrassed or ashamed of what they have done or of what has happened in their past – the house is a mess because of neglect, abuse or hoarding, etc and clearly there is a set of skills needed that can help to develop rapport quickly without creating dependency and providing an alternative to any negative behaviour present. Social workers, in tandem with colleagues, supervisors and managers, need to identify when their role and involvement ceases, and this is crucial in avoiding attachment and dependency, referring on to more appropriate input, ie support worker, befriender or neighbour as required.

To bring the required expertise to the professional role, social workers must have knowledge of and work to the relevant legislation (the Care Act 2014, Human Rights Act 1998 and the Mental Capacity Act 2005 being of significant importance); they must ensure that they keep up-to-date with current research and knowledge in the sector; that they empower and uphold the rights of those they work with; and they also need to build emotional resilience (Grant and Kinman, 2014) to cope with a range of experiences involving pain, courage, love, and the devastating impact of poverty on some service users' lives.

Alliance

Consider the people you are currently working with. How many are experiencing difficulties with their personal relationships, either with husbands, wives or partners, sons or daughters? Social workers have a pivotal role in attuning themselves with people to help repair and strengthen relationships. Forming alliances is basic to this. To do this well, understanding your own attachment patterns is critical to this process because understanding the nature, origin and significance of your relationship styles has the potential to help you more easily navigate adult relationships (Howe, 1995). Our ability to understand and identify these attachment patterns is significant for social workers in practice. We will all have experienced different connections, some positive, some that we struggle to understand and appreciate in detail and some that will be dysfunctional and unhealthy. The Dynamic Maturational Model of Attachment and Adaptation, developed by Crittenden (see Chapter 2), is a useful model for understanding attachment patterns as self-protective strategies that have been used across the lifespan to best achieve a sense of safety and predictability in relationships. Once more, the importance of supervision and critical reflection should not be underestimated as these issues are of significance and importance when endeavouring to understand relationships and build trust and effective alliances. We have all developed lifelong interpersonal strategies to respond to threats and danger and these reflect our intra-personal strategy for processing information. Individual attachment is basically the way in which we deal with a perceived threat, in the pursuit of comfort and avoidance of chaos. And we all deal with it slightly differently and there lies the value and significance of understanding the person you are and the one you are working with.

The so-called 'medical model' approach to well-being can be experienced as challenging to the social worker in the formation of effective alliances with medical professionals. For example, a medical professional may refer someone to social care with the advice that this patient 'is not fit to remain living at home' due to a medical condition, or 'this person needs palliative care and needs to be in a nursing home', etc. This approach denies many alternative solutions, eg support at home and enhanced social contact and can sometimes be prescriptive, often considering medication before looking at low-cost social alternatives. Furthermore, our society confers medical doctors with power and authority because of their specialist knowledge and longstanding professional status. Health Coaching and Social Prescribing are two more recent approaches seeking to fill the gap between the medical and social model of care and support. Health coaching has its origins in a solution-focused approach and social prescribing is one of the ten action points referenced in the General Practice Forward View (see NHS England, 2018).

Case Example

Emily is a White social worker of Irish background assigned to work with Alice, a White woman living in an isolated rural village who has been referred to Adult Social Care by her GP, who has stated that she needs to move into a more supportive environment. Alice has been diagnosed with a dementia-type illness and has become increasingly forgetful recently. Her daughter is particularly worried because her mother's diet is poor, she appears to be forgetting to take her prescribed medication and she is isolated. Her daughter suggested that it was time to get some help, although Alice denied that she needed assistance. Prior to visiting Alice, Emily phoned her to ask about her perception of her situation and subsequently wrote to her confirming when she would be visiting her with her daughter. Alice felt reassured and informed about what was happening and with Alice's permission, the social worker spoke to the GP and subsequently visited Alice, with the daughter present. By doing this, the social worker was able to gain much-needed insight from the GP, support from the daughter and some acceptance and credibility from Alice. And this provided the foundation that the social worker needed to develop a trusting relationship with Alice (and the daughter).

This example demonstrates how simple planning and basic collaboration can help to engage with people and develop trusting relationships. It helped to hand back some of the power and control to Alice, perhaps reassuring her that the people around her were working together to support her rather than conspiring against her. Nothing can be guaranteed to work well but the principles of effective communication and timely collaboration support better outcomes for individuals and are inclusive and informative.

Clearly, choice and control, as a policy development, is at the core of person-centred practice and runs as a golden thread through our work with people and into the heart of the Care

Act 2014. Respecting choice must involve helping people evaluate how they wish to improve their lives from an individual perspective, as what may be a perceived improvement, eg moving someone who lives in quite squalid or hoarded conditions to supported housing, may overlook the changes they may prefer, eg a funded blitz clean and enablement service of support to keep on top of things. It may be sufficient (and important for the service user) to maintain conditions at a safe level but not necessarily in a state which may reflect the wider family's values and standards. And social workers also need to be aware of very individual religious, cultural and spiritual beliefs and behaviours (Holloway and Moss, 2010) that can impact on an individual's sense of well-being.

We know that if a person is deemed as having mental capacity to make their own choices, the barriers to personalisation and self-directed support are often with the wider family and other agencies, such as housing, the police, ambulance services, and GPs, all of whom may be more risk averse. The challenge for the social worker is to ensure people have the information they need, the capacity to make decisions for themselves and to take informed risks, accessing services when needed, to plan and create innovative care and support plans. For example, the quick-fix response to hoarding might be to book a skip and clear the house and yet this is likely to fail and the hoarding will most likely return because the behaviour and actions of the hoarder have not been analysed and understood. This can only be effectively achieved through the development of a collaborative and respectful relationship. We need to evaluate patterns of behaviour and underlying feelings and this can be largely achieved by developing a relationship with the person and by making connections, eg when is the behaviour better or worse, what are the triggers and attachments, what's working well, etc?

Another health profession with which social workers working with older people often work in collaboration is Occupational Therapy, which has a crucial role to play in supporting older people to maintain day-to-day functioning in their environment, with the assessment and provision of, eg equipment/adaptations to increase safety, as does the utilisation of assistive technology (ie personal alarms and falls sensors). Part of the social work role is to explain the benefit of such interventions; to help reduce risk, increase choice and control and to support a more collaborative approach.

Personal budgets provided through local authorities rarely meet the full care and support needs of an individual as they are designed to meet 'minimum outcomes'. Within the bounds of their profession, social workers have become adept at individualising care and support plans to help maximise packages of care outside of resource allocation systems. Creativity is important in this aspect of the role, through networking and linking with family and community resources to find appropriate support and skills locally, where possible, with minimal financial outlay. Understanding the person in context, their likes, knowledge and skills are all crucial to this conversation built around effective networks and alliances.

Social workers need to consider the factors that influence professional judgements and decision making and how best they can support the development of these in practice (Helm and Roesch-Marsh, 2017). And after an assessment has been made, they need to reflect on how responsibilities and outcomes have been understood by those involved in the decision-making process, ensuring that a collaborative approach with collective responsibility remains at the heart of the care and support plan.

Support

The seventeenth-century English poet John Donne said that 'no man is an island' and social workers are no exception, requiring the support of others to help them develop the resilience and self-awareness from which they benefit to practise their profession well. Relationships in the office and team, whether uni-professional or multi-professional, are therefore important, especially the relationship between practitioner and supervisor/manager. In supervision, social workers benefit from and need guidance, support and regular formal discussion, and not just about their caseload. Supervision can take many forms, from coaching to mentoring, directing to nurturing and it can be especially important for newly qualified staff. Conversations in this environment need to consider how individuals develop resilience; what coping strategies they use; and how they navigate difficult conversations with the people they are working with, people who they hope will one day be able to make positive, potentially life-changing decisions for themselves.

Supervision that has its roots in solution-focused practice (de Shazer et al, 2007) can be key to this journey, with the supervisor focusing on the supervisee's strengths and resources, asking questions rather than offering answers, listening and finding out what is already working well before exploring ways to do more. Asking the right questions at the right time can be a powerful way to help the practitioner explore their actions, attitudes and behaviours, for example, enquiring about how they managed a difficult situation and, given a similar set of circumstances, thinking about what they would do differently next time; encouraging them to learn from set-backs while validating and acknowledging the difficulty they have experienced. Enabling experiential reflection in this way can effect positive change within the supervisee, helping them to visualise outcomes and focus on noticing signs and indicators of change. Supervisors mirror good practice in terms of listening skills, building strengths and resilience, and also have a role with modelling behaviour, promoting a work–life balance and demonstrating genuine concern and empathy for the individual supervisee's well-being.

Outside of supervision, training has traditionally been lauded as the best way to 'give people the tools to do their job'. A classroom-based 'talk and chalk' approach relies on the social worker transferring their new-found knowledge into the workplace, sometimes against the flow of existing practice and procedural methodology. Reflective learning in teams, modelling by managers, the application of consistent messages and the promotion of blended learning approaches will more likely effect positive change in the organisation. Formal training undoubtedly also has its place in enabling social workers to 'thrive and survive' and provide them with the tools, infrastructure and environment to do their job well, leading to better outcomes for all. This needs to be effectively planned in supervision too to ensure that the practitioner can plan, achieve and progress within the profession. However, indicators suggest that motivation to remain in the profession is compromised by stress and poor working conditions across the profession. An annual survey which started in 2017, conducted by researchers at Bath Spa University on the 'Working Conditions and Wellbeing of UK Social Workers' has found both in 2017 and in 2018 that working conditions are extremely poor and stress symptomology is high. High caseloads and repetitive administrative tasks, as well as hot-desking, are referred to as major stressors but also, relevant for this discussion, is the need for greater support from organisations in the form of reflective supervision for social work staff, in particular for complex and difficult cases (Revalier and Boichat, 2018, p 21).

Conclusion

Relationship-based social work has a focus on acceptance, genuineness and empathy (Rogers, 1957). Social workers need to reflect on their personal and professional boundaries when considering values and ethics in their work, as forming a working relationship can be compared to forming a friendship, especially when there is intensive support and frequent contact involved. Self-awareness and critical reflection are therefore crucial to the social worker in this instance; unravelling and considering their own thoughts and feelings, and being acutely mindful of the language they use and how this will be interpreted. They need to have an awareness of power in a relationship and what this means to individuals when working towards change and improvement, so that individual agendas are explicit.

Social workers need to consider culture, faith and generational differences in their professional relationships. What are the noticeable similarities in attitude, behaviour and approach between you and the people you are working with and how can these presumed positive connections make a difference and impact on your ability to form a strong and trusting relationship with them? The ability to observe and tap into this core of rapport will provide social workers with something to build on, perhaps with small steps initially. Forming strong relationships with all service users may be an unrealistic aim but working to the person's agenda builds momentum, and active listening, good supervision and effective reflection will most likely bring about some useful change for the person concerned.

References

Association of Directors of Adult Social Services (2017) *Financial Abuse and Scams: Guidance for Councillors, Directors, Managers and Social Work Practitioners.* [online] Available at: www.adass.org.uk/media/5799/top-tips-financial-abuse-and-scams.pdf (accessed 25 April 2019).

Age UK (2018) *Behind the Headlines: The Battle to Get Care at Home.* London: Age UK. [online] Available at: www.ageuk.org.uk/globalassets/age-uk/documents/reports-and-publications/reports-and-briefings/care--support/rb_jun18_-the_struggle_to_get_care_at_home.pdf (accessed 31 May 2019).

Age UK (2019) *Changes to State Pension Age.* London: Age UK. [online] Available at: www.ageuk.org.uk/information-advice/money-legal/pensions/state-pension/changes-to-state-pension-age (accessed 25 April 2019).

Alibhai-Brown, Y (1998) *Caring for Ethnic Minority Elders: A Guide.* London: Age Concern.

Bamford, T (1990) *The Future of Social Work.* London: Macmillan.

Beckett, C, Maynard, A and Jordan, P (2017) *Values and Ethics in Social Work* (3rd edn). London: Sage.

Boichat, C and Ravalier, M (2018) *UK Social Workers: Working Conditions and Wellbeing.* Bath: Bath Spa University.

Bailey, R and Brake, M (eds) (1975) *Radical Social Work.* London: Edward Arnold.

Care and Support Statutory Guidance (2018) London: Department of Health and Social Care.

Covey, S (2006) *The Speed of Trust: The One Thing That Changes Everything.* New York: Free Press.

de Shazer, S and Dolan, Y with Korman, H, Trepper, T, McCollum, E and Berg, I K (2007) *More than Miracles: The State of the Art of Solution-focused Brief Therapy.* New York: Routledge.

Gilleard, C and Higgs, P (2007) The Third Age and the Baby Boomers: Two Approaches to the Social Structuring of Later Life. *International Journal of Ageing and Later Life,* 2(2): 13–30.

Grant, L and Kinman, G (2014) *Developing Resilience for Social Work Practice.* London: Palgrave Macmillan.

Hafford-Letchfield, T (2014, updated 2018) *Working with Lesbian, Gay, Bisexual and Transgender Older People. Practice Guidance.* Community Care Inform. [online] Available at: https://adults.ccinform.co.uk/practice-guidance/social-work-lesbian-gay-bisexual-transgendered-older-people (accessed 19 February 2019).

Helm, D and Roesch-Marsh, A (2017) The Ecology of Judgement: A Model for Understanding and Improving Social Work Judgements. *British Journal of Social Work,* 47: 1361–76.

Holloway, M and Moss, B (2010) *Spirituality and Social Work.* Basingstoke: Palgrave Macmillan.

Howe, D (1995) *Attachment Theory for Social Work Practice.* Basingstoke: Macmillan Press Ltd.

Howe, D (2013) *Empathy: What It Is and Why It Matters.* Basingstoke: Palgrave Macmillan.

Ingram, R (2015*) Understanding Emotions in Social Work. Theory, Practice and Reflection.* Maidenhead: Open University/McGraw-Hill.

International Federation of Social Workers (2014) Global Definition of the Social Work Profession. [online] Available at: www.ifsw.org/what-is-social-work/global-definition-of-social-work (accessed 25 April 2019).

Jones, C, Ferguson, I, Lavalette, M and Penketh, L (2004) Social Work and Social Justice: A Manifesto for a New Engaged Practice. [online] Available at: www.liv.ac.uk/ssp/Social _Work_Manifesto.html

Langham, M (1998) Radical Social Work. In Adams, R, Dominelli, L and Payne, M (eds) *Social Work: Themes, Issues and Critical Debates* (pp 207–17). London: Macmillan.

Lymbery, M (2004) Managerialism and Care Management Practice with Older People. In Lymbery, M and Butler, S (eds) *Social Work Ideals and Practice Realities* (pp 157–78). Basingstoke: Palgrave.

Maslow, A (1954) *Motivation and Personality.* New York: Harper.

NHS England (2018) *General Practice Forward View.* [online] Available at: www.england.nhs.uk/gp/gpfv (accessed 25 April 2019).

O'Connell, B (2012) *Solution-focused Therapy* (3rd edn). London: Sage.

Office for National Statistics (2015) National Population Projections for the UK, 2014-based. London: ONS.

Revalier, J M and Boichat, C (2018) *UK Social Workers: Working Conditions and Wellbeing (August 2018). Bath: Bath Spa University.* [online] Available at: www.basw.co.uk/system/files/resources/Working%20Conditions%20%20Stress%20%282018%29%20pdf.pdf (accessed 25 April 2019).

Rogowski, S (2013) The Dog that Needs to Bark. *Professional Social Work,* January 2013: 14–15.

Rogers, C R (1957) The Necessary and Sufficient Conditions of Therapeutic Personality Change. *The Journal of Consulting Psychology,* 21: 95.

Smale, G and Tuson, G with Biehal, N and Marsh, P (1993) *Empowerment, Assessment, Care Management and the Skilled Worker.* London: Department of Health and National Institute for Social Work.

Stepney, P (2006) Mission Impossible? Critical Practice in Social Work. *British Journal of Social Work*, 36(8): 1289–307.

The Guardian (2016) A Guide to Radical Social Work. May 2016. [online] Available at: www.theguardian.com/social-care-network/2016/may/24/radical-social-work-quick-guide-change-poverty-inequality (accessed 25 April 2019).

The Kings Fund (2013) Time to Think Differently. London: Kings Fund. [online] Available at: www.kingsfund.org.uk/projects/time-think-differently/trends-public-attitudes-expectations-services (accessed 25 April 2019).

Turnell, A and Murphy, T (2017) *Signs of Safety Comprehensive Briefing Paper* (4th edn). East Perth, Australia: Resolutions Consultancy Pty Ltd.

Woodcock Ross, J (2016) *Specialist Communication Skills for Social Workers. Developing Professional Capability* (2nd edn). London: Palgrave.

Chapter 5 | Working with people with learning disabilities

Sue Hollinrake

Thanks also to Dumitru Puscaru, Team Manager, West Learning Disabilities and Autism Team, Adult and Community Services, Suffolk County Council, and Liz Whitby, formerly Head of Engagement and Co-production, Adult and Community Services, Suffolk County Council for their contributions to this chapter.

Introduction

This chapter will look at the context in which services for people with learning disabilities are delivered – the wider societal context, the organisational context and the influence of both of these on the context of the working relationship. The first part of the chapter will look briefly at the changing context of social work with people with learning disabilities and their families and carers. More detailed policy and legislative changes have already been presented in Chapter 2, which needs to be read in conjunction with this chapter. The discussion will then move on to look at the IDEAS model and its application within a relationship-based approach to practice.

As it is a term used in most policy documents, people with a 'learning disability' will be the preferred term in this chapter, but it is important to consider first just what is a learning disability and to whom the term refers? The Equality Act 2010 defines disability broadly as '*a physical or mental impairment that has a "substantial" and "long-term" negative effect on your ability to do normal daily activities*' (HM Government, 2010). Some people may take issue with the use of the word 'negative' as it implies a measurement or comparison against an assumed norm of 'ability' which is characterised as positive. According to Public Health England (2018), a learning disability is a label given to a group of conditions that are present before the age of 18 years. These affect development in all core areas of life. Williams (2009, p 7) notes the difficulties in providing an adequate definition. Using the term 'difficulties' rather than 'disabilities', he provides the following definition which has a more positive, less 'deficit model' quality:

A person with learning difficulties is someone who has been labelled as having difficulties in cognitive understanding, but is someone with rights, including the right to maximum control over decisions that affect them, and who may need help and support to claim and exercise those rights.

It must also be recognised that people with learning disabilities, having been dis-abled, can experience multiple oppressions such as isolation, social exclusion and poverty, as well as having multiple identities, including ethnicity, gender, class and age, and this will also be taken into account in the discussion that follows. The self-advocacy movement for people with learning disabilities has a proud tradition of challenging discrimination and oppression, and campaigning for social and human rights. It has been part of a celebratory and affirmative approach to redefining the identities of people with learning disabilities and the redefining of service approaches. Personalisation and co-production as policy and practice approaches (see Chapter 2) have to be embedded in a culture of collaboration led by the needs and aspirations of people with learning disabilities.

In practice, social workers working with people with learning disabilities can be working with a wide range of individual needs, some of which are complex, such as those of people within the autistic spectrum, those with a moderate learning disability who may have chaotic lifestyles characterised by homelessness, drug-taking and offending behaviour, and those with high-dependency needs arising from complex or multiple disabilities, often continuing to live with their parents into adulthood and seeking to integrate more into their local communities. Some of the complexities will emerge through the discussion that follows in this chapter, in terms of social work practice and building relationships with adults with learning disabilities.

Influence

Personalisation and co-production have been major influences on changing services for people with learning disabilities. In practice, common characteristics in co-production and personalisation point to important shifts in organisational culture and professional practice that characterise people who use services as citizens and active asset-holders rather than passive consumers. The relationships between people with learning disabilities using services and professionals should be affirmative, collaborative, personalised and not paternalistic, with a focus on meaningful outcomes for people. Work with individuals, as the Care Act Statutory Guidance 2.18 (HM Government, 2014, updated 2018) states, should be holistic in its focus, considering *'the person's skills, ambitions and priorities'.* And in relation to assessment, when *'a genuine conversation'* is referred to, in the Statutory Guidance (4.12), there should be reference to what *'a good life'* might look like and how this might be achieved. This reflects a personalised approach, which, as Sanderson commented in the early days of the development of personalisation, is:

a process of continual listening, and learning: focused on what is important to someone now, and in the future.

(Sanderson, 2000, p 2)

Similarly, according to a SCIE research briefing (Needham and Carr, 2009), co-production is a potentially transforming way of thinking about power, resources, partnerships, risks and outcomes. Power and responsibility are shared within a relationship, which will be discussed in this chapter. So, in this discussion, the baseline is for influence to be a shared endeavour wherever possible, with the influence of both sides of the relationship counting.

The skills that build the relationship to make this possible are explored under Alliance, but here we need to consider the influence that the social worker brings and develops out of their skills in relationship-building and relationship-maintaining to ensure that they can influence effectively and fairly, to support people to meet challenges and make changes, on a one-to-one level, but also at a group and community level. They are working to assess individual service users (some with capacity and some without), while working with advocates, family carers, formal carers, health professionals and, potentially, also across providers from the Private, Voluntary and Independent (PVI) Sector, involving businesses and organisations providing services as well as local councils and the National Health Service (NHS). Here social workers may need to influence and support the health and care sectors to tailor their services to accommodate the wide diversity of need presented by people with learning disabilities and autism to ensure a personalised approach based on community presence. Indeed, the Care Act Guidance (2015, 4.25) states that:

When arranging services themselves, local authorities must ensure their commissioning practices and the services delivered on their behalf comply with the requirements of the Equality Act 2010, and do not discriminate against people with protected characteristics; this should include monitoring delivery against the requirements of that Act.

As a prerequisite for effective practice with adults with learning disabilities, practitioners need to be mindful of their own personal values as well as professional values that underpin influence within an open, honest and respectful relationship with the individual service user. Negative societal attitudes towards people with learning disabilities still feature in interactions within wider society (see Chapter 2). Social work students who have not had much contact in their upbringing with people with learning disabilities may have absorbed unconsciously and retain social attitudes that are negative and discriminatory, so critical self-reflection during training and the opportunity to work with adults with learning disabilities will be important in challenging negative belief systems, to be able to recognise these in self and others and challenge accordingly, and to promote the development of anti-discriminatory services that truly include people with learning disabilities as partners.

Person-centred skills, communication tools and strategies, and a willingness to work at the pace of the person using the service are important when explaining the social worker's role and responsibilities and the powers that these may bring, according to the practice context (eg in a safeguarding referral when the priority is to protect the individual using a service, even if they are initially reluctant to cooperate).

Case Example

Peter is a White male aged 30 and lives with two other people with learning disabilities in a shared flat, with a team of support workers helping them with some personal care, cooking and household management. He has severe learning disabilities but enjoys going out for a drink at the local pub. A support worker, named Joe, accompanies him to the pub once a week and has a drink with him. They socialise with other pub-goers during the evening. After a few months, Peter's parents, who visit regularly, notice that Peter's finances seem to be very limited and his account is overdrawn. Peter is reluctant to talk about what is happening but another support worker, Anne, has noticed that Peter has been withdrawing money from his account every week prior to going to the pub and seems to be spending quite a lot of money in the pub. A social worker from the local team is visiting to conduct a review of Peter's care package around this time and the support worker shares her suspicions that her colleague may be complicit in the withdrawal of these sums of money.

The White female social worker, Kate, who is known to Peter, after clearly establishing the reason for her visit and outlining her role as reviewer of Peter's care and support, asks him about different aspects of his life. Peter can communicate verbally, but appears hesitant when talking about his visits to the pub. Kate uses her interpersonal skills and emotional intelligence (Howe, 2008) to point out to Peter that he seems worried about something when she mentions going to the pub with Joe. Gradually, using probes, she makes a connection between Joe's finances and his spending at the pub. Peter slowly admits that he is regularly buying drinks for Joe and gives Joe money to pay for them. He says he enjoys going to the pub and doesn't want to stop. Kate reassures him that he can continue to go to the pub but, using her authority, says she will have to investigate further and this investigation may involve Joe, service managers and the police. Using her professional role and influence, she explains, in a straightforward way, that an investigation will be undertaken to see if he is being financially abused. Kate's honesty and openness, clear presentation of the issues with patience and reassurance, help Peter to accept, albeit with some reluctance, that it is his interests that she is seeking to protect. The required relationship skills of empathy, attentiveness and emotional intelligence seek to achieve what Beresford, et al point to as respect, liking and a degree of mutuality (Beresford et al, 2008). At the end of her visit, Kate also summed up, in plain English, what her concerns were, what tasks she needed to carry out, what Peter had expressed about the situation and recapped on what the end goal of her intervention was. She checked Peter's understanding, by asking him what they had agreed for their plans to keep him safe and reassured him that he would still be able to go to the pub. In this way, she was 'clear, upfront and collaborative' (Howe, 2014, p 186). It was important in terms of the Care Act 2014 that she used a personalised approach, as described, in any safeguarding enquiry (Lawson et al, 2014; SCIE, 2016).

These skills can be used when working at a more strategic level, where appropriate, within an organisation. This may not be an everyday experience for the busy practitioner, but opportunities are 'out there' where professional influence can be used within the organisational context, supporting the changing of attitudes to a positive and asset-based way of thinking and planning services. This may be useful at a team level, in ensuring colleagues are working in this way, but is particularly so in relation to co-production at a strategic level. For this to be successful, it has to be recognised within the organisation that the influence and expertise of people with learning disabilities who use services are invaluable and can help to improve those services. This requires a shift in culture from more traditional approaches to service organisation and resource provision.

Case Example

The account that follows considers the development of a Strategy within a local authority, which drew on the accumulating understanding of what co-production is, as described in Chapter 2. With the pending implementation of the Care Act 2014 at the time, and, in particular, in view of the personalisation indicators of this Act, the County Council's and Clinical Commissioning Groups' Joint Learning Disability Strategy 2015–2020 needed to mark a different approach to service planning and delivery. The priority had been to move people from day services to community-based services to enable maximisation of independence, in line with national policy and based on the recognition that to achieve different and better outcomes that actively promote independence, choice and control, commissioners and service providers needed to work together and work differently with people, families and social networks to build on the rich and diverse assets of people with learning disabilities living in the local authority area, harnessing the resources of people, places and communities, by ensuring their full inclusion. It was agreed early on that co-production would drive the development of the Strategy and the changes to services that resulted. People with learning disabilities, their service user-led organisations, local authority commissioners and managers, specialist social workers, and providers of services all worked together on the Strategy and at its heart was the vision, developed through co-production, of people with learning disabilities living good ordinary lives. This is in line with the now expected planning practices in the Care Act Guidance (4.66):

Local authorities should ensure that active engagement and consultation with local people is built into the development and review of their strategies for market shaping and commissioning ...

(HM Government, 2014, updated 2018)

Leading into the development of the Strategy, the local Learning Disability Partnership Board began to collaborate with adult social care managers and a consultancy group commissioned by the local authority. Initially this collaboration identified potential strengths and began to build on these. A local self-advocacy organisation put forward its views with members meeting together and electing spokespeople to present their views and exert influence. A working group consisting of family members, self-advocates, provider representatives, adult social care and health colleagues was created. The group designed a series of highly interactive, challenging and creative engagement events which brought together all the relevant people, and was well supported by a wide range of stakeholders. These events sought, in a number of different ways, to maximise involvement and influence. An online survey was conducted and a social media campaign initiated, as well as a workshop arranged through the local Learning Disability Partnership. Approximately 450 people shared their thoughts, concerns, hopes and ideas for the future. All information gathered was collated and circulated as widely as possible, including through workshops, to give people the opportunity to review, amend and strengthen the recommendations. A final draft was presented to the local Health and Well-being Board. The aspirations of and for people with learning disabilities were unsurprisingly the same as for the rest of the population: to be listened to as individuals, to have choices about where to live and who to live with, to have relationships and pets, to choose the people who support them and to have opportunities for work and participation in their communities. A recurring theme of the engagement events was that the lives of people with learning disabilities were frequently treated in a risk-averse, protective way – eg protecting people from the right to relationships or having feelings following a bereavement, compared to the roller coaster of life experiences that most of the population experiences – ie the deficit model that prioritises a safeguarding duty but overlooks the whole person and their more general social rights.

The strategy has been implemented for nearly four years, at the time of writing, and has made some impact on local services for the better. The process of engaging all involved in the designing and delivery of services to examine what works well and what needs to change, harnessing the influence of both individuals with learning disabilities and professionals working together and sharing expertise, can produce a change in culture for the better, albeit slow, as cultures do not change overnight. But progress can be measured in a variety of ways, noting the benefits of relationships that are created, based on increasing participation and trust. The use of Appreciative Inquiry events (Hammond, 2013), when the local authority needed to carry out some market engagement before making changes to commissioned services, looked at what people thought worked well in organisations, focusing on the positives to promote change and to build a vision for the future that can then be co-produced.

The professionals involved in co-producing the strategy talked about 'lightbulb moments', when they experienced the benefits of the shift from their traditional ways of working or responding to a workload, to this new approach, co-production. Confidence and trust increased for the people involved, across the board, as trusting relationships were established. For self-advocates and professionals, this meant the opportunity to really hear the issues being worked on from many different perspectives, and to be influenced by the learning this afforded.

In the above scenario, in terms of the exercising of professional influence, a reflective and mindful approach was really important to ensure that the bigger picture is captured to encompass the interactions between the lives of people using services, the practices of those who work with them, departmental policies and strategies (their opportunities and constraints) and the wider political climate. As Howe (2014, p 191) states:

The critically reflexive, mindful worker sees more clearly and more widely. Her options increase. Her potential to be creative becomes greater.

Delivery

An important consideration in the delivery aspect of the IDEAS model, when working with adults with learning disabilities, is that the social worker should have an understanding of the boundaries of policy and legislation so that she/he can support service users, their families, and service providers to focus on what can be achieved creatively, within the community, in line with the appropriate legislation, policy strategy and resources available, with accountability to all parties.

Assessment must be strengths-based (Department of Health and Social Care, 2019) (see also Chapter 1). As stated earlier, it should start from a position of what sort of a life does the person want. An approach to this that has gained ground in practice with learning disabled people is Appreciative Inquiry's (AI) 4D cyclical approach (Discover, Dream, Design and Deliver) (Cooperrider and Whitney, 2005; Hammond, 2013) to highlight what is working well, identify positive aspects in the present time in the individual's life, and use these to plan a way forward towards the desired goals of change (see Chapter 2 for discussion of AI). In therapeutic practice, this approach has been criticised as potentially overlooking and avoiding 'shadow' areas that we avoid or deny (Reason and Bradbury, 2001) but which need to be addressed to move forward towards meaningful change. However, asking the right 'positive' questions in an assessment to avoid focusing on negatives, at least at the relationship-building stage, is important to avoid hopelessness and 'stuckness', and to build motivation. Stage 2 of the AI 4D cycle – describing dreams and wishes, can be useful in not only identifying what might be achieved, but also what is currently lacking. From here, stage 3 follows with a discussion about working together to develop what might be, and then stage 4, destiny, which involves experimenting with what can be – a stage which requires support and encouragement to maintain motivation and monitor risk. To maintain this cycle, there must be partnership and a common understanding of the '*purpose, nature and extent of professional involvement*' (Wilson et al, 2011, p 273). Parents of adults with learning disabilities and autism can receive a lot of criticism from unaware members of the public when their sons or daughters exhibit challenging behaviour in public spaces. They may continue to have many medical appointments to attend where the focus is on what the problems are (often arising from the application of the 'medical' model which focuses on what needs fixing or curing, which offers a 'deficit' approach to their situations, even though some issues do require medical interventions). A strengths-based approach does not deny problems that need to be addressed or managed, but it does lighten the perceived load, giving parents and carers an opportunity to reframe and celebrate the positives and feel energised by doing this. In the foregoing case example, the use of AI was significant in building the confidence of people with learning disabilities to bring their strengths 'to the table' and work collaboratively to achieve change at an organisational and community level by envisioning new ways to address existing issues and to challenge the status quo.

For this group of people who require services, where dependency needs can be high, there is also the need to consider, as part of 'delivery', partnership work with family carers. As highlighted elsewhere in this book (Chapter 2 and Chapter 6), the dynamics of servicing and caring within the private sphere of family life have, for centuries, delivered a gendered expectation for women in the role of informal carer, critiqued by feminist writers. Working in partnership with parent carers, where the person with a learning disability lives at home into adulthood, can be a delicate balancing act, when families may be protective of their son or daughter and very aware of the discrimination and oppression that exists in the outside world, while professionals are seeking to promote increased community presence, which may involve, from the family perspective, risk-taking that they would prefer to avoid. This again requires the practitioner to use communication and, in particular, negotiating skills, to listen to the aspirations and the concerns of parents, but also, to keep to the fore of discussions, the perspective of the individual with a learning disability. Here, a two-pronged approach may be necessary – to promote a normalising approach to as independent a lifestyle as possible for the person with a learning disability, and also to influence the local community to become more disability friendly. This can be done through working in partnership with providers of care services to ensure that local resources are disability-friendly and deliver to expected standards, with access to mainstream services available, and that any discrimination is appropriately challenged.

Organisational frameworks for practice have to be adhered to, and timescales for working and achieving change have to be followed, as required by service managers. However, in relation to adults with learning disabilities, where building relationships takes time, because of internalised oppression (Goodley, 2017, p 108) and because trust may be slow to develop, due to negative experiences in the community, then working at the individual's pace is necessary to achieve inclusion and to ensure that the individual has time to process matters (Woodcock Ross, 2016, p 200).

Assessments also need to consider the input of other professionals involved to ensure that everyone is working together. Given the general concerns about the health care needs for this population where inequalities are significant, it is important to be aware of and in contact (with permission) with others in the health professional network, such as learning disability nurses, who can bring a health perspective into the assessment. An adult with a learning disability may have a health action plan or a health passport, which can provide a greater understanding of the person and their strengths and needs, to provide the right care and support. If the individual does not have capacity, then it will be important to ask the family or support workers about the passport, and ensure that individuals are prompted and supported to take up annual health checks. Capacity should be considered for every decision and action that is taken with a person with a learning disability and if capacity is doubted, then it should be tested and the five key principles of the Mental Capacity Act (2005) applied (see Brown et al, 2009, pp 5–6).

Expertise

Building expertise comes from training and from immersing oneself in practice – and reflecting in and on practice (Ingram, 2013; Ferguson 2018). The skills, which are important and pivotal to developing 'best practice', arise with the application of knowledge and with the development of a sound value base. Knowledge derives from the study of theoretical concepts and methods, from applying evidence from research to inform practice, and from legislation and policy relevant to working effectively, alongside the experiential learning that comes with the application of theory and knowledge, values and skills in practice.

Communication skills are of central importance to a social worker's expertise in working with adults with learning disabilities to ensure that a personalised and co-produced approach is achieved. Written communication needs to be 'accessible', as stated in the Care Act Guidance (HM Government, 2014, 3.28) in relation to provision of information and assessment. This may mean simplified language with pictures, and in Easy Read format. Social workers must be aware of different ways of communicating with people who do not communicate verbally or who have limited verbal communication. On both counts, attention to non-verbal communication (Lishman, 2009, pp 32–9) is vital. Some people with learning disabilities may use a sign language (eg Makaton) or may need reasonable adjustments, eg symbols or pictures to communicate their needs, wishes and preferences, or rely on their carers and advocates who know them well, to ensure their needs and preferences are communicated and understood in assessments. Clearly, in these instances, the significance of body language, of facial expressions and of very individual communication styles need to be represented by those who know the individual very well. Addressing directly the carer or support worker or another professional present, instead of the person with a learning disability, should be avoided (the 'does she/he take sugar?' approach), although their knowledge and understanding of the person may be helpful in supporting communication and interpretation, and in clarifying points. It may be important to ensure that the surroundings for the conversation are free from distractions, and speech should be clear and not rushed, using plain English, avoiding jargon, metaphors and figurative speech. Using short sentences and checking understanding at regular intervals are also vital, alongside repeating a question. Sometimes, the use of facial expressions to support communicating feelings may be useful. In relation to the use of the Mental Capacity Act 2005, it is important to remember that limited communication does not in itself mean inability or limited ability to consent.

Relationship-based practice demands a sound understanding of the theoretical knowledge outlined in Chapter 1, as the significance of theory is that it enables an analysis of what is going on for an individual and those who know and support them, leading to a way forward to enable change for the better. Research and knowledge deriving from research studies and from serious case reviews, to promote best practice, are also key in this part of the IDEAS framework, when assessing and making sense of what is going on in an individual's life and working out with them how to respond. The practitioner needs to be able to apply knowledge and evidence from research and evaluate its usefulness to their understanding of the situation of the person they are working with. In relation to risks that may be significant for people with learning disabilities and affect their well-being and quality of life, there are a number of areas that practitioners need to be informed about. One such area is disability hate crime (Mencap, 2007, 2010, 2011; Scope, 2008) – what it is, how it affects those who experience it and how to report it. To promote equal citizenship and human and social rights, then knowledge is required in key areas of daily living. For example, in relation to healthcare, recent reports have held that people with learning disabilities have died unnecessarily due to the ignorance and indifference of services towards people with learning disabilities and their families and carers, in areas such as lack of basic care, poor communication and failure to understand pain (see Mencap, 2007, 2012 and 2016; Department of Health, 2008). Housing is another important area where knowledge of trends and possibilities is important (see Mencap, 2012; Mencap and Housing LIN, 2018). While some people with learning disabilities live independently with no formal support, and others live in supported living or residential care, half of all adults with a learning disability live in the family home (Foundation for People with Learning Disabilities, 2019).

When looking at risk in relation to family carers and parent carers, it is important to note that, in 2013, eight out of ten families caring for someone with profound and multiple learning disabilities reported being at breaking point or close to it because of a lack of short break services (Mencap, 2013, p 4), and since then, 'austerity' policies have increased the pressure of local authority budgets and the stress on services. Practitioners need to undertake assessments with great care and attention to the levels of stress to ensure they record carers' needs either alongside the service user's assessment or through a separate carers' assessment, and use the expertise they acquire through knowledge and research to argue the case and advocate for the person using services or their carer.

Knowledge and information about local networks are also important, as for all adult service user groups, to help to match people with appropriate resources that meet their needs, and also, in relation to people with disabilities, it is important to ensure that, in line with the Equality Act 2010, reasonable adjustments are made to support access to services and resources.

Knowledge of the roles of other professionals is also an important element of 'expertise', to enable positive, successful co-working with others and to build joint professional expertise to work together for the benefit of people with learning disabilities. The following case example illustrates how risk can be managed in a multi-agency context, and how the expertise of the different professionals was engaged and mobilised to ensure that John received proper recognition of his needs, balancing the risks to John himself against the risks he might have appeared to pose to others.

Case Example

John is a 32 year-old White British man, with a moderate to severe learning disability and autism. He lives at home with his mother. His mother also has moderate learning disabilities and works as a cleaner. They live in a remote village, rurally isolated and with limited leisure and social opportunities.

John spends most of his time on Facebook and the internet in search for interaction and friendship. Through this activity, John was picked up by a member of a paedophile hunters organisation, pretending to be an underage girl and luring him into a Facebook conversation. Soon after, the member visited John at home and threatened him. They also reported John to the police for underage grooming.

The police arrested and interviewed John. During the interview they realised that John probably did not have the mental capacity to understand and participate in the interview. An assessment under the Mental Capacity Act 2005 was undertaken and the police referred John to the Adults with Learning Disabilities and Autism Services for support. A conversation took place with John's general practitioner (GP) to refer John for a psychological assessment to explore his ability to:

1. understand and express his sexual needs safely;
2. understand elements of internet safety and age-appropriate relationships;
3. socialise safely.

John's consent was sought beforehand and granted.

John was released by the police on bail conditions. A Short Term Enablement Plan (STEP) was put in place by Adult and Community Services and commissioned from a local specialist service to address the following issues:

1. support to stay compliant with the bail conditions;
2. a skills assessment with regard to his independent living abilities;
3. identification of suitable and safe opportunities to socialise and engage in appropriate relationships;
4. learning how to safely use the internet.

When completed, the STEP was reviewed involving the police, adult social care, the local health trust, the specialist learning disability service, and the GP. From a social work perspective, skills in communicating with other professionals, in building a trusting and non-judgemental relationship with John and in advocating on his behalf were key to professional practice that protected John. The social worker then went on to support him in engaging in safer and more suitable socialising opportunities in his local community. However, a psychosexual counselling service was not available for John and this may increase the risk of sexual offenses. Sexual needs are fundamental and without adequate psychosexual counselling John may not be able to understand his sexual needs, increasing the risk of him displaying inappropriate sexual behaviour with significant consequences for his safety or mental well-being.

Alliances

Forming a working alliance through effective relationship-building is the prelude to change. An assets-based approach within an Appreciative Inquiry framework (as described in an earlier section of this chapter) offers a good starting place in building an alliance. An important aspect of the relationship which a social worker offers here is that of hope. This does not minimise or ignore issues that require change, but it does acknowledge that some things are going well, and this characterises the assets-based approach which provides a positive basis for building a trusting alliance.

In developing the above approach to the relationship, the practitioner also needs to use their emotional intelligence (Howe, 2014, pp 82–6) as the following example illustrates.

Case Example

When working with older Asian parents Geetha and Bikram, who care at home for their adult daughter Meera, who has severe learning disabilities as well as challenging behaviours and little verbal communication, their White British social worker Amy's ability to listen to emotions will be a key feature of her assessment of how they are managing the demands of caring, and may also be of significance in understanding Meera's experiences too. In doing so, a number of processes are going on at the same time for Amy. Listening to her own emotional responses to the situation is key, and doing the 'emotion work' to manage these without communicating them to the parents. Tuning in (Taylor and Devine, 1993, pp 20–2) to the daughter's behaviours and feelings and to the parents' emotional states, especially if they are feeling angry, distressed and unsupported, and then building empathy and being able to give the parents the space to express their feelings in a contained way, and to think about their impact on relationships in the household, will provide a way of aiding them in managing the feelings while also recognising the need for a plan for change. Thinking about difficult feelings, such as allowing others to care for their daughter, when their long-held belief, influenced also by experiences of racism, is that no one else can be trusted to do it as well as they can, yet they are increasingly tired in their efforts. This enables them to examine, with the social worker, Amy, their fear of 'letting go' and involving other carers, that results from their experiences of the general population and its often negative attitudes towards people with learning disabilities (Mencap, 2015). As Howe states:

The ability to think about and manage feeling states, both in the self and others, defines the emotionally intelligent social worker.

(Howe, 2014, p 85)

In this case, too, recognising the expertise of the parents is also crucial in building the alliance, to enable planning for change so that Geetha and Bikram feel validated and involved as key partners. They have years of expertise in caring for their daughter and they know her better than any other likely carers, so listening to their worries and concerns, their hopes and fears and their experiences is the other component to 'alliance-building' as well as, in this case, heeding the responses of Meera to any changes to her routines and experiences so as to assess what will work and what will not work. Behind these recognitions is the social worker's value base of respect, warmth and integrity, which is expressed through the person-centred skills that communicate the alliance, such as active listening. Amy may, through tuning in to herself, identify feelings arising from a counter-transference she experiences in relating to Geetha and Bikram, which remind her of her own struggles to separate from cautious and protective parents during her adolescence, and thus identify with Meera to whom she will attribute feelings of frustration. This over-identification could cause her to undervalue the protective feelings of Meera's parents which are important to acknowledge, as they will carry forward the vigilance and care they feel for their daughter into future care arrangements. Self-awareness and self-regulation are, as alluded to earlier, important aspects of emotional intelligence which can be used effectively in maintaining an alliance. It is important, too, that commonly held cultural stereotypes, such as the one that might be unthinkingly applied in this case (that Asian or other BAME parents of children or adults with learning disabilities prefer to 'look after their own' and avoid using formal services) are debunked and an anti-discriminatory approach is taken. Hubert's study (Hubert, 2006) showed that social work support was often poor and that stereotypes of supportive family networks were largely unfounded.

Effective relationships also need to be formed and maintained with other professionals, and working alliances created. This is supported when different professionals are co-located in the same team or in the same building, which can be the case with services for adults with learning disabilities and closer integration of health and social care should aid this. Serious case reviews, however, have repeatedly highlighted the need for effective communication and partnership working. One such case involved the death of Steven Hoskin in 2005

(Cornwall Adult Protection Committee, 2007). He was tortured and murdered by others who had targeted him because of his learning disabilities. Steven had lived in supported housing on his own and before his death had repeatedly telephoned a range of agencies but lack of information sharing had prevented them from seeing the full picture of the danger Steven was in. A key message from the Serious Case Review held after Steven's death was that sharing information and partnership working between agencies is vital for the effective safeguarding of adults.

The Care Act 2014, which replaced the No Secrets Report (Department of Health, 2000) and provided a blueprint for the establishment of local safeguarding procedures for the abuse of vulnerable adults, including those with learning disabilities, has made some changes. It has introduced Safeguarding Adults Reviews (SARs), which were previously known as Serious Case Reviews. The Act also reinforces the need for good communication, partnership and sharing of information. However, while protocols, procedures and agency requirements for practitioners are important structures that clarify expectations of professionals, the significance of positive and effective relationships between different professionals cannot be understated. Training for practitioners across different professions is vital so that different organisational structures and cultures, different professional values and priorities can be understood by those who need to work together across boundaries. This helps to build trust and develop mutual understanding in order to create and maintain successful working alliances based on firm relationship foundations.

Support

This aspect of the IDEAS model refers to the support that organisations need to offer, to ensure that practitioners can manage the demands of the work expected of them and can experience the support of managers in a safe environment that enables them to develop as resilient professionals who can manage risk and challenging situations in a way that does not chronically affect their well-being. Effective supervision is a requirement of the Care Act 2014. Kittay's (1999) notion of 'nested dependencies' has been mentioned in several contexts within this book because it conceptualises so well concentric circles of support that are needed for practitioners to feel safe in order for them to work safely with people who use services. Translated into practice settings, this points to an organisational commitment to supervision throughout the hierarchy of the organisation.

This means that for supervision to be effective for the supervisee, the supervisor or manager must also have supervision that is characterised by a relationship-focused experience and not just a task-focused, brief encounter to ensure organisational priorities are being addressed. This is particularly so for first-line managers in statutory agencies who are at the interface between organisational demands and drivers, and practitioners' experiences (with their potential uncertainties and anxieties) of direct work with those using the service. These managers have to manage within the supervisory relationship and the 'organisational anxieties' within themselves alongside the tensions and anxieties experienced by the practitioners. If organisational anxieties take priority in the supervision agenda, then the agenda will become a checklist of tasks and targets. When intervening in the lives of people who have experienced or are experiencing strong emotions of anger, fear, hopelessness or despair, then practitioners can feel caught up in the distress and experience their own powerful emotions. The 'out-of-control' feeling that this can provoke in the supervisor has to be contained at the next level up the hierarchy to avoid it being ignored and shut out of the practitioner's supervision, and out of the practice context.

Practitioners need to be aware of the impact that emotions may be having on their interventions. Ruch (2007) stresses the importance of practitioners being able to discuss the emotional impact of the work on them so that they can feel 'held' and their experiences made sense of within a reflective space that can tolerate confusion, chaos and uncertainty and make meaning from it. Averill (1994, cited in Ingram, 2013) warns that if it is accepted that emotions have a function, then suppressing or side-lining them is dysfunctional (and potentially dangerous in social work practice). To avoid this, and to promote effective practice, organisations and supervisors must make legitimate the discussion and exploration of feelings in supervision. By being curious and interested in these aspects of practice, a good supervisor can introduce new knowledge or can elicit knowledge from the practitioner that has become buried under the powerful emotions, and through calm reflection can identify strengths and barriers to finding a way forward. Over time, this builds confidence in the practitioner, as they recognise the incorporation of their own *internal supervisor* (Lawson, 2011), ie their ability to think and become their own internal supervisor as their ability to reflect 'in action' as well as 'on action' (Schön, 1983) develops.

An extension of this derives from the culture that exists within the practitioner's team. Biggart et al (2017) demonstrate the effectiveness of teams in providing a 'secure base' for practitioners to have their emotional needs, arising from practice, met, and in supporting the promotion of confidence-building and resilience, which takes the reader back to Kittay's (1999) 'nested dependencies' (see Chapter 1) and helps to elucidate this further.

Supervision is also key to anti-discriminatory practice. In a disabling society, processes of disablism are reproduced in relationships between people (Goodley and Lawthom, 2011), so that individual subjectivities take in socio-cultural knowledge and social arrangements consciously and unconsciously. Even if a practitioner has a conscious critical awareness of disabling social structures and attitudes, old attitudes and feelings associated with them, such as fear and guilt, can unconsciously affect their practice unless they are more consciously acknowledged. Shakespeare has suggested that non-disabled people's fears around disability are linked to their anxieties about death and physicality which they project on to people with disabilities (Shakespeare, 2000). Negative stereotypes can reduce practitioners' expectations of individuals with a learning disability. So, providing a safe environment in which to explore the possible unconscious manifestations in practice of such stereotypes is important to raise awareness of discriminatory attitudes and actions that undermine inclusion and lead to oppressive practice.

Conclusion

Celebrating disability, using an affirmative approach, as described earlier through the IDEAS model is an important stance to take in all sections of the model to combat the history of oppression and marginalising of people with a learning disability, both in wider society and in the use of social care services. Combating the 'personal tragedy' model (Swain and French, 2008) and accepting difference and diversity as an important aspect of the human condition (eg Trivedi, 2009) has to be part of the professional value base of the practitioner in order to use the IDEAS model to promote social justice and to ensure the moral quality of interventions. Empowering professionalism that creates a collaborative and personalised approach with the person with a learning disability at the centre is key to ensuring choice and control, so that they have the time and space to explore what is important to them in their life and can co-create their own individual support plan to overcome disabling barriers and access opportunities in the community according to their needs and aspirations.

References

Averill, J (1994) Emotions Are Many Splendored Things. In Ekman, P and Davidson, R (eds) *The Nature of Emotion* (pp 99–103). New York: Oxford University Press.

Beresford, P, Croft, S and Adshead, L (2008) 'We Don't See Her as a Social Worker': A Service User Case Study of the Importance of the Social Worker's Relationship and Humanity. *British Journal of Social Work*, 38: 1388–407.

Biggart, L, Ward, E, Cook, L and Schofield, G (2017) The Team as a Secure Base: Promoting Resilience and Competence in Child and Family Social Work. *Children and Youth Services Review*, 83: 119–30.

Brown, R, Barber, P and Martin, D (2009) *The Mental Capacity Act 2005: A Guide for Practice* (2nd edn). Exeter: Learning Matters.

Cooperrider, D L and Whitney, D (2005) *Appreciative Inquiry: A Positive Revolution in Change.* San Francisco, CA: Berrett-Koehler Publishers.

Cornwall Adult Protection Committee (2007) The Murder of Steven Hoskin: A Serious Case Review. Executive Summary. [online] Available at: www.cornwall.gov.uk/media/3633936/Steven-Hoskin-Serious-Case-Review-Exec-Summary.pdf (accessed 25 April 2019).

Department of Health (2000) *No Secrets: Guidance on Developing and Implementing Multi-Agency Policies and Procedures to Protect Vulnerable Adults from Abuse.* London: Department of Health.

Department of Health (2008) *Healthcare for All: Report of the Independent Inquiry into Access to Healthcare for People with Learning Disabilities.* London: Department of Health.

Department of Health and Social Care (2019) *Strengths-based Approach: Practice Framework and Practice Handbook.* London: Department of Health and Social Care. [online] Available at: https://assets.publishing.service. gov.uk/government/uploads/system/uploads/attachment_data/file/778134/stengths-based-approach-practice-framework-and-handbook.pdf (accessed 6 March 2019).

Dzur, A W (2008) *Democratic Professionalism, Citizen Participation and the Reconstruction of Professional Ethics, Identity and Practice.* University Park: The Pennsylvania State University Press.

Foundation for People with Learning Disabilities (part of the Mental Health Foundation) (2019) *Statistics.* [online] Available at: www.mentalhealth.org.uk/learning-disabilities/help-information/statistics/learning-disability-statistics-/187696 (accessed 17 February 2019).

Gates, B and Mafuba, K (2016) Use of the Term 'Learning Disabilities' in the United Kingdom: Issues for International Researchers and Practitioners. *Learning Disabilities: A Contemporary Journal*, 14(1): 9–23.

Goodley, D (2017) *Disability Studies: An Interdisciplinary Introduction* (2nd edn). London: Sage.

Hammond, S A (2013) *The Thin Book of Appreciative Inquiry* (3rd edn). Bend, OR: The Thin Book Publishing Company.

HM Government (2010) *Equality Act.* Part 2, Chapter 1, Section 6 Definition of Disability. [online] Available at: www. legislation.gov.uk/ukpga/2010/15/section/6 (accessed 25 April 2019).

HM Government (2014, updated 2018) *Care Act Statutory Guidance.* [online] Available at: www.gov.uk/government/publications/care-act-statutory-guidance/care-and-support-statutory-guidance (accessed 25 April 2019).

Howe, D (2008) *The Emotionally Intelligent Social Worker.* Basingstoke: Palgrave.

Howe, D (2009) *A Brief Introduction to Social Work.* Basingstoke: Palgrave.

Howe, D (2014) *The Compleat Social Worker.* London: Palgrave.

Hubert, J (2006) Family Carers' Views of Services for People with Learning Disabilities from Black and Minority Ethnic Groups: A Qualitative Study of 30 Families in a South London Borough. *Disability and Society*, 21(3): 259–72.

Ingram, R (2013) Emotions, Social Work Practice and Supervision: An Uneasy Alliance? *Journal of Social Work Practice*, 27(1): 5–19.

Kittay, E F (1999) *Love's Labor: Essays of Women, Equality and Dependency.* New York: Routledge.

Lawson, H (2011) Effective Supervision: What Is It and How Can Supervisors Ensure They Provide It? [online] Available at: www.ccinform.co.uk/practice-guidance/guide-to-effective-supervision-what-is-it-and-how-can-supervisors-ensure-they-provide-it (accessed 8 March 2019).

Lawson, J, Lewis, S and Williams, C (2014) Making Safeguarding Personal: Guide 2014. [online] Available at: www.local.gov.uk/sites/default/files/documents/Making%20Safeguarding%20Personal%20-%20Guide%202014.pdf (accessed 8 March 2019).

Lishman, J (2009) *Communication in Social Work* (2nd edn). London: Palgrave Macmillan.

Mencap (2007) *Don't Stick It, STOP IT! Bullying Wrecks Lives.* London: Mencap. [online] Available at: www.mencap.org.uk/sites/default/files/2016-07/Bullying%20wrecks%20lives.pdf (accessed 25 April 2019).

Mencap (2007) *Death by Indifference.* London: Mencap. [online] Available at: www.mencap.org.uk/sites/default/files/2016-07/DBIreport.pdf (accessed 25 April 2019).

Mencap (2010) *Don't Stand By: Ending Disability Hate Crime Together.* London: Mencap. [online] Available at: www.mencap.org.uk/sites/default/files/2016-08/Don%27t%20stand%20by-research-report%20%281%29.pdf (accessed 25 April 2019).

Mencap (2011) *How to Stand by Me: Sharing Achievements in Tackling Disability Hate Crime.* London: Mencap. [online] Available at: www.mencap.org.uk/sites/default/files/2016-07/Bullying%20wrecks%20lives.pdf (accessed 31 May 2019).

Mencap (2012) *Housing for People with a Learning Disability.* London: Mencap: Available at: www.mencap.org.uk/sites/default/files/2016-08/2012.108-Housing-report_V7.pdf (accessed 25 April 2019).

Mencap (2013) *Short Breaks Support Is Failing Family Carers: Reviewing Progress 10 Years on from Mencap's First Breaking Point Report.* [online] Available at: www.mencap.org.uk/sites/default/files/2016-07/Short%20breaks%20support%20is%20failing%20family%20carers.pdf (accessed 25 April 2019)

Mencap (2016) *Getting It Right Charter.* London: Mencap. [online] Available at: www.mencap.org.uk/sites/default/files/2016-07/Getting%20it%20Right%20charter.pdf (accessed 25 April 2019).

Mencap and Housing LIN (2018) *Funding Supported Housing for All. Specialised Supported Housing for People with a Learning Disability.* London: Mencap/Housing LIN. [online] Available at: www.housinglin.org.uk/_assets/Resources/Housing/Support_materials/Other_reports_and_guidance/Funding-supported-housing-for-all-Specialised-Supported-Housing-for-people-with-a-learning-disability.pdf (accessed 25 April 2019).

Needham, C and Carr, S (2009) *Co-production: An Emerging Evidence Base for Adult Social Care Transformation.* Social Care Institute for Excellence Research Briefing 31. London: SCIE.

New Economics Foundation (2004) *Co-production Works! The Win:Win of Involving Local People in Public Services.* London: NEF.

O'Brien, J (1986) A Guide to Personal Futures Planning. In Bellamy, G and Wilcox, B (eds) *The Activities Catalog: A Community Programming Guide for Youth and Adults with Severe Disabilities* (pp 171–90). Baltimore: Paul H. Brookes Publishing Company.

Public Health England (2018) *Guidance. Learning Disabilities: Applying All Our Health.* [online] Available at: www.gov.uk/government/publications/learning-disability-applying-all-our-health/learning-disabilities-applying-all-our-health (accessed 7 March 2019).

Reason, P and Bradbury, H (2001) Inquiry and Participation in Search of a World Worthy of Human Aspiration. In Reason, P and Bradbury, H (eds) *Handbook of Action Research: Participative Inquiry and Practice* (pp 1–14). London: Sage Publications.

Ruch, G (2007) Reflective Practice in Contemporary Child-care Social Work: The Role of Containment. *British Journal of Social Work*, 37: 659–80.

Sanderson, H (2000) *Person-centred Planning: Key Features and Approaches.* York: Joseph Rowntree Foundation.

SCIE (Social Care Institute for Excellend) (2016) Making Safeguarding Personal. [online] Available at: www.scie.org.uk/care-act-2014/safeguarding-adults/safeguarding-adults-boards-checklist-and-resources/making-safeguarding-personal.asp?gclid=CjwKCAjw27jnBRBuEiwAdjQXDF5Vwu6dY5RF5ye4gF41EmcPa7497RNDMtkuS-EXgcy-ivWy56H-aRoCNXgQAvD_BwE (accessed 3 June 2019).

Scope (2008) *Getting Away with Murder. Disabled People's Experiences of Hate Crime in the UK.* [online] Available at: www.scope.org.uk/scope/media/images/publication%20directory/getting-away-with-murder.pdf (accessed 20 January 2019).

Shakespeare, T (2000) *Help.* Birmingham: Venture Press.

Schön, D (1983) *The Reflective Practitioner.* London: Temple Smith.

Swain, J and French, S (2008) *Disability on Equal Terms.* London: Sage.

Taylor, B and Devine, T (1993) *Assessing Needs and Planning Care in Social Work.* Aldershot: Arena.

Trivedi, B (2009) Autistic and Proud. *New Scientist*, June: 36–40.

Williams, P (2009) *Social Work with People with Learning Difficulties* (2nd edn). Exeter: Learning Matters.

Wilson, K, Ruch, G, Lymbery, M and Cooper, A (2011) *Social Work: An Introduction to Contemporary Practice* (2nd edn). Harlow: Pearson Education.

Wolfensberger, W (1969) The Origin and Nature of Our Institutional Models. In Kugel, R and Wolfensberger, W (eds) *Changing Patterns in Residential Services for the Mentally Retarded* (pp 59–172). Washington, DC: President's Committee on Mental Retardation.

Woodcock Ross, J (2016) *Specialist Communication Skills for Social Workers Developing Professional Capability* (2nd edn). London: Blackwell.

Introduction

This chapter will look at how the IDEAS framework relates to work with people with caring responsibilities (referred to as carers), who in the context of the Care Act are called 'adults with support needs'. The chapter makes links between the legislative framework, theory and practice through use of case examples to illustrate how a relationship-based approach can be effective in understanding the lived experience of carers and in supporting purposeful outcomes. Within this chapter, the term 'carer' will be used to maintain consistency with the academic literature.

Theoretical approaches such as psychodynamic, person-centred, strengths-based and narrative methods and skills interventions will be used to consider how supportive relationships can be built with carers to understand how they manage the practical demands and their feelings, particularly when conflicting feelings of love, reciprocity, duty, satisfaction, sacrifice and burden can characterise the caring role (Barnes, 2006; Stalker, 2003). Moreover, consideration will be given to how the legislative and policy frameworks influence the way in which we form positive and meaningful relationships. Forming positive relationships with carers has always been a fundamental part of social work practice. The recent Department of Health (2014) guidance on whole family approaches under the Care Act 2014 also highlights the need for adult social care to work systemically, understanding the needs of families in the round, as well as working across organisational boundaries to join up practice through integrated and co-ordinated assessment arrangements. This suggests perhaps that adult social workers need a good understanding of systemic theory (narrative approaches being one example), to be effective communicators working together with families, rather than individuals (White and Epston, 1990). Either way, building empathic, authentic relationships that value and validate the experience of carers, viewing them as equal partners in care is an essential element in achieving the spirit and ethos of the Care Act and is at the heart of relationship-based practice.

The discussion will now continue with specific reference to the IDEAS Framework, looking at how the different aspects of this framework can be applied to relationship-based practice when working with carers.

Influence

We can conceptualise authority in several ways (Fook, 2002). One way concerns the authority vested in us by our employing organisation and as public office holders on behalf of a public body (local authority [LA]), if we are working in a statutory setting. As such, this refers to the duties and powers we enact on behalf of our employer, such as the assessment and eligibility decision-making duties that people with care and support needs are owed under the Care Act. The other is our own personal relationship with authority and power. The way in which we relate to people who hold power over us or vice versa is influenced to some extent by the way in which we experienced authority figures in our formative years and we need to be aware of the effects of this on current relationships, whereby we may transfer feelings and behaviours from past relationships with authority onto current relationships and also project these onto others, unconsciously, unless we bring awareness to such processes (Hennessey, 2011, pp 46–51). Having that self-awareness helps us to work in an anti-oppressive way because we are better able to share our own professional power with carers if we have a good understanding of how we personally relate to power.

Understanding of and use of self are critical components of both reflective practice and the ability to develop meaningful and positive relationships with carers that lead to purposeful outcomes. This places an emphasis on reciprocity in relationships (Hermsen and Embregts, 2015) and being able to work alongside carers, knowing what issues may need to take priority over others and being honest about what may be possible in relation to organisational constraints, such as timescales for assessment and support plans. Our influence as social workers is based upon our ability to communicate in an open, transparent and honest way, within the boundaries of our professional role.

Many statutory adult settings now use panels as a means of rationing funds. Although an administrative, as opposed to legal, function for social workers, they can be a daunting place to set out the rationale for the personal budget requested. One way of exerting influence is through legal literacy, used with confidence and clearly linked to the cared-for person's needs, established through a relationship-based approach, as characterised in the following extract.

Case Example

You are advocating on behalf of an adult with care and support needs, who has early-stage dementia and becomes anxious easily. In your professional opinion, you think their needs would be better served by a home care agency, that costs more than others, but is able to provide consistency of care. They can offer the same carer each day, which contributes not only to the well-being of the person using the service, but also to that of the carer, because they are able to leave the cared-for person, assured in the knowledge that the paid carer is able to develop a rapport and build a relationship, thus helping to reduce anxiety and offering the carer a break without being overly anxious of what they might find on their return home.

This is a sound rationale for requesting an increase in funds and one which takes account of the 'reasonable preference' principle contained within the Act. LAs must take account of the preferences, wishes and feelings of adults and those that care for them when considering the cost implications of support plans. Legal literacy allows you to influence those with budgetary decision-making responsibilities and to assert your assessment outcomes based upon a good working knowledge of the regulations and guidance (Department of Health, Care Act guidance, 2014, paragraph 11.24). The idea of taking account of wishes and preferences illustrates the importance of actively listening to families or friends and involving them in the assessment and support planning processes. Person-centred approaches to assessment can also reflect the importance of being able to influence others in different ways, illustrated by the following example.

Case Example

Mary (a White British woman) is main carer to her husband Bill (a Black African-Caribbean man), who was recently admitted to hospital following a fall at home. Bill has been referred for a social work assessment to facilitate a safe discharge from hospital. The social worker meets with Bill and Mary together and immediately Bill is resistant to the conversation. He is adamant he does not require any help or support at home and insists his wife can manage, although health colleagues have expressed concern about her ability to cope both to the couple and to the social worker.

Recognising that stressful life events can trigger a range of difficult emotions is a helpful starting point. Psychodynamic theories can provide useful explanations of how people can use a range of defensive behaviours to protect themselves from painful, distressing feelings, by employing, for example, projection, denial or avoidance strategies (Howe, 2008). Opening up with Bill about the fear and loss of control he may be experiencing from falling and being hospitalised helped to bring those feelings out in the open. At the same time, being open and honest about the limits of the role of the social worker and respecting his agency and right to choose whether to accept help as a capacitated adult reduced the emotional 'temperature' in the room. Bill decided not to accept an assessment of need. However, a conversation with Mary, in private, revealed a story of a challenging home environment where she was carrying out the majority of Bill's personal and practical care (bathing, personal hygiene, cooking, shopping and housework) and finding it increasingly difficult to manage. Her own life had taken 'a back seat', and her social space had shrunk, leading to feelings of isolation and loneliness. She is not in good physical health. She admits to the social worker privately that she is finding caring a struggle, physically and emotionally, but cannot admit that to her husband.

Offering carers a separate assessment of need, in private, away from the person being cared for, on the face of it does not sound like systemic practice. However, some carers do not always feel able to speak openly and honestly in front of the person they care for. Complex feelings of guilt, resentment, fear and helplessness can be mixed with satisfaction, love, duty and obligation. Narrative methods, with a 'tell me your story?' style of questioning can open up with carers how the nature of their relationship with the cared-for can influence how they feel about caring. Talking with Mary about her life before her husband's ill-health and increasing frailty revealed a story characterised by caring. Giving up a promising career once she married, to care for family and home, which she felt was her duty and obligation as a woman, wife and mother was tinged with resentment that social norms of the day expected that of her. She felt she should care for her husband but found the physical and emotional stresses and strains she now encountered difficult to manage. While both men and women can be carers, traditionally, it has been seen as a woman's role, reflected in Mary's sense that she should care as a reflection of how she sees herself, and Gilligan (1993, p 17) has commented that women *define themselves in a context of human relationship (and) judge themselves in terms of their ability to care'*. Giving carers the opportunity to talk freely about themselves can be an effective way to contextualise the current situation. This must be facilitated within a trusting and containing relationship context. With Mary's consent, the social worker spoke with Bill about how she was feeling, and he agreed that some support to help his wife would be an acceptable compromise to their situation. One of Bill's fears stemmed from a concern that home carers may try to 'take over' their lives or invade their privacy.

Narrative approaches or story telling are effective methods applied by systemic practitioners. People can experience problems when the stories of their lives (as they themselves or others have constructed them) do not represent their current reality. 'Re-storying' is considered a therapeutic way to re-tell or reconstruct a narrative that better fits with reality (White and Epston, 1990). In the foregoing example, the social worker could assist Mary through a narrative approach to unpick how social constructions of women's roles have influenced how she has attributed meaning to her role, which has prevented her from taking care of herself as well as her husband. This may help her to appreciate the potentially oppressive nature of societally determined roles for women and help her to achieve more agency. This can be done through a series of questions that can draw attention to how the problem (her sense of duty and obligation arising from social norms and expectations) has affected her relationships, her view of herself and how helpful or unhelpful this has been for her. By externalising the issues, the sense of guilt or failure can be mitigated (White and Epston, 2005).

Delivery

Delivery is concerned with the nuts and bolts of law and policy in relation to practice with carers. It is important to understand what public bodies can and cannot do when acting within the social work role as a public officer of the State. Legal literacy is complementary to relationship-based practice because a good working knowledge of the legal framework supports the ability to be transparent, honest and open about expectations, rights and needs. Here we see the relationship between influence and delivery. If influence is about our use of authority (personal and professional), then delivery is about the way in which we put that authority into practice to ensure an effective service.

It is important in assessment terms to view the carer in the context of their wider networks. Systems theory is helpful in explaining how people are part of systems, for example, couples, family, work and society, all with permeable boundaries that are interdependent (Bronfenbrenner, 1994; Ruch, 2010). For example, many working carers find that the stress of juggling a job with caring commitments, particularly if an employer is not particularly understanding, can have a significant impact upon their well-being.

Promoting well-being is one of the overarching duties and golden threads that runs throughout the Care Act 2014. Carers' assessments must consider the impact caring has upon a person's well-being and the Act provides a list of indicators for social workers to consider. The challenge with providing well-being as a list of indicators that can be measured in an objective sense is that it does not account for its inherently subjective nature and any objective measure of well-being cannot speak for every individual circumstance (Bache et al, 2014). In this context therefore, the assessment is an opportunity to have a conversation with a carer about their own aspirations and hopes for the future. The following example illustrates how a relationship-based approach may support this to happen.

Case Example

For several years, David, a White British man, has been caring for his wife Sue, also White British, who has chronic fatigue syndrome. Her condition fluctuates such that her level and intensity of need can change week by week. Some days she can require help with personal care and other days not so. The chronic fatigue meant she had to give up her job in teaching which she loved. Their social circle has shrunk as friends and activities have diminished over the years. David, too, made the decision to give up work last year to become Sue's full-time carer. The pressure of combining work with caring responsibilities has taken its toll on David's physical and mental health; and he now regrets the decision to give up his job in IT.

Carers' assessments under the Care Act 2014 must take account of:

>> whether a carer is, and is likely to continue to be, able *and* willing to care;

>> whether a carer works or wishes to;

>> whether a carer is participating in or wishes to participate in education, training or recreation.

(Department of Health, Care Act Guidance 2014, paragraph 6.18)

What David hopes to get out of the carer's assessment can be a helpful starting point, using person-centred practice to acknowledge and respect that David may have a very clear sense of what he would like to achieve. This involves using person-centred skills such as active listening, reflecting and summarising (Egan, 2009), to gain a shared clarity about David's thoughts and feelings about his current situation and his hopes and fears for the future. The Guidance also emphasises the importance of considering the assessment process in terms of outcomes, which means that an assessment includes identifying with a person's *'outcomes and how these impact on their well-being'* (Department of Health, 2017, para. 6.85). Finding out from David what matters most to him and what his own aspirations and hopes are for his own future recognises that he has a right to social inclusion as much as Sue and any other citizen, while giving him the space to articulate what may need to change to make his aspirations a possibility. It also recognises that he has needs beyond the caring role. If returning to work is an outcome he wishes to achieve, then the support planning process must consider ways in which that can be facilitated. The use of person-centred skills is clearly of crucial importance in determining David's needs and wishes in this respect.

In conducting the assessment, David's well-being has to be explored and whether and how the caring role has a significant impact on his well-being. What constitutes *significant impact* is not defined in law and this is where the professional skills of the social worker have an important role to play. The professional skill of the social worker can make what seems, on the face of it, an 'expert', objective, rational decision of eligibility into one that takes account of the subjectivity of what well-being means to the individual and how caring and its effects are unique in every sense.

For David, his decision to give up work was having a significant effect upon his well-being and this is identified following assessment. He has sourced a course at his local college which he felt would help him brush up on his IT skills and make him more employable. He has no savings, and their only income comes from Sue's disability benefits and his carers allowance. The outcomes-focused conversation with his social worker leads to a support plan which proposes a personal budget to help David get back on the road to employment through a direct payment to fund part of his IT course, with the remainder being sourced from grant funding.

It is possible to see from the language of the Act that needs must be considered in current but also in future time. For many carers, returning to employment may not be an aspiration in their current caring role, but may very well be in the future. The inclusion of the word *willing* is suggestive that social workers must not take for granted the contribution of the carer, even if carers themselves make that assumption.

Understanding the legal limits of the role and the duties and regulations imposed by the Care Act is central not only to defensible decision making, but also to the establishment of trust in the efficacy of the profession and the influence we may exert. Being able to justify the decisions made, for example, why one carer meets the eligibility criteria for support while another does not, must be based upon a sound knowledge of the law, so that reasoning can be articulated and justified, based on solid rational thinking within a relationship established on the values of trust, honesty and respect.

Expertise

This aspect of the IDEAS model refers to the knowledge and expertise that professional practice draws on when assessing and intervening in the life of a carer who may require support from services. The credibility of a practitioner is reliant on his or her ability to competently draw on the knowledge and skills that the profession has built up and which defines its professionalism, importantly linked to its value base. The values of the profession lie in its human rights-based approach, where person-centred planning is at its core. Equally, service user and carer involvement and participation are fundamental aspects of provision and people are valued and viewed as experts by experience (Beckett, 2015), bringing their expertise to complement that of the professional.

Two distinct themes emerge from the academic research literature on the experience of caring. First, there is a significant emphasis on the health and well-being effects of caring from physical, emotional, psychological and financial health perspectives (eg Burton, 2008; Thompson, 2009; Pickard et al, 2015; Carmichael and Ercolani, 2015; Greenwood and Smith, 2016). Second is the political and social construction of caring that emphasises the gendered nature of caring (eg Barnes, 2006), alongside a consideration of caring from an equalities and human rights-based perspective (eg Clements, 2013). Considering the way in which carers are 'constructed' politically and socially will help to shape the way in which the social worker is able to develop a positive relationship. Although dated, Twigg and Aitkin's typology of caring suggests that services generally construct carers in one of two ways, either as a resource (what they can contribute towards the care of another), or as a service user in need of help and support (someone who is not managing or coping with their caring role). They are rarely viewed as 'co-workers' or colleagues with expertise, knowledge and skills to contribute towards the care and support planning arrangement of the 'cared-for', or as someone with their own training and learning needs to care effectively and safely (Twigg and Atkin, 2012). This construction of carers as 'co-worker' or 'person with expertise' is a valuable tenet of person-centred practice. The notion that people are experts on themselves and possess knowledge and skills that can help them to overcome difficulties in their life is arguably an important element of a relationship-based approach. Carers frequently become 'expert' in their own field of knowledge, and, caring around the clock, they develop a knowledge base unique to their situation. An example to illustrate this is as follows.

Case Example

John, a White British man, had been caring for the last 15 years for his wife Elizabeth, a White British woman with a chronic muscular degenerative illness, which had left her unable to communicate verbally. Frequent hospital admissions meant that John accompanied and often stayed with Elizabeth that he could advocate on her behalf. During a discussion to consider discharge arrangements, ward staff complained to the hospital social worker about John's 'interfering' approach. He tells them how to do their job and complains if he thinks they are not properly understanding his wife's feelings or wishes. The hospital social worker (a Black British woman, originally from Nigeria) gains the impression that they feel John questions their knowledge and expertise about his wife's care needs.

A different narrative emerges from John when the social worker meets him. John is exhausted by his caring role. He feels the nurses take advantage of him staying with his wife and assume he will provide 'round-the-clock nursing care'. Because he knows his wife's needs intimately and understands through her non-verbal cues and expression how she is feeling, he can communicate this to ward staff. He feels he complements their role; however, at times, he also thinks that certain staff members are defensive about his suggestions and comments, which he feels are well-meaning attempts not only to advocate for his wife but also to make their jobs easier.

Understanding psychoanalytical theories in relation to unconscious processes has value in informing relationship-based practices because it allows the social worker to consider the complexity of human interaction, behaviour and personality and how defensive practices emerge in cultures of anxiety and uncertainty (Higley-Jones and Ruch, 2016). Being able to explore these feelings openly can help to reduce conflict and return a sense of equilibrium and mutual understanding (Ruch et al, 2010). Projection, transference and counter-transference are defensive behaviours that protect us from feeling anxiety and painful emotions. Avoidance is a good example of a defensive behaviour. Note how the nurses in this case scenario go to the social worker rather than John to raise the issue. Avoiding John directly, in the hope that the social worker can deal with their concern, protects the nurses from any potential conflict and anxiety that may arise from interacting with John directly. The nurses' response to John can also be thought of in terms of a projective process. Rather than accepting his comments as a well-meaning attempt to support their nursing care, they were internalised as criticism of their ability. This can elicit painful feelings of inadequacy, guilt or failure on the part of the nursing staff, particularly in a working culture that expects them to cope, and undervalues the emotional element of their labour (Theodosius, 2013). These can be difficult emotions to engage with as they require attention through self-reflection and a safe supervisory space to examine one's sense of self and professional identity. Projecting those unwanted difficult feelings onto John by labelling him as obstructive and interfering is an effective way to avoid the possible guilt and inadequacy the nurses may feel.

Self-awareness and self-reflection are crucial to relationship-based practice and are part of the professional expertise that social workers use in practice. A social worker's own construction of carers will be influenced to some extent by her/his own cultural and social norms. For example, whether caring is considered to be something that families should do as a duty, or whether there should always be a choice about whether to care, will inevitably be shaped by an individual's own experiences of being a member of a particular family and culture. It is critical that practitioners are aware of the assumptions they are making and at times be prepared to challenge their assumptions, in order to work in an anti-oppressive manner. This is imperative if the lived experience of carers is to be understood in a non-judgemental way. An example of oppressive practice would be to make a value judgement that an adult daughter would want to care for her ageing parents if they required care and support because that is 'what caring daughters do'. For her to reject a caring role may leave one feeling judgemental about her love and commitment to her parents. It is important to remember the social norms which dominate the discourse of caring in our society and how these norms influence our thinking and practice and ability to build strong relationships with carers.

Sociological perspectives importantly inform practice. Caring prevents women from entering the labour market and masks the labour dimensions of unpaid work. Thompson (2009) locates free agency within a feminist critique of welfare policy which suggests that society's view of caring as women's work continues to be the site of women's oppression and social exclusion from society. Feminist social work offers an important perspective on how to work in a woman-centred way (see Teater, 2014, pp 91–107).

One way of combating the risk of exclusion for carers is to utilise a practical ethical framework which emphasises interdependency and supports the relational aspects of caring based on an 'ethic of care' which sits well within a relationship-based approach to practice. Arising from this, Stalker (2003) and Burton (2008) propose an alternative construction of caring as relational or reciprocal. This position suggests that carers' needs should be considered in relation to the needs of the cared-for. Locating them separately does not account for the interdependence that exists in many relationships. Stalker (2003) argues that the rights of carers must not be at the expense of the rights of people with disabilities. It requires that the practitioner works with both perspectives – of carer and cared-for – in an attempt to support both by making sense with them of the feelings and emotions that caring or being cared for evokes, through the application of the person-centred skills of active listening (Egan, 2009), empathic understanding (Howe, 2013) and identification of needs (eg using Taylor and Devine's concept of 'tuning in' [Taylor and Devine, 1993, pp 20–2]) that may then lead to further practical or emotional support to relieve the difficulties faced.

To sum up, expertise can be thought of as a blended approach comprising both formal knowledge (of the Care Act duties and powers in relation to assessment and supporting planning); how you may incorporate knowledge from research (theories and models) to understand people's situations and how you apply this within a value base congruent with the values of the profession; and informal knowledge (that which is gained from peers, experience and interacting with the social environment). Informal knowledge will be influenced strongly by one's personal value base and the way in which reality is constructed from one's own life experience and cultural reference points. Awareness of self – how past relationships influence present ones and when one's own personal value base may conflict with professional and/or organisational values – is a crucial component in maintaining honesty and transparency in practice.

Alliance

This element of the model asks us to consider how the relationship itself can be a lever and a catalyst that brings about meaningful change. This is where person-centred principles of the humanist tradition and its values of positive regard, warmth, empathy and respect come to the fore (Egan, 2009). Treating people with dignity and respect irrespective of one's own emotional response demonstrates an emotionally intelligent practitioner. In terms of practical application, co-production as a model of practice best illustrates this approach (see Chapter 1). Active listening skills are an essential ingredient in developing a working alliance with carers. Use of non-verbal (body language) and verbal cues (paraphrasing, summarising and empathising) help to shape our understanding of carers' lived experiences. Awareness of self is critical to the formation of an effective alliance, through tuning in to one's own defensive thoughts and behaviours, for example, in response to the person's communication style. Considering one's own feelings and emotional responses to situations will help to make sense of what may be difficult or conflicting feelings towards people using services and their carers by being aware, for example, when someone is projecting their unwanted negative feelings towards the social worker and suggesting she/he is the problem as illustrated in the following case example.

Case Example

David has chronic obstructive airways disease (COPD) and a student social worker has been asked to assess what support he may need at home to maintain his independence. On arrival, he makes comments about her young age and questions her knowledge base of COPD. She is not medically trained, and he wants to see someone who is medically qualified who would know more about his condition and what support he should have. She talks in supervision with her manager about another older more experienced worker taking over the assessment as she feels unable to move the conversation away from this topic and David became angry and frustrated at her seeming lack of respect for his wishes.

The manager acknowledges how the situation made her feel but challenges the view that another worker may be able to carry out an assessment any better. They discuss how his projected feelings about her competence left her feeling inadequate but also how his feelings may be evidence of unconscious fears about a condition that renders breathing laboured and the possible feelings of crisis and panic that shortness of breath can bring in acute episodes. She then recognises that one way to remove this block may be to acknowledge how he is feeling and not allow her own emotional response to cloud her critical and constructive thinking skills. Critically reflective and emotionally resilient practitioners (Grant and Brewer, 2014, pp 54–6) can regulate and keep in check their own emotional states. The student agrees to go back, with another colleague, and carry out a joint assessment.

Support

In this aspect of the model, the role of supervision and training is crucial for the proper support of individual practitioners. Organisations have a duty of care towards their employees, which means that they should take all steps which are reasonably possible to ensure their health, safety and well-being (ACAS, 2012). Employers need to recognise the value and business case in investing in high-quality supervision that may support the retention of staff and reduce 'burn out'. This is an investment both of time and money. Demonstrating concern for the physical and mental health of employees can be shown in many ways, including the nature and culture of the supervisory relationship. Supervision is a crucial component in the development of professional expertise and practice. For expertise to flourish, social workers require a space where they can talk openly about their practice, and share ideas and concerns in a non-judgemental way. There is an argument for performance management conversations to be kept separate from the practice discussions (Munsen, 2002). Warmth, care, empathy and respect are just some of the elements within the values of social work, going back to delivery and the idea of reciprocity in relationships and the notion of an 'ethic of care'. The support that social workers provide for people using services and their carers, building and maintaining working relationships with them to promote change, involves 'emotion work' that has an impact on the social worker, which needs to be recognised in supervision. Managerial approaches to supervision tend to ignore this. In recognising the emotional aspects of social work, it is important that social workers are supported by their managers and organisations, using the same care ethic, which focuses not just on organisational accountability, but on the impact of emotional labour on the individual worker. The concept of 'nested dependencies' (Kittay, 1999, pp 66–8) is useful here, in emphasising the importance of providing a caring container within the organisation for those (ie the social workers) caring for others.

Reflective practitioner groups also offer the opportunity for workers to be supported and develop their practice, learn from others and consolidate their existing knowledge base. Informal sources of support, which may often be below cost/no cost options, while not replacing formal support and training, offer an alternative source of support, learning and development that enrich knowledge, understanding and ultimately practice.

Conclusion

In summary, this chapter has demonstrated that a relationship-based approach to social work practice requires not only skills in making and sustaining relationships (and the theories and values informing these skills), but also knowledge of the legal framework and research evidence, showing that legal literacy alongside knowledge from research and practice wisdom form the bedrock of practice rooted in principles of equalities and human rights. Understanding the limits of the role, both in terms of legal and moral authority together with self-awareness and an appreciation of emotional intelligence, will support real partnership working and co-production. Having an awareness of the way in which carers are constructed in society and one's own values and beliefs about caring will support working in an anti-oppressive manner that will develop and maintain positive working relationships for the benefit of service users and their carers.

References

ACAS (Advisory, Conciliation and Arbitration Service) (2012) An Employer's Duty of Care. [online] Available at: www.acas.org.uk/index.aspx?articleid=3751 (accessed 25 April 2019).

Bache, I, Reardon, L and Anand, P (2014) Happiness, Well-Being and the Role of Government: The Case of the UK. Paper presented at Well-being 2013 conference, 24–25 July.

Barnes, M (2006) Caring and Social Justice. Basingstoke: Palgrave.

Beckett, C (2015) Essential Theory for Social Work Practice. London: Sage.

Bronfenbrenner, U (1994) Ecological Models of Human Development. In International Encyclopedia of Education (Vol. 3, 2nd edn). Oxford: Elsevier.

Buckner, L and Yeandle, S (2011) Valuing Carers. [online] Available at: http://circle.leeds.ac.uk/files/2012/08/110512-circle-carers-uk-valuing-carers.pdf (accessed 25 June 2018).

Burton, M (2008) Grounding Constructions of Carers: Exploring the Experiences of Carers through a Grounded Approach. The British Journal of Social Work, 38(3): 493–501.

Carmichael, F and Ercolani, M G (2015) Unpaid Caregiving and Paid Work over Life-courses: Different Pathways, Diverging Outcomes. *Social Science & Medicine*, 156: 1–11. Available through Albert Sloman library (accessed 9 September 2017).

Clements, L (2013) Does Your Carer Take Sugar? Carers and Human Rights. *Washington & Lee Journal of Civil Rights and Social Justice*, 19(1): 397–434.

Department of Health (2014) *Care Act Statutory Guidance.* [online] Available at: www.gov.uk/government/publications/care-act-2014-statutory-guidance-for-implementation (accessed 25 June 2018).

Department of Health (2017) The Care and Support Statutory Guidance (revised 2017). [online] Available at: www.gov.uk/government/publications/care-act-statutory-guidance/care-and-support-statutory-guidance (accessed 25 April 2019).

Egan, G (2009) *The Skilled Helper* (9th edn). London: Cengage Learning.

Fook, J (2002) *Social Work: Critical Theory and Practice.* London: Sage.

Garlo, K, O'Leary, J, Van Ness, P H and Fried, T R (2010) Caregiver Burden in Caregivers of Older Adults with Advanced Illness. *Journal of American Geriatrics Society*, 58(12): 2315–22. [online] Available at: www.ncbi.nlm.nih.gov/pmc/articles/PMC3058825 (accessed 25 April 2019).

Gilligan, C (1993) *In a Different Voice: Psychological Theory and Women's Development.* Cambridge, MA: Harvard University Press.

Goldstein, H (1990) The Knowledge Base of Social Work Practice: Theory, Wisdom, Analogue, or Art? *Families in Society: The Journal of Contemporary Human Services*, 71: 32–43.

Grant, L and Brewer, B (2014) Critical Reflection and Reflective Supervision. In Grant, L and Kinman, G (eds) *Developing Resilience for Social Work Practice* (pp 54–72). Basingstoke: Palgrave Macmillan.

Greenwood, N and Smith, R (2016) The Oldest Carers: A Narrative Review and Synthesis of the Experiences of Carers Aged over 75 Years. *Maturitas*, 94: 161–72. [online] Available at: http://eprints.kingston.ac.uk/36345/3/Greenwood_N_36345_VoR.pdf (accessed 25 April 2019).

Hennessey, R (2011) *Relationship Skills in Social Work.* London: Sage.

Hermsen, M and Embregts, P (2015) An Explorative Study of the Place of the Ethics of Care and Reflective Practice in Social Work Education and Practice. *The International Journal of Social Work Education*, 34(7): 815–28.

Hingley-Jones, H and Ruch, G (2016) 'Stumbling through'? Relationship-based Social Work Practice in Austere Times. *Journal of Social Work Practice*, 30(3): 235–48.

Howe, D (2013) *Empathy: What It Is and Why It Matters.* Basingstoke: Palgrave Macmillan.

Jessup, N, Bakas, T, McLennon, S M and Weaver, M T (2015) Are There Gender, Racial or Relationship Differences in Caregiver Task Difficulty, Depressive Symptom and Life Changes among Stroke Family Carers? *Brain Injury*, 29(1): 17–24. Available through Albert Sloman Library (accessed 21 July 2017).

Kittay, E (1999) *Loves Labor: Essays on Women, Equality and Dependency.* New York: Routledge.

Munsen, C E (2002) *Handbook of Clinical Supervision* (3rd edn). New York: Howorth Social Work Practice Press.

Pickard, L, King, D and Knapp, M (2015) The 'visibility' of Unpaid Care in England. *Journal of Social Work*, 16(3): 263–82. doi: 10.1177/1468017315569645 (accessed 25 April 2019).

Pivodic, L, Van den Block, L, Pardon, K, Miccinesi, G, Vega Alonso, T, Boffin, N, Donker, G A, Cancian, M, Lopez-Maside, A, Onwuteaka-Philipsen, B D, Deliens, L; EURO IMPACT, Van den Block, L, De Groote, Z, Brearley, S, Caraceni, A, Cohen, J, Francke, A, Harding, R, Higginson, I J, Kaasa, S, Linden, K, Miccinesi,G, Onwuteaka-Philipsen, B, Pardon, K, and Pasman, H P (2014) Burden on Family Carers and Care Related Financial Strain at the End of Life: A Cross National Population-based Study: 1–8. Available through Albert Sloman Library (accessed 21 September 2017).

Ruch, G, Turney, D and Ward, A (2010) *Relationship-based Social Work: Getting to the Heart of Practice.* London: Jessica Kingsley.

Schön, D A (1973) Beyond the Stable State (pp 30), 116–79. The Norton Library, W.W. Norton and Company INC, New York reprinted as Chapter 1 in Blackmore, C (ed, 2010) *Social Learning Systems and Communities of Practice*. Milton Keynes/London: The Open University/Springer.

Stalker, K (ed) (2003) *Reconceptualising Work with Carers: New Directions for Policy and Practice*. London: Jessica Kingsley.

Taylor, B and Devine, T (1993) *Assessing Needs and Planning Care in Social Work*. Aldershot: Arena Ashgate.

Teater, B (2014) *An Introduction to Applying Social Work Theories and Methods* (2nd edn). Maidenhead: Open University Press/McGraw Hill.

Theodosius, C (2013) Emotional Labour. In Gabe, J and Monaghan, L F (eds) *Key Concepts in Medical Sociology* (2nd edn). London: Sage.

Thompson, D (2009) *The Social and Political Construction of Care: Community Care Policy and the 'Private' Carer*. University of Bedfordshire. Available through the British Library (accessed 24 July 2017).

Twigg, J and Atkin, K (2012) Who Cares? Managing Obligations and Responsibility across the Changing Landscapes of Informal Care. *Ageing and Society*, 33(5): 888–907.

White, M and Epston, D (1990) *Narrative Means to Therapeutic Ends*. New York: Norton.

White, M and Epston, D (2005) Externalising the Problem. In Malone, C, Forbat, L, Robb, M and Seden, J (eds) *Relating Experience: Stories from Health and Social Care* (pp 88–94). Oxon: Routledge.

Wenger, E (2012) *Communities of Practice: Learning, Meaning and Identity*. Cambridge: University Press.

Yeandle, S and Buckner, L (2011) *Valuing Carers 2011*. London: Carers UK.

Keeping the relationship in mind: using the IDEAS model in mental health practice

Dee Mustin

Introduction

I plan to start this chapter by considering what we mean by the terms 'mental illness' and 'mental capacity', before looking at the role of relationships and the way we can use the IDEAS framework as a model to support best practice in mental health social work.

Mental health has been defined by the World Health Organisation (2014) as *'a state of well-being in which every individual realises his or her own potential, can cope with the normal stresses of life, can work productively and fruitfully, and is able to make a contribution to her or his community'*. Although the term 'mental health' is often used by the media interchangeably with 'mental illness', these terms are not synonymous. However, defining mental illness is not straightforward and there is debate regarding how useful concepts of mental ill health are as there is often disagreement between professionals and people as to whether they are experiencing mental illness (Lishman et al, 2018). While acknowledging individual experiences, there is a general acceptance that mental illness, specifically mental disorders, share common characteristics that have been robustly evidenced and which affect a person's behaviour, psychological or biological functioning (DSM-V, 2013).

Mental capacity relates primarily to the ability to make decisions, and includes the ability to understand information; to retain it long enough to make a decision; to weigh-up the information and to communicate the decision (Mental Capacity Act, 2005). One of the principles of the Mental Capacity Act is that there should be an assumption of capacity, and therefore, even when someone is acutely mentally unwell, it should not be assumed that they lack capacity to make a decision (eg whether or not they agree to a specific treatment).

One of the major criticisms of psychiatry down the years has been that mental illness was seen as primarily biological in nature, and that this masks the social and material causes of distress in society (Parker et al, 1995). The disease model of psychiatry began to be challenged in the 1960s within the profession itself by psychiatrists including R D Laing (1960). Psychosocial models of mental illness are now far more prominent, recognising the primary influence of social factors and the environment on mental ill health (Tew, 2011). Within current mental health practice, which is often multidisciplinary, the model that arguably works best to inform a holistic approach to treatment and care is one that combines biological and social models such as the biopsychosocial model (Engel, 1980).

As mental health social workers, we are working with people who are frequently distressed, often vulnerable and possibly in crisis. Developing and using an effective relationship-based approach as a foundation for change will always be important. In this chapter I aim to show that the IDEAS framework provides a helpful structure for ensuring that people are kept at the forefront of service delivery, and that the relationships we develop with them and with colleagues or partner agencies can be an effective precursor for change.

Influence

Generally, when working in a community mental health setting, it can be assumed that the person is choosing to receive services; and where there is choice, and the professional has something worth offering in terms of progress towards recovery, there is potential for the development of an alliance between the person accessing services and the professional (Lacay, 2013). However, there will be many situations where the person has limited or no choice about receiving services, for example, when detained in hospital under the Mental Health Act (1983), or when compelled to accept treatment under a Community Treatment Order (CTO) (Section 17, Mental Health Act, 1983), with the threat of recall to hospital if they do not comply with the conditions. In these situations, the need for transparency is very important and if, as a practitioner, you support the need for containment and control, you need to have an open, honest dialogue with the person (when they are well enough to be able to cope with the discussion), explaining the reasons for the intervention and how they might be supported to avoid admission in the future, or (in the case of a CTO), work towards the possibility of the Order being discharged (Mental Health Act Code of Practice, 2017).

Case Example

Care co-ordinator Andrea, who is White British, is due to attend a pre-discharge ward review for Peter, a 29 year-old White British man living with schizophrenia, who has had three admissions to psychiatric hospital within three years. He has relapsed on each occasion having stopped taking the prescribed medication, and he is currently detained under Section 3 of the Mental Health Act (1983) for treatment. The consultant psychiatrist has asked the care co-ordinator and an AMHP to attend the ward review to discuss the plan to apply for a Community Treatment Order (CTO) prior to Peter's discharge, which, it is hoped, will provide a framework for effective treatment as Peter can be recalled to hospital if he does not accept depot medication.

Andrea discusses this plan in supervision and argues that although she agrees that a CTO is necessary, she should not attend the ward review because by doing so Peter will see her as part of the system, and she will lose any therapeutic alliance that she has developed with him. Her supervisor persuades Andrea that being open about her agreement with the treatment plan is demonstrating honesty and transparency, which is equally important within the therapeutic relationship. She persuades her therefore to attend the review.

By attending and contributing to the ward review discussions, Andrea is acknowledging the power differential in a way that will hopefully promote honest dialogue with Peter around the reasons for the treatment plan. Although the social worker is implicated here in the exercise of power over the individual, their loss of control and any feelings that this engenders may be ameliorated through a careful explanation of the reasons for the decision (that treatment decisions were made in his best interest and to optimise his chance of recovery). This does not negate Andrea's continued attempt to build a therapeutic relationship with Peter and using person-centred skills of genuineness, empathy and unconditional positive regard (Rogers, 1961) can assist this. Honesty and transparency clearly link to the Rogerian idea of Congruence (Rogers, 1957), which is the need for practitioners to present as real and genuine as a way of getting alongside people; attending the ward review and having an open conversation with Peter demonstrates respect, which is fundamental to the development of trust.

Conversely, Andrea may not have agreed with the necessity for a CTO, and she may have cogent clinical and therapeutic arguments for avoiding coercive treatment of this kind. In this instance she will need to use the legitimate authority inherent within her social work role to question and challenge this decision.

Case Example

Andrea attends the ward review, at which Peter is present, and suggests that he is prepared to take oral medication because he has begun to recognise the relapsing nature of his illness. She says that he has stopped taking medication previously because he hates the side effect of weight gain, but with his agreement she plans to apply for funding for gym membership for him, to better manage the impact of increased appetite. She argues that being forced to take medication, whether depot injection or oral, will leave Peter feeling disempowered and lacking in control, which is likely to impact on his mood and levels of stress (Stress Vulnerability Model of Psychosis, Zubin et al, 1977).

Andrea's arguments may or may not prevail, but adopting a feminist 'ethic of care', where she is focusing on the identity of Peter and understanding how he views himself by listening to his 'story' (Morgan et al, 2016, p 16), enables her to represent his wishes and to advocate for him. This may be even more necessary if Peter cannot easily express his own views in what can be a formal and intimidating setting.

If the clinical team decide to apply for a CTO in this case, it will be important that Andrea explains the reasons for this decision and continues to support Peter to comply with conditions in the interest of his mental health and to try and avoid further hospital admissions. By so doing she is being realistic about the legal regulations imposed upon him, and representing the decision reached by the multidisciplinary team, of which she is a part.

At the same time, Andrea can support Peter to appeal to the Mental Health Review Tribunal (Section 66 MHA 1983), as well as providing arguments for revoking the CTO (if appropriate), at the point of renewal. The importance of advocacy for people whose lives are impacted by Mental Health Act orders is formally recognised by the introduction of independent mental health advocacy services (Mental Health Act, 1983: Code of Practice, Chapter 9). However, the social worker as care co-ordinator also has an important advocacy role within the wider service. The relationship we develop with the person should enable us to support them to represent their views and wishes in the clinical context, and there may be times when we can use the influence inherent within our role to ensure their thoughts and feelings are heard. For example, when a parent who is mentally ill is attending a case conference for their child following safeguarding concerns, our mental health knowledge may assist an argument in support of the child remaining with the parent where we believe that concerns about their mental health do not sufficiently impact on the child's safety and well-being.

Delivery

Social workers are required to operate within a statutory framework which defines professional responsibility and prescribes codes of conduct. This includes the Care Act 2014, the Mental Health Act 2007, the Mental Capacity Act 2005 and the Mental Health Act 1983, among others. Most mental health care is provided within primary health care settings such as General Practitioner (GP) surgeries or by health visitors or community pharmacists. Staff working in these areas know that long-term physical health conditions and chronic pain can have a detrimental impact on an individual's mental health, and lead to depression and anxiety (Chapman et al, 2004). Equally, GPs will sometimes see patients presenting with physical health concerns which could be linked to unrecognised underlying mental health issues. Therefore, GPs need to understand mental health conditions and be able to effectively treat the majority of these in primary care. Medication may be the first line of treatment, but the Department of Health's Improving Access to Psychological Therapy (IAPT) programme (Department of Health, 2007), enables GPs to also prescribe psychological therapies such as Cognitive Behavioural Therapy (CBT) within primary care for patients with mild to moderate depression and anxiety. There is an increasing emphasis on the use of other holistic approaches such as 'social prescribing' where a link worker helps a person to connect to existing groups and resources in the community to provide 'practical and emotional support' (NHS England online).

It is well recognised that early diagnosis and treatment is key to improving people's chances of staying well, and effective treatment at an earlier stage may avoid the need for referral to secondary mental health services, which are primarily aimed at chronic and severe mental illness that cannot be managed in primary care (NHS England, 2016). My focus in this section will be on how services are delivered within secondary care, and on the relevance and importance of using a relationship-based approach at every stage, despite the arguably bureaucratic nature of many aspects of service delivery.

Although arrangements for the management of secondary mental health referrals vary in different areas of the country, the processes basically cover triage, assessment and crisis response. At any of these stages the outcome might be signposting to other services or referral back to primary care. The clear majority of non-crisis referrals come from GPs (British Medical Association, 2017) and in some areas of the country these may be referred to the GP after an initial telephone assessment (triage) with the person referred, with advice about suggested further treatment or support provided.

Even at the stage of telephone triage however, the professional can make the interaction positive and meaningful by using a person-centred approach (Rogers, 1961); listening and using empathic understanding to accurately check-out and identify the primary issues that have brought the person to services. If the conclusion of the triage assessment is that secondary services are not required, the worker needs to develop an ability to explain the decision and the reasons for it in a meaningful way that minimises the risk that the referred will simply see it as a rejection. 'Signposting', where relevant, is an important part of this process because the worker is identifying more helpful ways for the person's needs to be addressed; utilising a narrative approach (Kearney and Williams, 1996) to listen to and understand the person's story is necessary before the worker is then able to use their knowledge of services to redirect the person appropriately.

It could be argued that assessment is more important than any other single social work intervention, in that it forms the basis for all subsequent care planning and service delivery (Milner et al, 2015). Assessment is not necessarily a single intervention; indeed, Coulshed and Orme (2012) and Turnell and Murphy (2017) suggest that assessment is continuous in order to fully understand people within the context of their environments (Coulshed and Orme) and to understand and effectively manage risk (Turnell and Murphy), and within mental health settings, assessment is both an initial intervention and an ongoing process. The ongoing approach acknowledges that the needs of people change over time, especially following critical events (Crisp et al, 2005). Crisp et al (2005) also argue that assessment is inseparable from intervention and service delivery.

An effective, holistic assessment within the field of mental health covers all aspects of an individual's life, including early history; family situation; physical health; social situation; finances; relationships; symptoms; sleep; appetite; mood; spiritual/religious beliefs and so on (Golightly, 2014). The skill of the assessor lies in an ability to ask relevant supplementary questions to add detail in relevant areas, thereby enabling a full and accurate picture to be painted: one that the person will recognise but, in some cases, with details that they had not previously noticed. For example, a person may present with depression and issues in the workplace may be where they see their problems starting. Exploration of their history may highlight a link between the bullying they experienced at school and their difficulties at work now, where there is perceived bullying behaviour. Making the link may be the starting point for deciding how best to manage the situation.

We now recognise that many cases of adult mental illness are linked to childhood trauma, including sexual abuse (Jonas et al, 2010). We have thankfully moved forward from the 1990s when mental health care professionals were generally reluctant to ask questions of this nature for fear of 'opening up a can of worms', and it is now a question routinely asked at initial assessment. Even though the person may not want to disclose abuse at that stage, by asking the question we are normalising this as a subject for enquiry as well as recognising the validity of these experiences in connection with current experience of mental illness (Spataro et al, 2004).

It is fundamental to the IDEAS model that services are delivered in partnership with people. In order to do this, however, it is also important to acknowledge differences in societal and cultural contexts and to have an understanding of anti-discriminatory practice within the specialism of mental health, and the influence that racism within society, for example, may have had on an individual. It is also vitally important to acknowledge both the social and cultural context within which the person is living. For example, *'The marginality and social exclusion experienced by minority ethnic groups in the UK are likely to be significant in understanding the mental health experience in these communities and their access to mental health services'* (National Institute for Mental Health in England, 2003, p 9). The Independent Review of the Mental Health Act 1983 (Modernising the Mental Health Act, 2018), details steps to tackle the disproportionate number of people from minority ethnic communities detained under the Mental Health Act. This includes the development of an organisational competence framework which is designed to *'improve mental health service access and outcomes in ethnic minority people'* (p 56).

Although cultural knowledge does not equate to cultural competence (Ben-Ari and Strier, 2010), it is important to gain specific knowledge to equip us to meet the needs of individuals within their cultural context. For instance, a social worker may think that by placing a young Ethiopian refugee in a hostel with other young Ethiopian men, they are meeting his needs for contact with his own community. However, there is more than one Ethiopian language commonly spoken and there are likely to be significant issues for a man from the Oromia community living with others from the Ethiopian Somali community due to recent violent conflicts between these communities in Ethiopia (BBC News, 2017).

We cannot talk about assessment within mental health without considering risk assessment, which is generally a stand-alone part of the assessment process. There has been huge pressure on public authorities to adopt defensive risk management policies in recent years (Power, 2004), and one outcome has been a focus on learning from serious incidents and near misses. Moreover, secondary mental health services are funded by clinical commissioning groups (CCGs) and Key Performance Indicators (KPIs) are used to measure timely completion of assessments, allocation of work and routine completion of care plans, reviews, clustering and outcome scoring etc (Allen et al, 2016). As a consequence of this, there is a risk that practice becomes increasingly defensive and as a result, the person, in all their complexity, can become lost amidst all of the business processes and timescales designed to minimise risk, and evidence the work being undertaken. Using the analogy of the human body where Delivery is the skeleton, it is not always indicative of a healthy individual where there is insufficient flesh on the bones and you can see the framework of the skeleton beneath the skin. At times our practice does not feel very person-centred when there is an imbalance between time spent on bureaucracy and time spent working with the individual. Therefore, in order to be effective, workers need to ensure they are paying equal measure to other parts of the IDEAS model such as Influence and Alliance in order to truly engage in relationship-based practice.

I have focused a lot on assessment as part of the delivery of mental health services, but it is important to note the importance of care planning as the core role of the care co-ordinator under the Care Programme Approach (Department of Health, 2008). It is essential that care planning is done alongside the person and that whatever format is used, it includes identified needs, the actions agreed upon to meet those needs, and who is responsible for the actions. It should also include a timescale for review (generally a minimum of six-monthly), and a contingency or risk management plan for when things go wrong. Shared decision making is an important principle in working towards recovery because it recognises the person's expertise developed through their experience of mental illness (Morgan et al, 2016).

Risk management is an area of service delivery which can lead to cross-agency conflict, particularly where there is poor understanding of the reasons for positive risk-taking, which can be illustrated in the following case example.

Case Example

Wendy is a 28 year-old White British woman with a diagnosis of emotionally unstable personality disorder. She is a frequent attender at A&E following incidents of self- harm, and she has been brought to the local 'place of safety' in the psychiatric unit by the police on many occasions, having been picked up at the railway station with the stated intention of throwing herself beneath a train.

The care plan includes a risk management strategy which stipulates that admission to psychiatric hospital should be avoided. At a professionals' meeting held to discuss future risk management, the police and Wendy's GP are both present and they express frustration that mental health services do not admit Wendy to hospital for treatment.

The care co-ordinator and the community team psychiatrist explain that Wendy is seeking care in a maladaptive way and if she is 'rescued' and her needs are met in the short term by hospital admission, this is unlikely to reduce the risk of her acting in the same way next time she experiences emotional distress.

The care co-ordinator has understood the link between Wendy's early childhood trauma and rejection by trusted individuals, and her care-seeking behaviour now (Bowlby, 2005). The care co-ordinator is supporting Wendy to manage her emotional distress by demonstrating compassionate boundaries, and using a humanistic perspective to support her to manage her distress differently (Rogers, 1961). Good communication and cooperation between agencies is likely to promote a positive outcome for Wendy, which, it is hoped, will reduce the risky behaviours.

It will also be crucially important within the person/worker relationship that the rationale for the response is explained as being in her long-term interests, not a punitive response to difficult behaviour. The care co-ordinator will also need to demonstrate empathy by attempting to understand the reason for Wendy's distress when she engages in care-seeking behaviour, and they can look at alternative ways that she can be supported to manage her distress at these times.

Expertise

Expertise as described in the IDEAS model is extremely valuable for social workers as a way of underpinning the importance and relevance of 'practice wisdom' in the field of mental health: primarily because it is a field where medical ideas involving an evidence base for all practice have potentially led to an undervaluing of knowledge gained from experience. In the early years of community mental health teams, this emphasis sometimes contributed to a professional divide.

As a social worker I can recall times where my suggestions regarding intervention based on what I had seen to be helpful were effectively silenced by the question: 'but what is the evidence base?' However, while practice wisdom is of great importance, mental health social workers do need to have a good understanding of medical models of mental illness alongside other models, as well as a broad understanding of the history of treatment approaches. They also need to understand the range of treatment options, including medication and associated side effects. By understanding the range of approaches and treatments, we can avoid having a 'one-size-fits-all' response to treatment.

Mental disorders are broadly separated into two categories: organic and functional, although, as mentioned in the introduction, there is recognition of how the effects of biological, psychological and social factors interact to affect a person's well-being (Wade and Halligan, 2017). Organic disorders, like dementia or Korsakoff's syndrome, are generally identifiable by medical testing such as MRI scanning or blood tests (Arts et al, 2017). With functional illness, which includes depression, anxiety and psychotic illnesses, organic causes may need to be ruled-out. For instance, if an older person develops psychotic symptoms they should be checked for a urinary tract infection which could be causing delirium (Graham et al, 2014).

It has long been accepted that psychiatry is an inexact science, and there have been many developments in knowledge and changes of approach over the years (Rovinelli-Heller and Gitterman, 2011). This is particularly relevant with regard to our understanding of the possible causes of mental illness. These range from biochemical (eg excessive dopamine transmission in the brain of people with schizophrenia), to genetic causes (inherited predisposition to bipolar disorder, for example), and more recently, suggested physical causes such as theories concerning a link between gut bacteria and mental illness (Naseribafrouei et al, 2014), and the role of the immune system in certain cases of psychotic illness (Al-Diwani et al, 2017).

Understanding the range of possible causes is essential to providing effective treatment, and the mental health social worker has a role in helping the person to navigate through the psychiatric system and understand possible treatment options. However, the primary role of the non-medical professional is to balance medical perspectives with a focus on the psychological and sociological impact on a person's mental health. The psychiatrist Peter Breggin describes the major mental disorders such as schizophrenia and bipolar disorder: *'Each is an example of psychological overwhelm or, at least, hazardous stumbling along life's path'* (Breggin, 1993, p 33). Therefore, the role of the social worker is important as they focus on the wider social and environmental impact on an individual in order to address underlying causes of mental distress as well as tackling the stigma and discrimination commonly experienced by people with mental health problems (Allen et al, 2016).

The lived experience of people with psychosis has contributed to a relatively new approach to the experience of hearing voices, outside the medical model, developed by Professor Marius Romme and Sandra Escher (Romme and Escher, 1993). They focus on the relationship between the voices and critical events in the voice hearer's life, and use this knowledge to help them change their relationship with their voices. They believe that this is the only way to recover from the distress that the voices bring, and supporting people to follow this road is the only way to help them overcome their distress (Romme et al, 2009).

All of the different theories and approaches highlight the importance of the mental health professional needing to continually update their practice and knowledge by training and reading about new research, as well as using supervision and the shared experience of colleagues to decide which approaches are most applicable in a given situation. This knowledge can help in the development of a 'toolkit' for effective intervention. The person must be seen as an 'expert by experience', but very often, when it comes to knowing what will make a difference, they may know more about what has *not* worked than what *will* work, which is why they have come to services for help; it is a combination of the knowledge and experience the person brings, together with the professional knowledge and practice wisdom of the worker that can make a positive difference and support well-being (Mathews and Crawford, 2011).

Part of the professional's toolkit should be knowledge of written resources and relevant websites which might be helpful for the person such as the Royal College of Psychiatrists (RCP), National Institute of Clinical Excellence (NICE) or MIND, all of which provide helpful information about disorders, symptoms and the range of possible treatments. Being able to signpost people to self-help resources such online Cognitive Behavioural Therapy tools and self-help therapies (NHS Apps Library online) are also an important part of a practitioner's toolkit.

It is also important to have knowledge of behavioural approaches like anxiety management techniques and health coaching approaches. Some models of intervention have been adapted from techniques used in corporate coaching. For example, the GROW model (Goal, Reality, Options, Way Forward) created by business coaches such as Sir John Whitmore in the 1980s has been adapted by Myles Downey to include Topic as a first element (Downey, 2003) (see Figure 7.1). This approach can be particularly helpful because the person is encouraged to adopt the goal as their own, and by focusing on a desired outcome and reinforcing the possibility of change, it can help to motivate where the person may have been experiencing hopelessness.

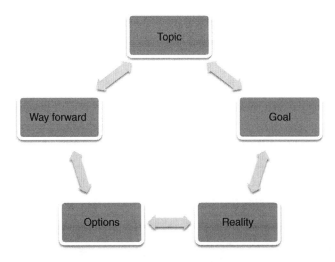

Figure 7.1 The TGROW model

The idea is that TGROW is not a linear process, but there will be interplay between the different stages. So when looking at options for change, the person will be encouraged to relate the options back to the issues listed under Reality, therefore avoiding unrealistic plans. The aim is to agree a simple plan at each session rather than a complex set of actions, and the process can be reviewed and repeated at further sessions.

Case Example

Geraldine is a White British 45 year-old mother of three school-age children. She has become increasingly anxious and depressed over the past five years. She now seldom leaves the family home and has stopped seeing friends or attending any activities. This has put a strain on her relationship with her husband, who is out at work all day. It has also led to the eldest child, aged 13, having to take her younger siblings to primary school before then going on to her own school. Geraldine has expressed very low self-esteem and feelings of hopelessness; she feels she is a burden on the family.

The social worker in the Community Mental Health Team (CMHT) has tried using an anxiety management ladder, or what Powell (2005) refers to as a graded practice target sheet, to support Geraldine to gradually expose herself to the anxiety-provoking activities such as leaving the house. However, she has not managed to do the homework tasks which will help with graded exposure, and her husband has not wanted to support her by accompanying her because he thinks it is a waste of time.

Clearly there are complex family and relationship issues for the social worker to consider, as well as potential risk issues. He decides to try using the TGROW model with Geraldine in order to help her focus on achievable change as a way of increasing her motivation.

Case Example

Geraldine identifies her inability to attend any school function as her biggest regret because it leaves her feeling useless as a parent. Geraldine and the social worker identify attending the school Christmas play as the desired goal, and by pinpointing all of the reasons why this currently feels impossible, they are able to start to addressing the barriers, and exploring options for overcoming them. Some of the options do not seem possible in reality, but Geraldine decides she would be able to start by enlisting the help of another mum at the school whom she has previously found supportive. They agree that Geraldine will phone this person and invite her round for a cup of tea as a way of starting the conversation.

The social worker used motivational interviewing skills (Miller and Rollnick, 2013) to support Geraldine to identify the goals and the obstacles herself, and to arrive at a manageable plan. He ensures that the goal is SMART (specific, measurable, achievable, relevant and time-based), and that he has taken into account where Geraldine is in terms of stages of change (Prochaska and DiClemente, 1984), thus optimising the chances of success.

As well as the expertise gained from knowledge acquired, it is important within relationship-based practice (where relevant) to share the knowledge gained from practice wisdom. So to say: 'I have worked with people who have had similar experiences to you, and they have found this approach helpful in this way' can provide some reassurance that change is possible.

The tools used in practice add relevance, can enrich the relationship between people and can deliver results, but it is the relationship which must come first to establish trust and thereby optimise the effectiveness of the interventions (Allen et al, 2016).

Alliance

Alliance within the IDEAS model is perhaps the area that most easily fits with traditional notions of relationship-based practice. Many people come into the caring professions because they have notions of working alongside individuals to 'make a difference'. So often nowadays this is difficult to equate with the role of social worker as a 'broker' of care and a care manager who allocates resources (Leece and Leece, 2011). However, within the specialism of mental health, the use of a relationship as a mechanism for change is still a really important part of our role.

As a 'care co-ordinator' we have a key role working with an individual. Admittedly, the care *co-ordinator* will sometimes do just that, 'co-ordinate', and the care provision may be primarily from a community support worker, a psychologist or other professionals. However, the role is very often central to the care being provided, and, where necessary, the care co-ordinator (whether social worker or mental health nurse), will have regular and frequent contact with the person, and will be the professional who knows them best and is best placed to respond in a crisis.

To facilitate the development of an effective trusting relationship, it is essential that the professional has something of value to offer the person. The following areas outlined below provide details of what this involves.

» *Being honest* and saying 'I do not have all the answers, but I will consult others with different experience, knowledge and skills, and we will use this information to inform decisions about treatment and care.'

» *An ability to collaborate*: Exploration with the person and, where appropriate, their carers, around the meaning of their experiences for them, and a testing-out of possible solutions and approaches.

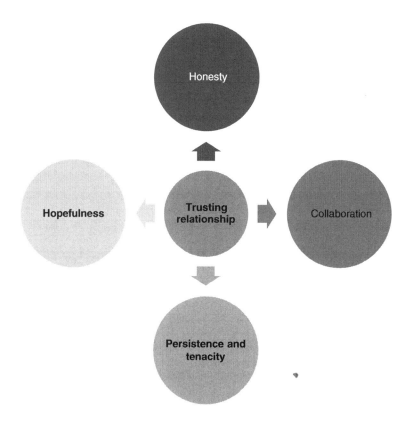

Figure 7.2 Components of a trusting relationship

» *Persistence/tenacity*: If something does not work in partnership with the person, be willing to find something that might work better.

» *Hopefulness*: We will keep trying because there will always be something that can help towards recovery or, at least, the better management of symptoms.

In Chapter 4, the importance of emotional intelligence is referred to in relation to the Alliance aspect of the model. When most of the people with whom we are working are suffering chronic or acute mental health problems, and many will be in crisis at some point during our intervention, being able to regulate one's own emotional responses will be vitally important. We will sometimes have to work with people who are behaving unreasonably or even aggressively, but if we can develop the skills to help us manage our emotions to enable us to help people to better manage theirs, this will also help in the process of developing a relationship with them (Taylor, 2011).

The theoretical perspectives discussed in Chapter 1 include discussion of the value of 'kindness' within a caring relationship, and the building of a connection through compassion and understanding. This can be a valuable starting point for the development of an effective therapeutic relationship. The development of an alliance begins at the very earliest stages of our work with individuals and even if the person is in crisis at the point of initial intervention, they are likely to be alert to expressions of empathy and understanding of their situation. They may also have come to services with unhelpful presumptions about the pointlessness of professional intervention based on previous experience, so as workers we need to offer positivity and hopefulness through the use of our language and behaviour. This demonstrates our belief that change can occur, which can provide an alternative more positive experience. At these points of intervention, the social worker may be faced with a lot of information to unpick, but by listening to the person's story and using empathic understanding, we can sometimes make an important connection with the individual.

Case Example

Nathan is a Black British man who has a diagnosis of schizophrenia alongside emotional and behavioural problems dating back to childhood. He has been referred back to services due to deteriorating self-care. Nathan struggles to cope with formal appointments, and walked out in frustration from the initial appointment with the psychiatrist and social worker. The social worker sees him at home for a second appointment, and after Nathan has explained at speed and at length about the intrusive nature of his voices, the social worker comments 'that must be exhausting for you'.

In this situation the social worker has demonstrated that they are listening, but more importantly, have an empathic understanding of the real impact on Nathan. At this stage it is probably unhelpful to start exploring the detail of what the voices are saying and what they mean to him, but it is more important to develop an alliance by demonstrating some understanding of the impact it is having on his life. Even if the social worker's observations are not accurate, it can be a starting point for checking-out the emotional impact and the meaning it has for him.

It is equally important to recognise the longer-term implications of our work with people. At times we may appear to be making no difference and having no noticeable impact in helping them to make changes or manage their mental disorder more effectively; but for some people, the very fact that a care co-ordinator has provided long-term, consistent support and accompanied them on their journey towards recovery can be extremely valuable to them. For example, remembering how they were historically and reminding them of the progress they have made can be reassuring, and remembering what they have previously told us shows that we are paying attention to them as an individual and have genuine interest and investment in their recovery.

Recovery as a principle within mental health perhaps needs some scrutiny here. It was developed as a guiding principle in the UK relatively late in the last century and followed the move towards closure of long-stay psychiatric facilities and the provision of 'care in the community' (Rose et al, 1995). Social inclusion is an important principle in relation to engagement and recovery, and the person is central to the process, and needs to be involved in developing their own recovery plan. The principles of co-production are also vitally important, so that the planning and delivery of services is not something that is simply 'done to you' but rather there is a sharing of power and influence. This also involves a focus on aspirations as an important aspect of care planning towards recovery (Morgan et al, 2016).

The recovery model focuses not just on managing symptoms, but on helping people with a mental disorder build resilience and *regain a meaningful life despite persistent symptoms* (Jacob, 2015, p 117). The thinking behind this concept is a move away from people becoming patients for life, but rather they are encouraged to develop self-reliance and resilience. The model has its critics who argue that it is primarily a way of managing scarce resources, and can lead to people being discharged before they are ready, and to setting clinical goals that are largely dictated by professionals (Slade et al, 2014). It is therefore crucial to develop a relationship with people that can be used as a mechanism for change. For recovery planning towards eventual discharge (where possible) not to be seen as dismissive or victimising, the care co-ordinator needs to work alongside the person to establish shared goals and a hopeful outlook.

Support

Organisational support to underpin safe and effective practice is fundamental within the statutory services where vulnerable adults or children are supported to maintain well-being and to stay safe. Although homicides are very rare, public protection has to be a concern in respect of a small number of acutely unwell people with whom we work. Far more often however, mentally ill persons are at risk of violence from others (Graves et al, 2005). The risk of suicide is frequently considered within teams. In order to avoid our practice becoming overly defensive with the avoidance of positive risk-taking, workers need effective and proactive support and supervision. The multidisciplinary team (MDT) model provides a variety of ways that this support can be provided, including managerial supervision, peer support or supervision and MDT meetings.

In many CMHTs there are daily clinical meetings where the whole team discuss clinical priorities and pass on information from day to day, focusing on people in crisis as well as organising the practicalities of allocation of work. This model provides a forum for management of risk, where the whole team to some extent shares responsibility for decisions made and where discussions are recorded. This can be a valuable justification for decision making in the unfortunate event that things do go wrong. There may also be opportunities for detailed discussion of complex cases where knowledge and ideas can be shared in the interest of informed and creative practice.

Case Example

Andy is a White British man brings the following case to the MDT meeting for discussion and advice: Peter is a White British is ex-professional rugby player who started to experience severe headaches, memory difficulties and non-epileptic seizures. When neurological investigations found no organic cause it was decided that it is a functional illness and he was referred to the CMHT, where he has been treated for depression. Neither painkillers nor anti-depressants have made any difference and Peter is now feeling hopeless, and says that he cannot live like this with no hope of change. Andy feels that he does not know what to do to help Peter.

The team ask Andy further questions about Peter's home life, his social contacts etc. Andy says that Peter lives alone and has no contact with his family. He is gay but not in a relationship, and his family and rugby friends do not know about his sexuality.

Some team members suggest that Peter's sexuality could be very relevant to his experience of depression, and that he may have felt he had to hide it from his fellow rugby players due to issues of stigma in the sporting field. Andy is advised to explore this further with Peter and he is given information about national and local advice agencies where Peter can go for support. Andy will also consider with Peter whether a referral for psychological therapy may be helpful.

Andy is being encouraged to consider using psycho-dynamic/psycho-analytic theories of repression to understand the possible impact upon Peter of repressing his sexuality, and whether this may be contributing to his current experience of depression as well as his somatic symptoms (Aybek et al, 2013).

An important principle within the MDT model of case work is mutual trust among colleagues such that we can feel safe in sharing our puzzlement or lack of expertise, and feel able to learn from others without feeling inadequate or judged. In a similar way, within professional or peer supervision we should be able to reflect on our practice and learn from others in order to develop our practice. This openness to learning and developing (however experienced we are and however many years we have worked) is dependent on both our own emotional intelligence and on the culture of the team and the organisation within which we work.

Arguably, all organisations need to reflect upon and learn from serious incidents and near misses. In mental health we potentially have more than most because we work with people who are at high risk of suicide. The death of someone we have been supporting and working with, particularly if it is by suicide, is likely to be the most difficult experience we have to deal with in our career. It can be made substantially worse if the subsequent internal investigation focuses on apportioning blame rather than open investigation into whether we can learn lessons from the incident in order to guide future practice within the organisation. Adopting a 'learning culture' (Senge, 1990) where everybody is encouraged to learn from situations and events that have occurred can be one way of an organisation offering a form of 'containment' (Bion, 1962). This can be achieved in relation to managing serious incidents, particularly the death of a person, through the provision of a forum, facilitated by a suitably experienced professional such as a psychologist, where those professionals who had been involved with the person can come together to share their thoughts and concerns.

Conclusion

In conclusion, relationships are at the heart of everything we do in mental health work; not only the relationships we develop with people and their carers, but also the relationships with colleagues and other agencies, both statutory and voluntary.

In order to be effective in developing these relationships we need to demonstrate a range of skills and qualities: We need to have relevant knowledge and expertise and the commitment and curiosity to find out what we need to know but do not know currently; we need to use our experience of what has helped others in order to provide reassurance of possible change; we need a positive and hopeful outlook and we need to value and use the experience of people and carers in a collaborative way that enables them to feel involved in finding solutions to their problems.

IDEAS is a model of service delivery that covers all aspects of collaborative, relationship-based work as well as looking at the context within which this work is provided. It allows us to focus on the impact of service delivery and organisational contexts to find ways of achieving positive change through meaningful relationships.

References

Al-Diwani, A, Pollak, T A, Irani, S R and Lennox, B R (2017) Psychosis: An Autoimmune Disease? *Immunology*, 152(3): 388–401.

Allen, R, Carr, S, Linde, K and Sewell, H (2016) *Social Work for Better Mental Health: A Strategic Statement.* London: Department of Health. Crown Copyright.

American Psychiatric Association (2013) *Diagnostic and Statistical Manual of Mental Disorder – DSM IV.* Washington, DC: APA.

Arts, N J M, Walvoort, S J W and Kessels, R P C (2017) Korsakoff's Syndrome: A Critical Review. *Neuropsychiatric Disease and Treatment*, 13: 2875–90.

Aybek, S, Nicholson, T, Zelaya, F, O'Daly, O, Craig, T, David, A and Kanaan, R (2013) The Neural Correlates of Freudian 'repression' in Conversion Disorder. *Journal of Neurology, Neurosurgery and Psychiatry*, 84(9): e1. [online] Available at: https://kclpure.kcl.ac.uk/portal/en/publications/the-neural-correlates-of-freudian-repression-in-conversion-disorder(b615973a-4be6-4198-843b-93e03b78c83a).html (accessed 25 April 2019).

BBC News (18 September 2017) *What is Behind Clashes in Ethiopia Oromia and Somali Regions?* [online] Available at: www.bbc.co.uk/news/world-africa-41278618 (accessed 4 March 2019).

Ben-Ari, A and Strier, R (2010) Rethinking Cultural Competence: What Can We Learn from Levinas? *British Journal of Social Work*, 40(6): 1–13.

Bion, W (1962) *Learning from Experience.* London: Heinemann.

Bowlby, J (2005) *A Secure Base: Clinical Applications of Attachment Theory.* London: Taylor and Francis.

Breggin, P (1993) *Toxic Psychiatry.* HarperCollins.

British Medical Association (2017) *Breaking Down Barriers – the Challenges of Improving Mental Health Outcomes.* London: British Medical Association.

Gower College Swansea
Library
Coleg Gŵyr Abertawe
Llyrfgell

Chapman, D, Perry, G and Strine, Tara W (2004) *The Vital Link Between Chronic Disease and Depressive Disorders.* Public Health Research Practice and Policy. [online] Available at: www.ncbi.nlm.nih.gov/pmc/articles/PMC1323317 (accessed 21 June 2019).

Coulshed, V and Orme, J (2012) *Social Work Practice: An introduction* (5th edn). Basingstoke: Palgrave Macmillan.

Crisp, B R, Anderson, M T, Orme, J and Lister, P G (2005) *Knowledge Review 08: Learning and Teaching in Social Work Education: Textbooks and Frameworks on Assessment.* London: Social Care Institute for Excellence.

Department of Health (2008) *Refocusing the Care Programme Approach*: Policy Practice Guidance. London: DH.

Downey, M (2003) *Effective Coaching* (3rd edn). Cengage Learning.

Engel, G L (1980) The Clinical Application of the Biopsychosocial Model. *The American Journal of Psychiatry*, 137(5): 534–44.

Galderisi, S, Heinz, A, Kastrup, M, Beezhold, J and Sartorius, N (2015) *Toward a New Definition of Mental Health.* [online] Available at: http://europepmc.org/backend/ptpmcrender.fcgi?accid=PMC4471980&blobtype=pdf (accessed 3 March 2019).

Golightly, M (2017) *Social Work and Mental Health* (5th edn). London: Sage Learning Matters.

Graham, K L, Carson, C M, Buckley, P F and Miller, B J (2014) Urinary Tract Infections in Acute Psychosis. *Journal of Clinical Psychiatry*, 74(4): 379–85.

Graves, R, Cassissi, J and Penn, D (2005) Psycho-physiological Evaluation of Stigma towards Schizophrenia. *Schizophrenia Research*, 76(2–3): 317–27.

Jacob, K S (2015) Recovery Model of Mental Illness: A Complementary Approach to Psychiatric Care. *Indian Journal of Psychological Medicine*, 37: 117–19.

Jonas, S, Bebbington, P, McManus, S and Meltzer, H (2011) Sexual Abuse and Psychiatric Disorder in England: Results from the 2007 Adult Psychiatric Morbidity Study. *Psychological Medicine*, 41(4): 709–19.

Kearney, R and Williams, J (1996) Narrative and Ethics. *Proceedings of the Aristotelian Society*, Supplementary papers, 70: 47–61.

Lacay, S (2013) *Breaking Boundaries with Empathy: How the Therapeutic Alliance Can Defy Client/Worker Differences.* [online] Available at: www.socialworker.com/feature-articles/practice/Breaking_Boundaries_With_Empathy%3A_How_the_Therapeutic_Alliance_Can_Defy_Client-Worker_Differences (accessed 3 March 2019).

Laing, R D (1960) *The Divided Self: An Existential Study in Sanity and Madness.* Harmondsworth: Penguin.

Leece, J and Leece, D (2011) Personalisation: Perceptions of the Role of Social Work in a World of Brokers and Budgets. *The British Journal of Social Work*, 41 (2): 204–23.

Lishman, J, Yuill, C, Brannan, J and Gibson, A (2018) *Social Work: An Introduction* (2nd edn). London: Sage.

Mathews, I and Crawford, K (2011) *Evidence-based Practice in Social Work.* Exeter: Learning Matters.

Mental Capacity Act (2005) [online] Available at: www.legislation.gov.uk/ukpga/2005/9/contents (accessed 7 March 2019).

Mental Health Act (1983) [online] Available at: www.legislation.gov.uk/ukpga/1983/20/contents (accessed 7 March 2019).

Mental Health Act (2007) [online] Available at: www.legislation.gov.uk/ukpga/2007/12/contents (accessed 7 March 2019).

Mental Health Act (1983) Code of Practice (2007) London: The Stationery Office.

Miller, W R and Rollnick, S (2013) *Motivational Interviewing: Preparing People for Change* (3rd edn). New York: Guilford Press.

Milner, J, Myers, S and O'Byrne, P (2015) *Assessment in Social Work* (4th edn). London: Palgrave Macmillan.

Modernising the Mental Health Act: Increasing Choice, Reducing Compulsion (2018). Final report of the Independent Review of the Mental Health Act 1983. Crown Copyright. [online] Available at: https://assets.publishing.service.gov.uk/

government/uploads/system/uploads/attachment_data/file/763547/Modernising_the_Mental_Health_Act__increasing_choice__reducing_compulsion__summary_version.pdf (accessed 6 March 2019).

Morgan, A, Felton, A, Fulford, B (K W M), Kalathil, J and Stacey, G (2016) *Values and Ethics in Mental Health: An Exploration for Practice.* London: Palgrave Macmillan.

Naseribafrouei, A, Hestad, K, Avershina, A, Sekelja, M, Linlokken, A, Wilson, R and Rudi, K (2014) Correlation between the Human Fecal Microbiota and Depression. *Neurogastroenterology and Motility: The Official Journal of the European Gastrointestinal Motility Society*, 26(8): 1152–62.

National Institute for Mental Health in England (2003) *Inside Outside: Improving Mental Health Services for Black and Minority Ethnic Communities in England.* Department of Health: Crown Copyright.

NHS Apps Library. [online] Available at: www.nhs.uk/apps-library/category/mental-health (accessed 24 February 2019).

NHS England (2016) *The 5 Year Forward View for Mental Health.* A Report from the Independent Mental Health Taskforce to the NHS in England. Mental Health Taskforce. [online] Available at: www.england.nhs.uk/wp-content/uploads/2016/02/Mental-Health-Taskforce-FYFV-final.pdf (accessed 21 June 2019).

Parker, I, Georgaca, E, Harper, D, McLaughlin, T and Stowell-Smith, M (eds) (1995) *Deconstructing Psychopathology.* London: Sage.

Powell, T (2005) *Mental Health Handbook* (revised). Bicester: Speechmark Publishing.

Power, M (2004) *The Risk Management of Everything: Rethinking the Politics of Uncertainty.* London: Demos.

Prochaska, J and DiClemente, C (1984) *The Transtheoretical Approach: Crossing Traditional Boundaries of Therapy.* Homewood, IL: Dow/Jones Irwin.

Rogers, C (1957) The Necessary and Sufficient Conditions of Therapeutic Personality Change. *Journal of Consulting Psychology*, 21: 95–103.

Rogers, C (1961) *On Becoming a Person.* Boston: Houghton Mifflin Company.

Romme, M and Escher, S (1993) *Accepting Voices.* London: Mind.

Romme, S, Escher, S, Dillon, J, Corstens, D and Morris, M (2009) *Living with Voices.* Ross-on-Wye: PCCS BOOKS Ltd.

Rose, S M and Black, B L (1995*) Advocacy and Empowerment: Mental Health Care in the Community.* London: Routledge.

Rovinelli Heller, N and Gitterman, A (eds) (2011) *Mental Health and Social Problems: A Social Work Perspective.* London: Routledge.

Senge, P M (1983) *The Fifth Discipline: The Art and Practice of the Learning Organisation.* London: Random House.

Slade, M, Amering, M, Farkas, M, Hamilton, B, O'Hagan, M, Panther, G, Perkins, R, Shepherd, G, Tse, S and Whitley, R (2014) Uses and Abuses of Recovery: Implementing Recovery-oriented Practices in Mental Health Systems. *World Psychiatry*, 13(1): 12–20.

Spataro, J, Mullen, P E, Burgess, P M and Wells, D M (2004) Impact of Child Sexual Abuse on Mental Health: Prospective Study in Males and Females. *British Journal of Psychiatry*, 184(5): 416–42.

Taylor, B (2011) *Working with Aggression and Resistance in Social Work.* Exeter: Learning Matters.

Tew, J (2011) *Social Approaches to Mental Distress.* Basingstoke: Palgrave Macmillan.

Turnell, A and Murphy, T (2017) *Signs of Safety Comprehensive Briefing Paper* (4th edn). East Perth, Australia: Resolutions Consultancy Pty Ltd.

Wade, D T and Halligan, P W (2017) The Biopsychosocial Model of Illness: A Model Whose Time Has Come. *Clinical Rehabilitation*, 31(8): 995–1004.

Whitmore, J (1992) *Coaching for Performance: GROWing Human Potential and Purpose: The Principles and Practice of Coaching and Leadership.* People skills for professionals. Boston: Nicholas Brealey.

World Health Organisation (2014) [online] Available at: www.who.int/features/factfiles/mental_health/en (accessed 3 March 2019).

Zubin, J and Spring, B (1977) Vulnerability: A New View of Schizophrenia. *The American Journal of Psychology*, 86(2): 103–26.

Chapter 8

Relationships and risk: utilising the IDEAS model with adult offenders

Jennifer Meade

Introduction

This chapter will look at how the IDEAS framework fits into work with adult offenders in the United Kingdom and consider some of the challenges of applying the model in this context. It will also attempt to explore the extent to which a relationship-based approach is effective in this setting. While recognising that work with adult offenders is structured differently and currently delivered by a number of organisations in different parts of the UK, for the sake of simplicity I will use the generic terms 'probation' and 'probation service' to describe the agencies and organisations which work with and supervise adults in the Criminal Justice System in the United Kingdom. I have also used the term 'offender' throughout.

It may be a surprise to find probation work included in a book on relationship-based practice. Questions about the extent to which the work of probation services is about care or control and what the balance should be between rehabilitation and risk management have a long history. Malcolm Vanstone points out that attempts to understand and resolve this tension, *'have been at the core of the Services' theory and practice since its inception'* (Vanstone, 2004, p 41). If the purpose of probation services is solely control and managing risk, then what is the point of building a relationship to use as a medium for change and rehabilitation?

The Practice Framework (MOJ and NOMs, 2015) includes reducing reoffending as part of the aims of sentencing and the Offender Management Community Cohort Study (Wood et al, 2015) found that those who rated their relationships with their supervising officer as excellent were less likely to reoffend. It seems therefore that the quality of relationships continues to be critical to the work with adult offenders and reducing reoffending.

The extent to which probation services remain part of the social work tradition is also debatable. *'In the UK at least, for most of the twentieth century, probation was a social work enterprise with a specialist interest in people who come before the courts'* (Raynor and Vanstone, 2016, p 1132). They summarise the history of the probation movement in the United Kingdom from its Christian missionary roots, through alignment with the social work tradition and into the 1980s, when political and societal influences on the service in England and Wales drove a change from probation services which delivered social work type interventions to an agency with a criminal justice emphasis. In Scotland probation work is organised differently and is still part of local authority social services. Practitioners continue to be social work trained and are called Criminal Justice Social Workers. Regardless of these differences in organisational structure and training, a comparison of practitioner accounts in England and Scotland found that *'the most striking observation we can make is of seemingly durable convergence of perspectives on the meaning of quality in supervision'* (Grant and McNeill, 2014, p 163). This included a consensus on the importance of values and ethical practice, suggesting that whatever the organisational structure, probation services in both countries retain a value base which is similar to that of social work.

Influence

Influence is connected to power conferred by role but also power to influence others through personal qualities. Inherent to the concept of influence is the recognition and acceptance of power differentials which are more significant in probation than in most settings. It is a reality that this area of practice involves working with people who are not there through choice and that practitioners in the field can make decisions (such as whether to breach) that have immediate consequences for offenders. In probation services, influence includes the effective use of authority (including *role clarification*), acting as a role model and using other pro-social modelling and reinforcement techniques.

Trotter sums up the process of role clarification as answering the following questions: 'What are we here for? What do we hope to get out of this?' and crucially 'What do we have to do? And what do we have a choice about?' (Trotter, 2015, p 78).

Case Example

The practitioner, Armani (mixed heritage Black Jamaican and White British), in early meetings with the offender, Mark (White British), tells him that they are both there to work together to stop Mark offending again. Armani also explains clearly that they have a dual role of offering support and help but also monitoring compliance and enforcing the order. Armani helps Mark to explore what will count as a breach of the order and engages him in identifying ways to avoid this and they also both explore how Armani can assist with this. Armani then goes on to establish with Mark what his 'best hopes' for the outcomes of their meetings are and how these fit in with the purposes of the order.

This process might take place over several contacts and it is likely that it will have to be repeated and reinforced at intervals. In terms of explaining what must be done, just explaining what is in a court order or license and what the penalties are for not complying is not sufficient. Other important but less obvious rules of engagement must also be made clear. For example, the practitioner might also need to help the offender to understand clearly what constitutes reasonable behaviour in a group setting or what factors will be taken into account when deciding whether to issue a warning for non-attendance.

Another important part of Influence is the ability to influence others. This can show itself in ways which are as simple as practitioners taking care to 'set a good example' to offenders and colleagues, ie not in fact behaving in ways which are not congruent with the ways in which they expect the offender to behave and not expressing views, however unintentionally, that would be unacceptable for the offender to also express; in fact, consciously acting as a positive role model. In addition by applying rules fairly and in ways which match the 'rules of engagement' which the practitioner and the offender have explored together, the practitioner starts to establish their own personal legitimacy and increases their influence over the offender. It is quite easy to unintentionally undermine this aspect of influence. For example, in working with an offender with alcohol problems, the following interaction might take place.

Case Example

Amy (White British) arrives late and flustered to meet Karen (also White British) and says she has not had time to prepare the session or contact the employment advisor as they had agreed at their last meeting. Karen says that she have been waiting for 20 minutes. Amy dismisses Karen's concerns and reminds her she must attend as directed. Later, Karen overhears Amy in the waiting room talking to a colleague about having got 'legless' last night at a party and being late for work.

The concept of pro-social modelling and reinforcement is one which is well used in probation work. Trotter proposes a broad definition of pro-social as *'actions and values which support and care for others'* and highlights its connection to the values of *'non-sexism, non-racism, openness and tolerance'* (Trotter, 2015, p 23). Pro-social reinforcement can be broken down into practitioners being clear about the values, actions and attitudes they want to promote and identifying, rewarding and reinforcing these while at the same time challenging pro-criminal or anti-social attitudes and behaviours as well as the positive role modelling outlined earlier. Trotter also points out that numerous research studies have pointed to the effectiveness of this approach in improving outcomes. It is important to distinguish between challenging and confronting anti-social and/or pro-criminal attitudes and behaviour, and criticising and blaming individuals. The focus should be on challenging a specific anti-social attitude or behaviour, while continuing to show respect for the individual because as Trotter has also pointed out, *'approaches which blame, punish and judge clients in the hope that their behaviour will change seem doomed to failure'* (Trotter, 2015, p 63). As do criticising, arguing and attempting to dominate and being confrontational and abusive. It takes a high degree of skill to get this balance right. Practitioners who understand the need to challenge unacceptable behaviour and attitudes but are uncomfortable about doing so may come across as personally blaming and confrontational in style. Practice and feedback with a peer or line manager can be helpful in these circumstances.

Case Example

Carlene, a practitioner of mixed heritage (White British and Black African) delivering an anger management group work programme, is running a session which includes Ronan (White British). Ronan says to the group that over the weekend he did not shout at a driver who cut him up as his wife and children were in the car. Carlene tells Ronan that it is positive he is thinking about his wife's and his children's feelings and putting the learning from the group into practice. Ronan then goes on to say that he doesn't know why he is in the group as the worst he has ever done is 'push someone about a bit'. Carlene says that she knows from police reports that Ronan has caused injuries in fights which led to the victim being hospitalised and this is more serious than his account of events and that is why he is in the group.

Perhaps the last word on influence can be left to some of those who were once on probation. An oral history study which looked at the experience of those who had been on probation in the 1960s concluded that *'the legitimacy of the practitioner – on which his or her influence for good depends – is hard won, easily lost and almost impossible to recover'* (McNeill et al, 2010, p 506).

Delivery

Delivery, with its technical and procedural aspects, is one of the most challenging aspects of IDEAS to deliver in a relationship-based way and one which has historically been overemphasised in a probation setting. Delivery is about understanding and using the technical and procedural aspects of the framework within which the practitioner works. It includes: working within local and national policies and procedures, standards and professional boundaries; understanding and using practice frameworks effectively; using the approved assessment tools; keeping to timescales and recognising that accurate and timely assessment, planning and record keeping are an essential part of effective practice, not an 'add on'. For many practitioners, this is not, at first sight, a particularly inspiring list. Delivery is perhaps the aspect of IDEAS in which accountability to an agency is most pronounced and the needs of the individual offender most easily overlooked.

However, the guidance, policies and procedures which underpin practice form an important safety net for both practitioner and offender. The framework within which practice is delivered is important to ensure accountability and fairness. Practitioners may hark back to a golden age of autonomy and freedom, but Worral (2015) spoke to *'experienced officers that thought that nostalgia was rather overrated'*. They pointed out that there was a lot of bad practice in the 'golden age' and abuse of the freedom and autonomy that came with the job (Worral, 2015, p 511). For example, I can remember cases where offenders were not seen for many months before national standards were introduced.

The main documents which summarise how probation services in England and Wales should be delivered currently is the 'Practice Framework – National Standards for the Management of Offenders 2015'. The Practice Framework is relatively light touch in terms of what it prescribes and this is to be welcomed. An up-to-date understanding of the standards and timescales which the practitioner should work to is important in terms of delivering the sentences of the court in an equitable way. Equally important is that practitioners recognise when and how to ask for the standards to be set aside and demonstrate their accountability through discussions with a manager.

As well as understanding standards and timescales, Delivery is also about the effective use of approved assessment and planning tools. The quality of assessments is critical as Moore has pointed out, *'The effectiveness and efficiency of interventions designed to reduce reoffending and protect the public is dependent upon accurate estimation of offenders' risks and needs. Within England and Wales, as elsewhere, good assessment is thus recognised to be the starting point for managing offenders'* (Moore, 2015, p 2), and therefore the ability to use approved tools effectively is a core practice skill.

As Kemshall has pointed out, the process of assessment has to take place within the context of a relationship in order to be effective: *'The risk assessor has to understand the individual in order to both personalise the assessment and work out how general risk factors apply in a particular set of circumstances to a particular individual'* (Kemshall et al, 2013, p 39). There is usually no reason in practice why both the assessment and planning process cannot be done in a collaborative way with the offender and significant others. They can not only provide information to inform the assessment but agree and disagree about the content as well as negotiating goals and objectives for change with the practitioner. The only time that this sharing process will not be an appropriate, or indeed an essential, part of effective supervision is when sharing information in whole or part will place someone else at risk.

Case Example

Practitioner Ahmed (a British male of Pakistani descent) is completing an assessment on offender Ben (White British). Ahmed has formed a hypothesis that Ben offends when drunk and binge drinks after supervised contact visits with his children because his offending pattern is closely associated with the weekly contact visits. Ahmed asks Ben to describe the events which led up his last offence, which was common assault. Ben talks through a sequence of actions, which starts with a visit to his father and ends in the off license. Ben thinks he drinks because his father is negative towards him and mocks him for not being able to look after his own children. Ahmed encourages Ben to tell him more about his relationship with his father and how it affects him and relates to his offending. He agrees with Ben what they will record in the assessment, which is that they have differing views about what prompts Ben's binge drinking but that both agree when he binge drinks, he is at much higher risk of offending.

The truth of why Ben drinks may be that Ahmed is right or Ben is right, or it may lie somewhere between the two. Ahmed has listened to Ben and taken his views seriously and this has helped them reach common ground that for Ben, binge drinking increases the risk he will re-offend.

Trotter (2015) outlines a collaborative problem-solving approach which involves working with offender-defined issues by asking solution-focused questions (Berg and Szabo, 2005) such as *'What would be different if everything was the way you wanted it to be?'* (Trotter, 2015, p 127), ranking the issues identified and choosing one or at most two to work on and then taking time to understand these in more detail and setting goals before developing detailed and specific tasks to achieve them. The stages are:

- » problem surveying
- » problem ranking
- » problem exploration
- » setting goals
- » developing a contract
- » developing strategies and tasks

(Trotter, 2015, p 126)

There is also an emphasis on ongoing reviews. While it is helpful to talk about things that the offender would like to change rather than problems, this model can help to ensure that offender goals are identified and part of planning, and information on what is significant to them is included in the assessment.

Assessment and planning are widely recognised as important but basic case recording can be an underappreciated area of practice. The day-to-day recording of when the offender was last seen, what happened, what work has been done, and how it went and what is now planned, is a skill in itself. This kind of summary helps both practitioner and offender engage in a process of frequent progress checking. Good recording should be focused, clear, concisely written in neutral straightforward language, and based on evidence. It should enable the reader to quickly understand the full picture, what work is planned and the intended outcomes. Case recording is a central part of accountable practice and an important part of Delivery. It is an essential part of the real job, not a distraction from it. And it can, like the assessment and planning process, be done collaboratively.

Case Example

At the end of a session on problem solving, practitioner Garfield (Black British) asks offender Esaie (Black British) what he has learnt and what should be recorded about the session. Esaie says he has learnt to stop and think about different solutions when he has a problem, not just do the first thing that comes into his head. Garfield asks Esaie to give an example from his life. Esaie is unable to do so. Esaie and Garfield agree that Garfield will record that Esaie has learnt he should stop and think about alternative solutions when he has a problem and at the next session they will look at some examples of real problems Esaie faces and practise both generating alternative solutions and evaluating them.

This approach has many benefits, not just checking out whether the offender has understood and absorbed the intended learning from the session, but also whether a different approach needs to be tried and what the offender's immediate priorities for the next session are. Shared recording in this way can also show progress to the offender and validate that is has been recognised.

While Delivery inevitably focuses on process, many elements of it can be done in a relationship-based way through adopting person-centred approaches to ensure that the voice of the offender is clearly reflected within the assessment and case records. Skills such as the respectful use of questioning, reflecting back, clarifying and summarising what the offender has said very much characterise this approach (Egan, 2009).

Expertise

I will now consider Expertise, which is basically about knowing and using the approaches to intervention with offenders that are most likely to 'work'. Something that at first glance might seem quite simple. Although in practice, identifying what this body of knowledge consists of is not always easy for the individual practitioner.

The history of trying to identify 'what works' in rehabilitating offenders has many twists and turns. Take the famous *What Works?* report (Martinson et al, 1974), which in essence concluded that nothing worked and, alongside other studies (eg Lipton et al, 1975), led to widespread pessimism about the value of efforts to rehabilitate offenders. Martinson et al's report has been criticised and Martinson himself had moved from the position that nothing worked as early as 1979, and *'wrote that, some treatment programs do have an appreciable effect on recidivism'* (Sarre, 1999, p 4), but his original view remained influential in policy and practice for many years. Throughout the 1980s, voices which dissented from the view that nothing worked gathered strength and the use of meta-analyses which *'enabled reviewers to combine findings from different experiments'* (McGuire et al, 1995, p 7) gave impetus to this and they became a *'sustained international movement, sometimes known as the "what works" movement, to promote "evidence-based, best practices in criminal justice"'* (Maruna and LeBel, cited in McNeill et al, 2010, p 65).

Over time, a near consensus has emerged about what types of approach are likely to work and while these will continue to be added to and refined, they provided a useful basis for practice. The analysis of the Skills for Effective Engagement Development (SEED) pilot in 2013 includes a useful summary of effective practice skills based on international evidence. Trotter (2015) proposed an evidence-based practice model for working with involuntary service users, which has many similarities. Andrews and Kiessling identified core correctional practices (CCP) in 1998 (cited in Dowden and Andrews, 2004), which again have common features. Short summaries of these are given in Table 8.1.

As well as research findings, expertise includes having the ability to reflect and learn from the practitioner's own practice and that of others, learning from feedback and from service user expertise. In addition, strengths-based approaches, and working with family and social networks are now also recognised as important and *Family interventions which are most effective are those that are consistent with the research about "what works" in offender rehabilitation'* (Trotter, cited in McNeill et al, 2010, p 298).

The Good Lives Model (GLM), originally developed by Tony Ward and colleagues for work with sex offenders, is a strengths-based approach by *'virtue of its responsiveness to offenders' core aspirations and interests'* (Ward, cited in McNeill et al, 2010, p 41). Its starting point is that as offenders must respect other people's rights and freedoms, they are also entitled to have their own rights and freedoms considered. It focuses on achieving offenders'

Table 8.1 Brief summary of promising approaches

SEED Pilot (Sorsby et al, 2013)	Trotter's Model (2015)	Core correctional practices (CCP) (Andrews and Dowden, 2004)
Motivational Interviewing (MI) interviewing techniques that promote readiness to change	Pro-social modelling and reinforcement	Appropriate modelling and reinforcement (effective modelling and reinforcement and disapproval)
Structuring sessions with a consistent framework for all sessions, which focuses on purposeful engagement	Problem solving	Structured learning
Cognitive Behavioural Techniques (CBT) addressing unhelpful thinking and behavioural patterns, teaching cognitive skills and providing opportunities to practise	Relationship building	Problem solving
Risk-Need-Responsivity (RNR) directing resources to those with the highest risks and needs, and matching intervention style to offender characteristics	Role clarification	Effective use of community resources
Pro-social Modelling (PSM) exemplifying pro-social behaviour, challenging anti-social statements and behaviour and reinforcing (eg through praise) pro-social statements and behaviour		Quality of interpersonal relationships

personal goals in legitimate ways while at the same time reducing and managing their risk of offending. GLM is now being used across wider offender populations and is in the process of being evaluated.

Desistance theory starts by asking what is known about why some people stay involved in crime and some do not. Then it considers what interventions will support or accelerate the process of ceasing to be involved in crime. *'Maruna identifies three broad theoretical perspectives in the desistance literature: maturational reform, social bonds theory and narrative theory'* (21st Century Social Work Review Group, 2005, p 5). The fact that offenders often grow out of crime as they mature is well established. In terms of social bonds theory, this suggests that establishing societal ties or bonds (to family or employment, for example) gives offenders something to lose by continuing to offend. Narrative theories rooted in the work of White and Epston (1990) stress the significance of changes to the offenders' perception of themselves and increased recognition of their ability to make choices and influence events as significant in the journey to rehabilitation. While some of these factors (such as getting older) are not something a practitioner can influence, supporting and/or creating social bonds and encouraging the development of a more positive identity are areas where interventions can be made. Relationship-based practice is clearly a 'container' for this kind of work, which involves challenging not only an offender's behaviour but also their self-perception, self-confidence and self-efficacy. This can only be done within a trusting, respectful relationship that progresses over time and creates an environment in which change can occur (Miller and Rollnick, 2013; Lewis, 2014; Rowe and Soppitt, 2014).

Case Example

Practitioner Fabio (Black British) is reviewing how to work with offender Gina (White British). Fabio has a CBT-based 1:1 programme which he has been using to try and improve Gina's decision making for the past three weeks. Fabio has become aware that Gina appears not to have taken any of it on board and has no examples of how she has put what she has learnt into practice between sessions. Fabio asks Gina why she thinks this is. Gina says she has recently learnt she is pregnant and has been thinking about this. Fabio has recently been reading about desistance and recognises that the pregnancy may offer an opportunity to help Gina to construct a new more positive identity. Fabio adapts his approach accordingly and combines this with continuing to deliver the CBT programme, changing the examples to fit around birth and becoming a parent.

In the probation services there are significant challenges to using Expertise. These include workloads and political and societal attitudes which tend to the view that 'lock them up and throw away the key' is the solution to offending and historically a top-down, risk-averse and overly managerial approach to what approaches and interventions were organisationally acceptable. Nevertheless, a practitioner with expertise will know what the current research about effectiveness consists of: including emerging and promising practice which has yet to be formally evaluated (such as GLM). They will also have the analytical and intellectual skills to understand the debates about what constitutes and who decides what that evidence base consists of and can critically consider why some areas of research seem to be favoured over others.

Alliance

This is the next element in the Framework and refers to the creation of a 'working' or 'therapeutic' alliance between practitioner and offender. Trotter (2015) defined core relationship skills as openness, honesty, empathy, optimism, capacity to understand and articulate the service user's feelings, coupled with self-disclosure and humour. To this list can be added techniques such as using open questions and values such as respect for the individual and their personal autonomy. The use of the professional relationship as a mechanism for change but also an important source of information is summed up by Wilson et al (2011, pp 7–8): *'The ... relationship is recognised to be an important source of information for the worker to understand how best to help, and simultaneously this relationship is the means by which any help or intervention is offered.'* The creation of this working relationship between practitioner and offender poses challenges in the context of probation services. One is that contact with probation is not something that offenders volunteer for; it is imposed on them through the criminal justice system and this is not the ideal way to start. Trotter (2015) suggests that one of the tasks of the practitioner working with an involuntary service user is to teach them how to accept and make use of professional help. Despite this unpromising start, the fact that some practitioners seem to be better than others at getting offenders to attend appointments and engage in meaningful work is well known and ' *"as easily recognisable as an elephant" according to some!'* (Raynor and Vanstone, cited in McNeill et al, 2010, p 113) and this is largely attributable to their skill in building relationships. As well as building relationships with offenders, engaging with families and social networks is also important because *'The literature on desistance elucidates how the motivation, encouragement and emotional support families and social networks provide acts to increase public safety'* (Shapiro and diZerega, cited in McNeill et al, 2010, p 244).

Another challenge posed by this group is that developing effective working alliances with offenders who can be *'hostile, unreliable, deceptive, disinterested, disrespectful and committedly antisocial'* (Ward et al, 2005, p 4) requires practitioners with a very high level of self-awareness and self-management skills. The impact of working with offenders whose presenting characteristics and offending history present a continual challenge to the practitioner's beliefs and values base is often not acknowledged and requires space for reflection and organisational and management support.

Case Example

Practitioner Helen (White British) has been working with offender Issac (Black British) who has been convicted for the rape of a young woman who was very drunk after a night out in a club. During each session Issac has continued to tell Helen that he is not getting anything from the sessions and he feels their backgrounds are so different that she doesn't understand him or the events that led to the offence, and he has started to talk about wanting another supervisor. Helen has continued to use her skills to try and build a basis with Issac on what meaningful work can be done but is starting to feel that she is failing personally and someone else would do better. Helen has a conversation with her supervisor Jess (White British) and explains the situation. Jess explores with Helen the impact Issac is having on her and together they recognise that Issac's remarks to Helen may be partly due to his attitude to women and his attempts to minimise his offence. Helen also makes a connection with her relationship with her own father, who she describes as a traditional male who did not see the value in women having a successful professional career. Helen has unresolved issues around her father's critical attitude towards her career development and the conflict between them. In this sense, Helen can begin to recognise possible transference and countertransference issues between herself and Issac, which make her feel devalued and this helps to take the sting out of Issac's criticisms of her work. Jess also talks to Helen about other cases where she has been successful in promoting change and helps her see that Issac's attitude to her is not justified. Jess offers to get someone else to take on the case but Helen decides to keep it for the time being.

While establishing and using an effective working relationship is an important part of being effective, it is not enough on its own. *'It does appear that while worker relationship skills are important in offender supervision they may only be valuable if they are combined with other effective practice skills such as pro-social modelling and problem-solving'* (Trotter and Evans, cited in McNeill et al, 2010, p 133). Bonta and Andrews also point to the importance of structuring skills: *'Effectiveness of interventions is enhanced when delivered by staff with high quality relationship skills in combination with structuring skills'* (Bonta and Andrews, 2010, p 22). Structuring practices include *'pro-social modelling, effective reinforcement and disapproval, skill building, problem-solving, effective use of authority, advocacy/brokerage cognitive restructuring and motivational interviewing'* (Bonta and Andrews, 2010, p 22). In addition, a sense of purpose and focus on outcomes is also important: *'It is possible to be well engaged with someone, enjoying an energetic conversation but without any clear sense of direction'* (Miller and Rollnick, 2013, p 93).

Perhaps the last word on Alliance should go to a critique of the implementation of the risk, need and responsivity model, which put most of the emphasis on programmes and very little on the contribution of individual supervision. The critique reclaims the importance of individual supervision and points out that however it was implemented, RNR was 'never intended to substitute for sensitive and attuned case work' (Poporino and McNeill et al, 2010, p 10). This is illustrated well in an article by McNeill et al (2018) where the need for practitioners to display 'humanity' in their work is highlighted as a necessary ingredient for constructive supervision.

Support

I have already mentioned several times the importance of Support, which is made up of the other elements (apart from what practitioners themselves contribute) that need to be in place to enable effective practice. Support is not just about the contribution line managers make to individual practitioners but the support local partnerships give to practice and central and local government to agencies. It is also about adequate resourcing. Creating positive and solution-orientated working environments is not only about the actions of local managers, though they do have an important part to play. Taxman and Sachwald (cited in McNeill et al, 2010, p 538) describe American studies that show that *'knowledge, commitment, belief and the creation of a "learning culture" … are more important than budget or size in determining whether evidence-based practices will be adopted'* (in an organisation).

The provision of high-quality reflective supervision, while not enough on its own, is a very important part of supporting practice. The line management role is described as critical in *'providing support to practitioners who are engaged in work with offenders'* (Ministry of Justice and National Offender Management Service, 2015, p 4), and the same document also promotes the use of reflective supervision. Kemshall et al (2013) talk about other aspects of support as essential, including time and space for informal discussions and support from peers, but also about more formal support, for example, ensuring supervision is focused on meeting targets: *'good risk practice does require clear accountability and an unambiguous sense of what is expected … Accountability is not enough however as practitioners also need to be able to take decisions confidently in situations of uncertainty, where correct solutions are debatable'* (Kemshall et al, 2013, p 160). Reflective supervision provides an environment in which these aspects of practice can be safely explored.

A study into the use of Appreciative Inquiry (AI) in a probation setting found that *'participants talked about having few opportunities to talk about their best work or their strengths'* (Robinson et al, 2012, p 12) but when they did have that opportunity they felt better about their jobs and invigorated about their work. The same study heard comments about supervision, which focused solely on cases that had gone wrong, targets missed etc. This balance can be changed even within a difficult resourcing climate. It does require a shift in focus, but very simple things like starting supervision with an AI, ensuring team meetings have staff bringing positive examples of work, supporting practice forums which use case examples of good practice, and a shift in thinking from learning from what went wrong to also learning from what went right are all possible and will help to maintain staff motivation in difficult times. Training and opportunities for skills development are also an important part of support.

Returning to resourcing issues, a study on OASys referred to earlier found that over 50 per cent *'of the assessors disagreed that they usually had sufficient working hours to complete assessments'* (Moore, 2015, p 18). As with other aspects of the IDEAS framework, this finding illustrates the interdependency of the different elements of the model. Without support, not just from immediate line managers but from adequate resourcing and leadership, the delivery of other elements is placed in jeopardy. Drawing common themes from serious case reviews across different spheres of social work, Kemshall et al talk about practitioners being overwhelmed by the nature and extent of their workloads. A lack of sufficient high-quality supervision is highlighted as an issue in many but so is a lack of resources which *'can have a significantly detrimental impact on practice'* (Kemshall et al, 2013, p 125).

The last decade has seen an almost continuous change to the working practices of the probation service by government, something that seems likely to continue (Deering, cited in McNeill et al, 2010, p 466). This prediction turned out to be true with widespread and sweeping reforms to the system in England and Wales brought about by the introduction of Transforming Rehabilitation (TR) and the split between a public National Probation Service (NPS) and mainly privately run Community Rehabilitation Companies in June 2014 in England and Wales. The following quotations are from HMI Probation and are on inspections which have taken place since TR. *'Probation services in London have long struggled with high workloads, and workload pressures have been a regular feature in the most notorious of cases where a supervised individual has committed a Serious Further Offence.'* Talking about the Community Rehabilitation Company (CRC) in North London: *'A combination of unmanageable caseloads, inexperienced officers, extremely poor oversight and a lack of senior management focus and control meant some service users were not seen for weeks or months, and some were lost in the system altogether ... Staff were sometimes working long hours and were often "fire-fighting" rather than enabled to deliver a professional service consistently or sufficiently well'* (HM Inspectorate of Probation, 2016, p 4). Similar issues were found in Staffordshire and Stoke: *'High individual caseloads are becoming commonplace in CRCs. Of course CRCs must manage within anticipated resource, but the public is at greater risk when officers are spread too thinly and if quality assurance is not robust'* (HM Inspectorate of Probation, 2017, p 4). There is all too much reason to fear that currently support is lacking in terms of the resources available to deliver probation work. While some of the effects of this can be mitigated through high-quality supervision, the cumulative effects of workload pressure should not be underestimated.

However, the situation does appear to be changing. In May 2019 the government announced that making private companies responsible for the management of low- to medium-risk offenders has not been effective. As such all offender management will return to the National Probation Service by spring 2021 (*The Guardian*, 2019). It is clear that relationship-based practice will be required to underpin the future success of this policy shift.

Conclusion

This chapter has attempted to show how the IDEAS framework fits into working in a proba-tion setting and where the tensions and challenges of working in a way which is consistent with it are. The framework is both helpful and widely applicable by individual practitioners with individual offenders, but is challenged in many ways by organisational structures and resourcing issues. Delivery models in some CRCs are designed in ways which for selected offenders minimise the role of the working alliance and may in practice mean individual offenders have very little face-to-face contact with one allocated practitioner in England and Wales. A retreat from local partnerships and work with family networks due to resource pressures may also undermine effective practice in this setting.

McNeil et al (2010, p 544) suggest that *'A narrow focus on the pursuit of effective methods without an awareness of context or of their meanings in the lives of supervised offenders runs the risk of repeating the experience of England and Wales, where promising developments drawn from international research on "what works" were compromised by an overcentralised and managerialist implementation process and a punitive political culture.'* IDEAS can help to form an antidote to this tendency to focus on one often easily measurable and control-lable aspect of practice at the expense of others, because it not only identifies the different aspects of practice which go to make up the necessary whole, but also emphasises their interdependence but it will never be enough on its own. Offending and the reasons behind it are a complex problem and the rush to the simple solution should be resisted.

All is not lost, however, as *'Probation is an honourable profession which has survived several governmental onslaughts on its integrity in recent years'* (Worral, 2015, p 508) and hopefully it retains the resilience to survive a little longer. There are certainly grounds for optimism in the development of new strengths-based approaches and in the increasing recognition of 'what works' (McNeill et al, 2010 , p 534). Practitioners in the system retain, in the main, a belief in the rehabilitative ideal and an understanding of the important role of relationships, which is remarkably resilient. IDEAS with its explicit emphasis on continual learning can also help the hard-pressed practitioners justify the time to look around them and consider what they can learn from international and local research and how this can best support them to remain positive and work in a way that is congruent with relationship-based practice.

References

Berg, I K and Szabo, P (2005) *Brief Coaching for Lasting Solutions.* New York: W W Norton and Company.

Deering, J (2010) The Purposes of Supervision: Practitioner and Policy Perspectives in England and Wales. In McNeill, F, Raynor, P and Trotter, C (eds) *Offender Supervision: New Directions in Theory, Research and Practice* (pp 451–70). Cullompton: Willan.

Dowden, C and Andrews, D (2004) The Importance of Staff Practice in Delivering Effective Correctional Treatment: A Meta-analytic Review of Core Correctional Practice. *International Journal of Offender Therapy and Comparative Criminology*, 48(2), 203–14.

Egan, G (2009) *The Skilled Helper* (9th edn). London: Cengage Learning.

Grant, S and McNeill, F (2014) The Quality of Probation Supervision: Comparing Practitioner Accounts in England and Scotland. *European Journal of Probation*, 6(2): 147–68.

HM Inspectorate of Probation (2018) *An Inspection of Probation Services in Staffordshire & West Midlands Community Rehabilitation Company*. Manchester: Crown Copyright.

HM Inspectorate of Probation (2016) *Quality & Impact Inspection: The Effectiveness of Probation Work in the North of London*. Manchester: CrownCopyright.

HM Inspectorate of Probation (2017) *Quality & Impact Inspection: The Effectiveness of Probation Work in Staffordshire and Stoke*. Manchester: Crown Copyright.

HM Inspectorate of Probation (2014) *Transforming Rehabilitation Early Implementation: An Independent Inspection Setting Out the Operational Impacts, Challenges and Necessary Actions*. Manchester: Crown Copyright.

Kemshall, H, Wilkinson, B and Baker, K (2013) *Working with Risk: Skills for Contemporary Social Work*. Cambridge: Policy Press.

Lewis, S (2014) Exploring Positive Working Relationships in Light of the Aims of Probation, Using a Collaborative Approach. *Probation Journal,* 61(4): 334–45.

Lipton, D S, Martinson, R and Wilks, J (1975) *The Effectiveness of Correctional Treatment*. New York: Praeger.

Martinson, R (1974) What Works?—Questions and Answers about Prison Reform. *The Public Interest*, Spring 1974: 22–54.

McGuire, J (1995) *What Works in Reducing Reoffending: Guidelines from Research and Practice*. Chichester: Wiley.

Maruna, S (2010) The Desistance Paradigm in Correctional Practice: From Programmes to Lives. In McNeill, F, Raynor, P and Trotter, C (eds) *Offender Supervision: New Directions in Theory, Research and Practice* (pp 65–89). Cullompton: Willan.

McNeill, F, Thomas, M and Thorndon-Edwards, K (2018) Helping, Holding, Hurting: A Conversation about Supervision. *The Howard Journal of Crime and Justice*, 57(1): 94–107.

McNeill, F, Raynor, P and Trotter, C (eds) (2010) *Offender Supervision: New Directions in Theory, Research and Practice*. Cullompton: Willan.

Miller, W and Rollnick, S (2013) *Motivational Interviewing: Helping People Change* (3rd edn). New York: Guildford Press.

Ministry of Justice and National Offender Management Service (2015) *National Standards Practice Framework*. Crown Copyright.

Ministry of Justice (2018) *Strengthening Probation, Building Confidence*. London: Crown Copyright.

Ministry of Justice (2013) *Transforming Rehabilitation: A Strategy for Reform*. London: Crown Copyright.

Moore, R (ed) (2015) *A Compendium of Research and Analysis on the Offender Assessment System (OASys) 2009–2013*. Ministry of Justice Analytical Series. London: National Offender Management Service.

Raynor, P and Vanstone, M (2016) Moving Away from Social Work and Half Way Back Again: New Research on Skills in Probation. *British Journal of Social Work*, 46: 1131–47.

Robinson, G, Priede, C, Farrall, S, Shapland, J and McNeill, F (2013) Doing 'strengths-based' Research: Appreciative Inquiry in a Probation Setting. *Criminology & Criminal Justice*, 13(1): 3–20.

Rowe, M and Soppitt, S (2014) 'Who you gonna call?' The Role of Trust and Relationships in Desistance from Crime. *Probation Journal*, 61(4): 397–412.

Sarre, R (2001) Beyond 'What Works?' A 25-year Jubilee Retrospective of Robert Martinson's Famous Article. *Australian & New Zealand Journal of Criminology*, 34(1): 38–46.

Scottish Government (2005) *21st Century Social Work: Reducing Re-offending: Key Practice Skills*. [online] Available at: www2.gov.scot/Publications/2005/04/21132007/20080 (accessed 23 February 2019).

Shapiro, C and DiZerega, M (2010) It's Relational: Integrating Families into Community Corrections. In McNeill, F, Raynor, P and Trotter, C (eds) *Offender Supervision: New Directions in Theory, Research and Practice* (pp 241–56). Cullompton: Willan.

Sorsby, A, Shapland, J, Farrall, S, McNeill, F, Priede, C and Robinson, G (2013) *Probation Staff Views of the Skills for Effective Engagement Development (SEED) Pilot.* Analytic Study 2013. National Offender Management. [online] Available at: https://assets.publishing.service.gov.uk/government/uploads/system/uploads/attachment_data/file/224308/probation-views-seed-pilot.pdf (accessed 21 June 2019).

The Guardian (2019) Probation Will Be Renationalised After Disastrous Grayling Reforms. 16 May. [online] Available at: www.theguardian.com/society/2019/may/16/part-privatisation-probation-sevices-to-be-reversed-offender-management-nationalised-chris-grayling (accessed 28 May 2019).

Trotter, C (2015) *Working with Involuntary Clients: A Guide to Practice* (3rd edn). London: Sage.

Vanstone, M (2004) Mission Control: The Origins of a Humanitarian Service. *Probation Journal*, 51(1): 34–47.

Ward, T (2010) The Good Lives Model of Offender Rehabilitation: Basic Assumptions, Etiological Commitments, and Practice Implications. In McNeill, F, Raynor, P and Trotter, C (eds) *Offender Supervision: New Directions in Theory, Research and Practice* (pp 41–64). Devon, UK: Willan Publishing.

Ward, T, Polaschek, D L L and Beech, A R (2005) *Theories of Risk, in Theories of Sexual Offending.* Chichester: John Wiley & Sons, Ltd.

White, M and Epston, D (1990) *Narrative Means to Therapeutic Ends.* New York: W.W. Norton.

Wilson, K, Ruch, G, Lymbery, M and Cooper, A (eds) (2011) *Social Work: An Introduction to Contemporary Practice.* Harlow: Pearson.

Wood, M, Cattell, J, Hales, G, Lord, C, Kenny, T, Capes, T and NatCen Social Research and Get the Data (2015) *Reoffending by Offenders on Community Orders: Results from the Offender Management Community Cohort Study.* Ministry of Justice Analytical Series: London: Crown Copyright.

Worral, A (2015) Grace Under Pressure: The Role of Courage in the Future of Probation Work. The *Howard Journal of Crime and Justice*, 54(5): 508–20.

Introduction

Drug and alcohol services deal with highly complex individuals, many of whom have had to cope with multiple episodes of trauma, abuse and neglect. These individuals develop coping strategies that can put themselves at risk with a possible consequence being that further trauma can be experienced. The 'self-medication' effect of the substance used can make these individuals feel safe, secure and in control, if only for a brief period. Anyone seen to be threatening these coping strategies will often be responded to with hostility, distrust and desperation. Therefore, overcoming barriers and prejudice, generating trust and acceptance are difficult tasks for practitioners operating in this area of social work. Helping these individuals to unpick their lives, dismantling the often unhealthy strategies that they feel have kept them alive and able to function are not easy achievements. Attempting to empower the person to initiate positive change, while keeping them and their family as safe as possible during this work is a challenge for even the most experienced and capable social worker.

While governments have, for centuries, recognised the usefulness of gaining income from taxation of substances that intoxicate or make us 'feel better', relax or cope better with unpleasant emotions, for example, taxing chocolate and coffee in the sixteenth century, and later, taxing alcohol, there has also been a long-time concern about the anti-social and physical and psychological harm that use or misuse of drugs and alcohol can cause. Over time, the drug user has come to be seen as an 'outsider', not 'one of us' and someone who potentially damages the community. Drug and alcohol misuse has been criminalised and as such, the legislation that is in place to deal with substance misuse is in the criminal justice arena.

The 1990s saw the introduction of Tackling Drugs Together (1995), the first drugs 'policy' in the UK. With partnership working at its core, the strategy had three main target areas – enforcement, prevention and treatment – and was meant to address the long-debated tensions between a focus on substance use as a public health issue, or as a criminal justice matter. More recently, the focus of work on drug and alcohol misuse continues to be based on these two policy agendas, the main aims of which are: to reduce demand by taking a whole life approach, using early intervention with vulnerable users; from a criminal justice perspective, to restrict supply by targeting criminal gangs; and to build recovery through a more holistic approach, looking at employment, housing and resilience-building factors for individuals. Here, a relationship-based approach can be seen as a significant component of treatment, holding together a range of interventions to support people in changing their behaviour.

This chapter will explore how the IDEAS framework can assist the practitioner to utilise a relationship-based approach when working with people who have contact with drug and alcohol services.

Influence

In order to promote positive change and utilise the potential influence that the worker can have, the appropriate use of professional confidence and authority is essential (Forrester et al, 2008). If a worker appears disorganised, unable to either give or find out the appropriate answers or are unreliable then it is unlikely that the person using services will continue to maintain trust. The loss of professional credibility and authority within the relationship can become a stumbling block and, left unchecked, the relationship is unlikely to be productive.

Many people who engage with drug and alcohol services have had negative role models within their lives, and they may have developed unhealthy coping strategies because they have not had the opportunity to learn appropriate skills from their caregivers and peers (Dayton, 2012). A significant number of people who access substance misuse services have been through the care system and will be familiar with social work intervention. Alderson et al, 2017) suggest that:

Looked After Children have multiple risk factors for substance use, poor mental health, school failure and early parenthood. These factors include parental poverty, absence of support networks, parental substance use, poor maternal mental health, early family disruption and, in the majority of cases, abuse and/or neglect.

Typical reactions to moderately stressful situations can be anger, fear, anxiety and a sense of helplessness for even minor, avoidable and common issues. This can quite often trigger drug/alcohol use or other unhelpful behaviours such as anger, shame, depression and anxiety (Fisher and Rogel, 2009). Being able to model appropriate responses and behaviours is a powerful tool, and pro-social modelling can influence a change in behaviour, especially when used alongside other interventions such as therapeutic counselling, motivational interviewing and strengths-based, task-centred work, all of which can increase self-esteem and self-worth. Being able to help somebody transform what has previously been viewed as a deficit into a strength can be a pivotal moment in the intervention journey. This can be something as small as helping them make a phone call to sort out a debt that in the past would have seemed impossible due to the feelings of shame as the money had been spent on substances rather than bills, or as large as supporting them in a Family Court Hearing. Modelling relaxation techniques can help people who are in a state of heightened anxiety and listening to their fears and reminding them of how far they have come can make a positive difference (Cherry, 2010).

Case Example

Yolanda, a mixed heritage (White British and Black Jamaican) 32 year-old divorced mother of two had an alcohol addiction for three years but had remained sober for the past 18 months. She was in the family court arena attempting to arrange unsupervised contact with her children who lived with their father as she had a history of self-harm and suicide attempts linked to her childhood experiences of abuse and rape. Yolanda was initially angry and frustrated with the court outcome, which was a further assessment period of six months; however, the worker supporting her reminded her of how much better she was at coping now and was able to describe how long Yolanda had been waiting so far and how six more months was not beyond her capabilities. Yolanda calmed down and felt that in fact the court had listened to her as she was being assessed rather than being simply told no.

Multi-agency working is an important factor in substance misuse work. Practitioners in this specialism can find themselves collaborating with general practitioners, nurses, teachers, police officers, solicitors, judges, health visitors, housing officers and occupational therapists among others. A person who uses services is often working with multiple professionals who each have a different agenda and culture to the other. This can be very confusing to a person who, as suggested earlier, may have pre-existing prejudices and perceptions. Demonstrating that other professionals are not 'the enemy' is vital. If the worker has a good positive, trusting relationship, modelling effective communication with all other professionals is likely to show that this interaction is normal and not hostile, potentially reducing anxieties and tension for them. This can encourage more positive relations where not only the person feels the relationship is better, the other professionals can also experience a more positive view of them (Cherry, 2010).

Case Example

James is a 33 year-old single White British male with two children who were initially living with his previous partner. James had a criminal record for theft and smoked cannabis daily. His children were removed from his previous partner due to her drug use and chaotic lifestyle and had been placed in foster care and James wanted to have custody of the children.

James struggled with authority figures. However, role-playing interactions with other professionals helped him to practise his new approach and reduced his stress levels, giving him the space to reduce his substance misuse and deal with day-to-day issues in a calm and positive way. His social worker said she was *'amazed'* at the change in James' presentation and cooperation as he stopped being hostile and took responsibility for his past actions, giving the social worker a chance to develop a positive relationship with him.

Delivery

The delivery of services within a statutory drug and alcohol agency are governed by the policies in place at a national level. Historically, the government direction has altered over time with the desirable outcome veering between a recovery agenda and harm reduction. Depending through which lens substance misuse is viewed, the user is either a person making a lifestyle choice or their addiction is the product of their environment and upbringing (Amull, 2014). There is a continuing tension between the medical model of treatment which includes the prescribing of substitutes for drugs and the gradual reduction of these and the social model which looks at the person as located within a set of ecological systems with each part influencing the other with treatment including holistic therapies. Experience suggests that both models have a vital role to play for many people and are best used together whenever appropriate.

Whatever the focus of the organisation, local policies and procedures are necessary and within this area of practice, data protection, information sharing and safeguarding are particular areas in which practitioners need to ensure they are following the necessary guidance. Practitioners need to be familiar with and clearly communicate their safeguarding responsibilities and this is a potentially difficult discussion to have. Being congruent, utilising motivational techniques and offering reassurance that any responsibilities the worker has to share information will be fully discussed before this happens.

Efficient delivery of a service often begins with a comprehensive and well-formed assessment of the needs of the person accessing services. Being able to see the person as soon as they express an interest in engaging can utilise the momentum of motivation, thus enabling a richer assessment. The assessment needs to include standard demographics such as ethnicity, age etc, and also contain tools which enable people to self-report their opinion on areas such as their mental health, physical health and their quality of life. Asking questions which provide the person with opportunities to express their view of their current situation is also an important part of the assessment. This may include a discussion about hopes, goals and motivation. Utilising solution-focused tools such as the use of scales can be helpful here (Macdonald, 2011). Following the assessment, an holistic plan needs to be co-produced with the person and their family and this may include the involvement of professionals from other organisations. Assessment and planning need to be fluid to allow for changes in lifestyle, life events or motivation. Ideally the assessment is completed over one or two sessions, but flexibility may be required as to establish the trust and rapport required in order to complete an accurate assessment.

To support and inform the intervention, a risk assessment is also required. This needs to cover areas such as overdose, sexual health, mental health, criminal history, risk of suicide, children, debt and self-care. This information not only informs the person, worker and the agency of potential risk areas that need to be managed; it also indicates potential strengths, areas for development and opportunities for change.

Record keeping is also an important consideration. Within the drug and alcohol field, the very nature of people who are potentially taking real risks with their lives means that there will be incidents where serious harm or even death can occur. The death of a person is a tragic occurrence and a well-kept set of recordings describing why decisions have been made and demonstrating that the correct procedures have been followed can be of great importance. This not only aids any investigation, but it can also provide comfort to the family of the deceased who may seek reassurance that their loved one was given adequate support prior to their death or injury.

Expertise

Within any setting social workers need to be able to draw upon on knowledge and understanding in order to intervene effectively. Experience within the author's agency suggests that the practical application of a wide range of theoretical concepts and models can improve outcomes for people and their families. It is not possible to list everything in detail within this chapter, so I intend to briefly consider three interconnected approaches.

The use of Transactional Analysis (TA) can be an effective catalyst for change within drug and alcohol work. It is described as '*a theory of personality and a systematic psychotherapy for personal growth and personal change*' (Stuart and Joines, 2012, p 3). It is also a theory and intervention that is potentially simple to introduce to the person themselves. The visual nature of the three ego state principles (Child, Adult, Parent) makes it possible to overcome barriers such as understanding and language. This sharing of aspects of a theory for understanding and explaining what is going on for a person can help build partnership by sharing expertise and insight without judgement. Often within sessions where TA is being utilised and explained in a visual manner, the person has exclaimed; '*That is so me!!!*' and couples have gone away from a session and returned a week later with real changes to their personal communication. For instance, it is not uncommon to hear comments such as:

'I never realised just how often I nagged her (partner) like a parent and now I understand why she acted like a kid being told off!'

'I now know why I was so angry with him (partner), my dad was horrible and abusive to me and feeling "told off" by a parent just put me back to being a kid waiting for a slap!'

An aspect of TA that is useful to keep in the forefront of the worker's thinking is the Drama Triangle (Weinhold and Weinhold, 2017). In essence, the drama triangle consists of three roles: the Victim, the Persecutor and the Rescuer. These roles can become interchangeable with the person often experiencing the role of the victim and is often a reason why many people feel that for them, things never change (Holden, 2013). Workers can also become part of this triangle, for example, the worker can become the rescuer for the individual using the service. However, they can easily find themselves placed in the role of the persecutor by people who use services if they do not fulfil their expectations. For workers, remembering the mantra of *'Never promise what you cannot deliver but always deliver what you promise'* can help to avoid this occurring.

Cycle of Change and Loop of Stasis

Every person is a unique individual and understanding why somebody is 'stuck' is a complex and involved process. The Cycle of Change (Prochaska and Diclemente, 1986) readily demonstrates the stages that a person goes through before change becomes sustainable. Typically, somebody will go through a phase of 'Pre-Contemplation' of change; in this stage there is no active thought of changing a behaviour, and this is followed by a period of thought regarding change or 'Contemplation'. The next stage is 'Preparation', where the person is ready to attempt to change; this is followed by the 'Action' stage where effort is taken to actually make changes. 'Maintenance' of this change will either lead to the change being sustained and 'Recovery' is achieved or the 'Relapse' phase is entered and a return to the pre-contemplation stage. The Loop of Perpetuating Stasis examines the areas between recovery and relapse that are contained within the Cycle of Change and helps to explore the experiences, behaviours and beliefs that keep the person within the Loop of Stasis. These are the potential root causes of behaviours and potential symptoms of problems that prevent many from breaking free and living lives that they feel are productive and happy.

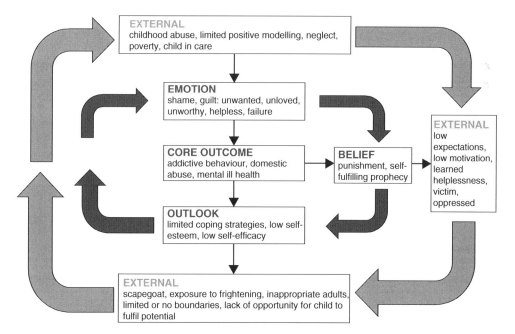

Figure 9.1 The Loop of Perpetuating Status

At the centre of the Loop are the behaviours that are of concern; these can be addictive behaviours, domestic violence, mental ill health or any other behaviour that requires change. Surrounding these are others that underpin the central issues and adjoining these are the experiences that may have contributed to behaviours or patterns of thinking. These stressors, triggers and experiences cannot be dealt with in isolation as they impact upon each other and simply concentrating on one aspect exclusively may not be productive.

Case Example

Charlie is a White British 38 year-old single mother of two. She has a past history of drug addiction and involvement in sex work. She entered the agency as her young children had child protection plans. She returned to drug and alcohol use and occasionally funded this with sex work. The Loop helps to illustrate the potential root causes of this. Charlie was sexually abused as a child and research suggests that childhood sexual abuse is often associated with substance abuse in later life (Kendler et al, 2000). Charlie would talk of her shame and fear; she described herself as worthless and said that her periods of sex work increased her feelings of shame. She felt worthlessness due to the fact that, even though she had children, she still returned to drugs and alcohol as a coping strategy. Following the Loop she felt she would never get better; she projected her own inability to improve onto others putting herself into the victim role with authority figures, which made it difficult to build effective relationships. Her parenting became ineffective and at times emotionally abusive. Simply stopping her using substances would not address the issues underpinning that behaviour. Examining her Loop with the worker gave them both the framework to consider what needed to be addressed.

The use of Motivational Interviewing (MI) (Miller and Rollnick, 2012) can help turn relapse into learning opportunities and makes successes the stepping stones to positive change. It requires the worker to establish a positive working relationship that is based on trust and respect and is built on a common purpose that allows the person to look at their own goals rather than the goals of an agency. Enabling and encouraging people to set their own targets, make positive changes and solve problems can be empowering.

Case Example

Yolanda had felt unloved, unwanted and worthless throughout her life. By using open questions such as 'Describe how you think things could be better?', 'Tell me what you could do differently?' gave her the tools and motivation to explore the reasons for her alcohol addiction. Slowly she dismantled the mindset that she would be unable to cope without alcohol. Her worker found that working in an MI-based partnership, which involved celebrating small victories and ensuring interventions were available at the appropriate time, was an effective course of action. For Yolanda this began with a supported session with a mental health professional, with the result that she felt listened to and validated.

It is important to remember that it is the person who defines what success, for them, looks like. Within many contemporary substance use services, there is a focus on abstinence and if this is not the choice for an individual, there is a potential for oppressive practice with the person feeling judged and blamed (Dominelli, 2002).

Alliance

Within the field of psychotherapy, a productive and strong working alliance between a person and worker can be seen as a mechanism that drives change from and underpins the desire to maintain that change (Horvath and Greenberg, 1994). This is transferable to social work. Empathy, warmth, congruence and genuineness are important qualities for relationship building (Rogers, 2003). Avoiding collusion, reinforcing the positive role of social work and not alienating the person using services are all important qualities required from first contact.

If the therapist seems to ignore the client's expectations of immediate relief from discomfort rather than realistically renegotiating them, the client's anxieties will be increased. The failure to develop a collaborative stance may also indicate that the client has externalised the locus of change and expects it to come from the environment or the therapist rather than from within. This unrealistic expectation implies that the therapist and the client have not established a workable framework for therapy and poor outcome is likely.

(Horvath and Greenberg, 1994, p 3)

Appropriate use of self with this group of people is potentially a very powerful tool. The humanisation of the practitioner within the relationship while maintaining boundaries and defined roles can significantly increase the likelihood of trust, belief and a willingness to work well together (Ruch et al, 2010). The substance misuse field has long championed the use of peer mentors as the shared experience that they bring can be the influence that some people who use services need to get them on the road to recovery (Galenter, 1999). The true empathy and understanding that a peer mentor brings and the fact they have experienced addiction and have been able to make the changes needed to be well into recovery gives the person hope, belief and confidence that they can recover. This often promotes a feeling of partnership with the mentor.

Many people accessing treatment services are from disadvantaged or chaotic backgrounds and have a fear of authority, which can lead to a 'projection' of these fears on to the allocated social worker. This reaction to their experience of authority figures, including parents, teachers and other adults in positions of power, can be interpreted as a defence mechanism and an internal unconscious response to previous experiences, which has become a repeated pattern of response when there is a threat from the external world (Grant and Crawley, 2002). Unwanted and uncomfortable internal feelings are externalised and displaced onto another person, and this displacement, or projection, 'infects' the relationship with the social worker who may well respond with their own unconscious 'internalised' pattern of response to a threat (this is often referred to as counter-transference, or the response to a person's transference of past experiences into the present [projection is one part of this process]). People can be angry, hesitant or even fearful of contact with social workers in a substance misuse service because of their perceived (and actual) authority and power. This dynamic can be exposed through the social worker's theoretical understanding, their self-awareness of their own past experiences and insight into how these can affect contemporary relationships, which can be used to illuminate the dynamic with the person accessing services. Supervision is useful for examining such dynamics and 'untangling' such issues within the relationship for therapeutic benefit and to develop insight.

How can this fear or anger be overcome? Many drug and alcohol-based social workers are located within the National Health Service or third sector agencies and establishing that the service offered is separate from social care services can be helpful to beginning a relationship. People often believe that practitioners working in these settings do not have the same statutory powers as social workers in social care services and thus it may be easier for this group to begin to trust (Healy and Darlington, 2009). The author has often heard comments from people such as the following: *'I trusted you because you weren't a "proper" social worker and so wasn't going to judge me as an unfit mother and take my children away from me.'* However, it does need to be communicated that all workers, regardless of their profession or organisation, all have the same responsibilities to safeguard and protect under relevant policy guidance and legislation. Creation of trust starts with honesty and it is important that workers share any worries or concerns they have. The previously mentioned defence mechanisms and projection of blame often results in social workers from children's social care services being a focus for the family to attack and the scapegoat for all the family's difficulties. Many users of drug and alcohol services have the perception that their past social workers have lied to them and deceived them in some way, possibly as a result of transference and projection, and an open and transparent relationship between a practitioner and a person using services, wherever the agency is situated, is central to overcoming this view.

Case Example

James did not have any trust in his children's social worker. While she believed that she had not been negative towards him, he described his previous experiences regarding social care as difficult. He stated that his expectation was that he would be lied to, patronised and inevitably judged to be unable to care for his children. These perceptions, as discussed earlier, may result from his defence mechanisms, with James projecting his fear, anger and disappointment upon the worker. Offering empathetic understanding without judgement while avoiding collusion, and listening to James's views and opinions and offering an alternative interpretation helped to develop his insight and withdraw the projections. Handled with sensitivity, while making connections with his early experiences of being parented and subsequent experiences with other authority figures, made him feel valued and acknowledged. Speaking with him at a review several months after his case was closed, James stated that:

It was like someone had switched a light on for me; there was someone in authority who wasn't telling me I was wrong and for once I felt that someone didn't think I was getting what I deserved because I had a bit of a past.

Showing 'Unconditional Positive Regard' (Rogers, 2003) helped James to stop seeing himself as a 'bad man' (and 'bad child') and assisted him to believe in his own potential for change. He was gently encouraged to take responsibility for his own actions and the consequences attached to them without deflecting the blame to others. He began to look for help in changing his attitude and addressing his own attitudes and behaviours and went on to undertake therapeutic counselling as well as attending parenting courses and a domestic violence perpetrator programme.

These courses utilised a Cognitive Behavioural Therapy model, encouraging the participants to examine how their emotions, influenced by their negative thoughts, led to negative actions and the effect that these actions and thoughts have on others (Scott et al, 2006). James felt that this really helped him to gain an insight into his thoughts and behaviours and, importantly, the local authority social worker was no longer blamed for intervening to protect the children.

Tuning in (Taylor and Devine, 1993) to how a person may be feeling, their experiences, hopes and fears is essential to forming a working relationship that is a true therapeutic alliance. An important aspect of tuning-in specifically involves the social worker imagining the world of the person, the external world of their immediate social networks – family and neighbourhood as well as the wider societal influences, all of which impact on their internal world. This imaginative exercise helps to develop empathic understanding of what it feels like to be that person and is an effective way of preparing for engaging with them. As part of this process, as referred to before, social workers also need to be aware of their own experiences and values and this is an important part of recognising the self and its impact on working relationships. Transference, as discussed earlier, is present in all interactions with people; it can be positive or negative, productive and counter-productive. Transference of a person's anxieties onto the practitioner can lead to anxiety about them and the person may place a great deal of reliance on that individual in order for their anxiety to be controlled. This can become an exclusive relationship for the person and no other practitioner can be as good. The counter-transference from this can lead the practitioner to believe that only they can undertake the work with this person and feelings of guilt and responsibility can be felt when they are not available or are unable to fulfil their wishes. This can create added stress and tension for all parties concerned, damaging the alliance and leading to poorer outcomes or even disengagement. Again, good supervision can be key to alerting the social worker to such dynamics, so that they do not become destructive to the working alliance.

Case Example

Veronica is a 21 year-old White British woman with a diagnosis of emotional disregulation. She was involved in casual sex work and drug use. Initially she became attached to one particular social worker, often saying 'I have never told anyone else this' and 'You are the only person I can talk to'. The practitioner, being aware of transference and counter-transference, discussed with Veronica a possible therapeutic intervention provided by somebody else within the agency. However, this triggered within Veronica her fear of rejection and she became extremely anxious at the thought that she would be seeing someone else. As a consequence, she attended only two sessions, was in a state of high anxiety at all times and the intervention was unsuccessful. The practitioner recognised that the 'failed' intervention was eliciting feelings of guilt in herself that she was the only person that Veronica would work with and so introduced a different worker to work jointly with her, thereby gently allowing her to step back without making Veronica feel rejected. This process was repeated until Veronica was working with the appropriate mental health team.

Support

Support from an organisation is an essential component within the helping professions and the drug and alcohol field is no exception. Practitioners are often hearing people's experiences of fear, abuse and trauma on a daily basis, which can elicit anger and sadness in the worker themselves. Emotional labour (Hochschild, 1983) is an unavoidable element of social work as practised in drug and alcohol treatment settings. This 'vicarious trauma' (Izzo and Carpel Miller, 2010) can be psychologically exhausting, cause burnout, stress disorder and compassion fatigue. Research suggests that 50 per cent of professionals working with trauma report feeling distressed (Meichenbaum, nd). The experiences of a person may mirror personal experiences for the worker, which in turn can trigger issues arising from personal trauma in their own lives. Being aware of the potential for this and recognising when it is happening is important for the continuing mental health of the social worker. The use of supervision is an established method for exploring these situations for therapists and social workers alike. However, if these traumas are happening daily and supervision is a monthly event, how is the practitioner to hold on to these feelings and emotions? One way, particularly in therapeutic environments, is to have a group meeting every morning in which it is expected that staff will discuss any issues they have and receive support from their colleagues. This provides what Kittay (1999) refers to as 'nested dependencies', a concept that highlights how those caring for others also need care and support established within their own organisational culture to manage the feelings (positive and negative) that work involving the care of others can induce. Without this, stress and burnout can become established features of practice. Developing a culture of mutual respect and recognition when a member of the team is struggling with a situation evokes a culture of kindness and caring for each other. Ensuring that regular breaks are taken, including time for lunch rather than just pressing on due to the pressure of work, are examples of this care which can help to cement a team together and foster an atmosphere of respect, acceptance and support, which is vital if social workers are to maintain healthy and productive professional working relationships with people who use services.

Developing resilience is also part of professional development. Being resilient as a professional social worker not only protects the worker themselves but also allows them to be more effective (Grant, 2014). Resilience development can be helped by following effective steps already discussed such as having a support network and a good work–life balance and enjoying activities outside of work. Having a healthy work–life balance can be very beneficial for both the practitioner and the person using services and experience suggests that a practitioner who is feeling mentally well and not exhausted, jaded or burnt out is more likely to be able to deliver an effective, responsive experience. Where significant personal experiences are re-awoken, the practitioner may require therapy with a counsellor provided as part of clinical supervision to keep themselves mentally healthy.

Managing time and workload effectively relieves stress and anxiety; assertiveness skills may also be required in order to advocate for time to develop effective relationships (Grant, 2012). As a social worker it is possible to open doors for people; however, it is ultimately the person who chooses to walk through them.

Conclusion

The relationship is at the very core of work with substance users: it promotes a person's perception of 'doing with' rather than 'being done to', and it is an essential element when trying to promote sustainable, positive change in individuals and families who have experienced harm and oppression in their lives. Therefore, the IDEAS model is well suited to this area of social work. As mentioned at the start of this chapter, people who use substances have complex histories and multiple stressors. Careful use of influence can enable a person and their family to develop the confidence and self-belief required to make positive change. The delivery element of the framework includes the assessment and adherence to legislation, policies and allows the effective management of risk involved in making any change and underpins the development of a transparent and adaptable working alliance. The expertise required to listen to, acknowledge and accept people's lived experiences and deliver effective interventions within the context of a therapeutic relationship where people feel that practitioners genuinely care about them, all require effective support to be provided by the organisation. Social workers will often see and hear traumatic stories and events and may even experience the death of somebody; therefore, robust and compassionate support mechanisms need to be in place to assist them to do their job effectively and safely.

References

Alderson, H, McGovern, R, Brown, R, Howel, D, Becker, F, Carr, L, Copello, A, Fouweather, T, Kaner, E, McArdle, P, McColl, E, Shucksmith, J, Steele, A, Vale, L, and Lingam, R (2017) Supporting Looked After Children and Care Leavers in Decreasing Drugs, and Alcohol (SOLID): Protocol for a Pilot Feasibility Randomised Controlled Trial of

Interventions to Decrease Risky Substance Use (Drugs and Alcohol) and Improve Mental Health of Looked After Children and Care Leavers Aged 12–20 Years. *Pilot and Feasibility Studies, 2017*, 3: 25. Newcastle University.

Amull, E (2014) *Understanding Substance Use Policy and Practice.* Northwich: Critical Publishing.

Cherry, S (2010) *Transforming Behaviour: Pro-social Modelling in Practice.* London: Willan.

Dayton, T (2012) *The ACOA Trauma Syndrome: The Impact of Childhood Pain on Adult Relationships.* Deerfield Beach, FL: Health Communication Inc.

Dominelli, L (2002) *Anti Oppressive Social Work Theory and Practice.* Basingstoke: Palgrave.

Fisher, G L and Rogel, N A (2009) *Encyclopedia of Substance Abuse Prevention, Treatment, and Recovery.* London: Sage.

Forrester, D, Kershaw, S, Moss, H and Hughes, L (2008) Communication Skills in Child Protection: How Do Social Workers Talk to Parents? *Child and Family Social Work*, 13: 41–51.

Galenter, M (1999) *Network Therapy for Alcohol & Drug Abuse.* Milton Keynes: Guilford Publications.

Grant, J and Crawley, J (2002) *Transference and Projection: Mirrors to the Self.* Maidenhead: Open University Press.

Grant, L (2014) *Developing Resilience for Social Work Practice.* Basingstoke: Palgrave.

Grant, L (2012) *Emotional Resilience Expert Guide*, Community Care. [online] Available at: www.communitycare.co.uk/emotional-resilience-expert-guide (accessed 21 June 2019).

Healy, K and Darlington, Y (2009) Service User Participation in Diverse Child Protection Contexts: Principles for Practice. *Child and Family Social Work*, 14: 420–30.

HM Government (1995) *Tackling Drugs Together: A Strategy for England 1995–1998.* London: HMSO.

Holden, C (2013) *The Drama Triangle (Transactional Analysis in Bite Sized Chunks Book 2).* London: Whole Deen.

Horvath, A O and Greenberg, L S (1994) *The Working Alliance: Theory, Research, and Practice.* New York: John Wiley & Sons.

Izzo, E and Carpel Miller, V (2010) *Second-Hand Shock: Surviving & Overcoming Vicarious Trauma.* Scottsdale: HCI Press.

Kendler, K, Bulik, C M and Silberg, J (2000) Childhood Sexual Abuse and Adult Psychiatric and Substance Use Disorders in Women: An Epidemiological and Cotwin Control Analysis. *Archives of General Psychiatry*, 57(10): 953–9.

Kittay, E F (1999) *Love's Labor: Essays of Women, Equality and Dependency.* New York: Routledge.

Macdonald, A (2011) *Solution-Focused Therapy: Theory, Research & Practice.* London: Sage.

Meichenbaum, D (nd) *Self-care for Trauma Psychotherapists and Caregivers: Individual, Social and Organizational Interventions.* [online] Available at: www.wfmt.info/wp-content/uploads/2017/08/Meichenbaum-SelfCare_Global-Crises-Intervention-Resources.pdf (accessed 21 June 2019).

Miller, W and Rollnick, S (2012) *Motivational Interviewing, Third Edition: Helping People Change (Applications of Motivational Interviewing).* New York: Guilford Press.

Prochaska, J O and Diclemente, C C (1986) Toward a Comprehensive Model of Change. In Miller, W R and Heather, N (eds) *Treating Addictive Behaviours* (pp 3–27). Applied Clinical Psychology, vol 13. Boston, MA: Springer.

Rogers, C (2003) *Client Centred Therapy: Its Current Practice, Implications and Theory.* London: Constable.

Ruch, G, Turney, D and Ward, A (2010) *Relationship Based Social Work.* London: Jessica Kingsley.

Scott, K, Francis, K, Crooks, C and Kelly, T (2006) *Caring Dads: Helping Fathers Value Their Children.* Oxford: Trafford Publishing.

Stewart, I and Joines, V (2012) *TA Today: A New Introduction To Transactional Analysis.* Chapel Hill, NC: Lifespace.

Taylor, B and Devine, T (1993) *Assessing Needs and Planning Care in Social Work.* London: Routledge.

Weinhold, B and Weinhold, J (2017) *How to Break Free from the Drama Triangle and Victim Consciousness.* Asheville, NC: Circle Press.

Introduction

Domestic abuse is a complex, insidious and hidden phenomenon present within all societies. In the UK the cost of gender-based violence to both victims/survivors and society is approximately £66 billion per year (Home Office, 2019) and is reported to be a major health problem. Each year in England and Wales approximately 2 million adults experience domestic abuse (ONS, 2018). Although, the actual figure is likely to be significantly higher as the current statistics do not fully take account of the relatively new coercive and controlling behaviour offence alongside the well-known underreporting of domestic abuse and recording by the police (ONS, 2016).

Terminology and definitions of domestic abuse are varied and represent our understandings of both what is included and what is excluded. For example, the Women's Aid (2015) definition of domestic abuse includes online and digital abuse, and although it is not included in the Home Office draft Domestic Abuse Bill (2019), the government will be producing a White Paper called *Online Harms* (Home Office et al, 2018), which will explore the use of technology and social media in perpetrating domestic abuse. This emerging area has wide-ranging implications for victims/survivors and requires social workers to build a framework of understanding which includes developing contemporary knowledge, language and skills.

Kelly and Westmarland (2016) argue that language is key and found to contribute towards reducing and obscuring the reality of men's violence towards women. Rooted in social inequality, domestic abuse is seen as a gendered crime as we know that a disproportionate number of victims/survivors are women, although any person can experience domestic abuse irrespective of ethnicity, sexuality, religion, class or disability. Some people who experience other forms of oppression and discrimination face additional barriers to disclosing abuse and accessing services, and this chapter will encompass some of the issues faced by marginalised individuals.

Influence

Domestic abuse is often misunderstood; surrounded in stigma it is an area involving many myths and stereotypes which can lead to the abuse remaining unidentified, and a disconnection between the protections and victim/survivor (Stark, 2007). To fully understand the dynamics of domestic abuse, practitioners need to develop insight and better understandings of power constructs. For example, a useful starting point in social work practice may involve an exploration of Lukes' (2005) typologies of power involving coercion, influence, force, authority and manipulation. During supervision, the practitioner may visually map these power relationships to further understand the presenting dynamics through developing their professional understanding in relation to the people causing harm and supporting the victim/survivor to make sense of the situation. Although victim/survivor well-being and safety should always be prioritised, social workers need to work alongside and develop deeper understandings of perpetrators and power dynamics for meaningful change to take place.

To build on these understandings further may involve social workers recognising their urge to 'rescue' the victim/survivor to ensure their safety. This connects to the influence of invisible power involving socialisation and institutions of control (Hinson and Healey, 2003). For example, this represents how victims/survivors are understood and viewed within broader society: disenfranchised, powerless, with little recognition. As practitioners we can often recognise feelings of powerlessness as evidence suggests that social workers may represent the groups that they work alongside, reflecting and mirroring them (Dominelli, 1993). Practitioners may experience feelings of ambivalence towards their power and the concept can be complicated, often associated with social workers' possession of power and their relationship with and responsibility to create change. However, this element of the IDEAS model suggests that to be effective in this area of practice it is important that we develop our understanding of power as this supports practitioners to build and demonstrate the necessary skills to model positive interventions.

Within the sphere of domestic abuse, a strong sense of agency and pro-social modelling are encouraged. It is important for practitioners to be mindful of their influence and not to be oppressive in their behaviours to further revictimise the victim/survivor and participate in the cycle of abuse (Watson, 2017). As discussed in previous chapters, social workers are well positioned to be role models and use their legitimate power (French and Raven, [1959] 2001) to provide education to improve understanding of domestic abuse and challenge its acceptability and responses. For example, social workers should not be afraid to ask the 'Why?' question: Why does our organisation respond in this way? Why do I respond in this manner? Why do my colleagues respond using a particular approach? Is it effective? Is there a different approach? Is there evidence to support this?

When considering pro-social modelling, power and domestic abuse, it may be helpful to think about bystander intervention (Latané and Darley, 1970). A bystander is someone who observes a problematic event and a decision is made to intervene (pro-social/active bystander) or not (passive bystander) (Powell, 2011) (see Figure 10.1). In situations where the bystander chooses to do something, they send a powerful message to the perpetrator and other bystanders that their behaviour is socially unacceptable, thus connecting the private issues of domestic abuse to the public sphere and reinforcing domestic abuse as 'everyone's business' (HMIC, 2015). The more that these boundaries are challenged, reinforced and made visible by bystanders, the more social norms about what is acceptable

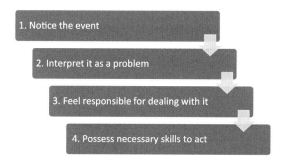

Figure 10.1 Four stages to becoming a prosocial bystander (Fenton et al, 2016, adapted from Berkowitz, 2009, p 10)

and the narrative around domestic abuse will shift. This emphasises the importance of individual agency influencing how society operates with social workers possessing the necessary skills to challenge attitudes, stereotypes and assumptions, and support the widening shift in public narrative for better understanding and recognition of domestic abuse. A toolkit (Public Health England, 2014), theoretical rationale (Fenton et al, 2014) and theory of change (Fenton et al, 2016, p 55) is available for practitioners to support individual changes as well as move beyond this, to create system and community change. More recently, bystander approaches have been viewed as an effective approach in changing attitudes around domestic abuse in universities, particularly in the USA, and although well-received in the UK further evaluation is required.

Finally, the concept of advocacy is integral within the social work profession. As agents of change, social workers work closely with the experiences and voices of victims/survivors and can effectively support the visibility of different groups of marginalised people who experience domestic abuse. Practitioners can address the stigma and recognise the different barriers individuals face, while challenging the misunderstandings, the myths and the status quo. Social workers can be activists and trailblazers in the dynamics of domestic abuse, fighting for better access to services and encouraging a consistent public dialogue around domestic abuse. However, it is acknowledged that awareness-raising skills such as these are not without their challenges in the current political and austerity climate, with reduced resources and increasing demand (Ferguson and Lavalette, 2013). One way of practitioners overcoming this is to build relationships with groups, communities and specialist services involved in activism, which is discussed further in Alliance.

Case Example

You have just finished attending a meeting and are on your way to a home visit with a colleague. A 24 year-old Chinese gay man is loudly harassing and pushing a 21 year-old White gay man outside in the street. No one is doing anything.

As a bystander and social worker, a positive and inclusive intervention involves noticing the event, chatting with your colleague about whether there is a problem and questioning if it is safe to say something. For example, a brief focused observation of the environment, a quick assessment of the urgency of the situation and consideration of whether the behaviour is non-mutual, harassment or abusive. The next stage involves questioning your feelings of responsibility to act and intervening with your colleague's support. Interrupt the situation through distraction and separation techniques, asking the perpetrator, 'Excuse me, do you have the time?' With your colleague, use this time to separate the victim/survivor and check in with them or saying to the perpetrator 'we see what you're doing and it's not okay'. Further considerations may include seeking assistance if necessary, eg contacting the police and providing contact details for specialist services to the victim/survivor and perpetrator.

Delivery

The government's approach to domestic abuse is framed within the Violence Against Women and Girls Strategy 2016–20 (HM Government, 2016). The draft Domestic Abuse Bill (Home Office, 2019), statutory guidance (Ministry of Housing, Communities & Local Government, 2018) and other national policy will shape local policy, systems and processes. In the context of domestic abuse, the element of Delivery involves practitioners needing to skilfully navigate these frameworks and legislation, which can be useful to understand and ensure people's rights are upheld. For example, as a first step practitioners can develop their knowledge and discuss the Code of Practice for Victims of Crime with victims/survivors (Ministry of Justice, 2015). Social workers can develop their understanding of a human rights-based approach as a conceptual framework and could draw on the Human Rights Act 1998, Article 3 and use this legislation meaningfully in practice. The connection between social work's values and human rights is clearly evident through its definitions, ethical principles, official statements and publications (UN, 1994; Healy, 2008). However, human rights in social work practice is often seen as rhetoric, with practitioners struggling to make sense of how they can effect change through its implementation and perhaps considering human rights to be too politicised for mainstream social work (Hessle, 2014).

Delivery also involves the tools and systems which support practice and when involved with domestic abuse these may include accessing different measures within the civil and criminal justice systems. Social workers demonstrate a critical role in facilitating access to and communication of these systems. However, this can often be wrought with complexities and challenges due to the nature of domestic abuse being unlike other crimes, in that it takes place within an intimate relationship. This is alongside the operation of legal systems and remedies which aim to support and protect the victim/survivor but can unintentionally affect their safety and allow further and new ways of revictimisation (Douglas, 2018). Social workers need to understand the impact of accessing the legal systems, in terms of the personal and material resources that may be required by the victim/survivor to navigate the complex legislative processes, and realise the potential of the law to deliver both negative and positive outcomes. This may be particularly applicable to marginalised groups of victims/survivors who are located outside of the mainstream. Examples of the tools and systems in place may involve the Domestic Violence Disclosure Scheme (DVDS), also known as Clare's Law (Home Office, 2016); Domestic Violence Protection Notices (DVPNs) and orders (DVPOs), under sections 24 to 33 of the Crime and Security Act 2010; and restraining orders within the Protection from Harassment Act 1997 and provided though the criminal courts. Victims/survivors can also apply to court for civil remedies, such as a non-molestation order and an occupation order, both of which are types of injunction. All of the above will require practitioners to recognise the effectiveness and challenges of engaging with such protections, able to identify the systemic barriers that prevent participation in the legal system, provide consistent support to navigate the complexities of legal responses and balance the ongoing process of safety and risk (Laing et al, 2013).

Social workers need to have knowledge in relation to existing risk assessments, such as the Domestic Abuse, Stalking and Honour Based Violence (DASH) (DASH, 2009) Risk Identification, Assessment and Management Model, an instrument which is used to support decision-making processes and aid clear communication of risk. Social workers need to also understand the processes and different roles of Multi-Agency Public Protection Arrangements (MAPPA) (Ministry of Justice et al, 2012) and Multi-Agency Risk Assessment Conferences (MARAC). MAPPA is a mechanism which involves agencies working together and using their statutory powers to manage the risk of violent offenders within the community. MARACs are focused on victim safety and involve multi-agency meetings where information is shared about the top 10 per cent of victims most at risk of harm or homicide (McLaughlin et al, 2018). Although it is important for social workers to be clear about their roles within these processes, practitioners also need to be open to and aware of the critiques that exist. For example, Grace (2015) argues that *'greater information sharing over time will create more knowledge about risk(s) but does not necessarily improve responses to risk(s) per se'*, while Steel et al (2011) questions the effectiveness and sustainability of MARACS and Almond et al (2017) highlights DASH's limited evaluation and evidence-base. As such, this suggests the need to work within the existing systems and frameworks in which practitioners operate, and do so through a critical lens, being aware of the limitations of such approaches ensuring that practitioners do not undertake and follow processes and approaches without question, but instead be curious about practice and the different contexts in which it operates.

Expertise

It is argued that domestic abuse is increasingly synonymous with child protection (Peckover, 2014) and as such, women are seen as mothers rather than victims/survivors. Social workers working within adult services also have access to fewer resources and may be unclear about their role and powers (Robbins et al, 2016). As a result, there are concerns about how social work practice responds to victims/survivors who do not fit with the constructions of domestic abuse. For example, Lazenbatt et al (2013, p 28) outline that *'service providers and policy makers often assume that DV stops at around 50'*, highlighting a continued prevalence of damaging stereotypes and harmful attitudes towards domestic abuse victims/survivors, and potentially leaving older people at significant risk of being unidentified with access to little resources. To address working with marginalised groups such as this and others, SafeLives (2018) outline that there is a need for social workers to be 'culturally competent' in their response to domestic abuse and demonstrate an understanding of the victim/survivor experience. For example, when working with older people or the LGBTQIA community, it is important for practitioners to understand the differing abusive experiences, the differences in societal attitudes towards victims/survivors, the lack of inclusion, access to services and additional barriers individuals face. Although there is much controversy around cultural competence as a concept (Beagan, 2018; Danso, 2018) with suggestions for alternatives such as cultural humility and other terms, in essence it is important for practitioners to fully commit and embed anti-racist, anti-discriminatory and anti-oppressive practice. Social workers need to understand and respond to both the *personal* and *structural* elements of these (Dominelli, 2018), in the context of a changing society as forces such as racism, oppression and discrimination continue to evolve and grow. A twenty-first-century social worker needs to understand and respond to such areas as technology facilitated domestic abuse and control, and the issues which this brings. For example, recognising when texting and social networking is used to harass, stalk or intimidate a victim/survivor, the importance of understanding the law around matters such as revenge porn and responding to impersonation and doxing violations. Doxing involves perpetrators researching and publishing an individual victim/survivor's personal identifiable information, or perhaps even those of the social worker. As such, practitioners are required to be capable and literate in their use of technology, seeking guidance from the Code of Ethics (BASW, 2014) in their digital social work practice.

Expertise encourages practitioners to draw on their knowledge of research and theory in relation to domestic abuse, particularly around violence, power and control, victimology, trauma and feminist perspectives. However, theory may appear 'invisible' (Thompson, 2017a, p 14) to practitioners who struggle with this aspect of practice. Theory is used to shape and evaluate practice, and to develop practitioners' expertise in this area may involve clearly naming theories while in supervision sessions. Although, as social workers it is important during these discussions to be mindful of what is not known, be open to different approaches and recognise the limitations of some theories and policies.

Building on the discussion in *Delivery*, regarding the creation of a *'human rights culture'* (Wronka, 2008, p 292) practitioners may also consider making explicit links between their daily professional practice, eg behaviours, values and skills, and knowledge, eg human rights principles, social justice and social work (Steen, 2018) (see Figure 10.2). To support this approach Androff (2015) outlines five core principles embedded within a human rights framework:

1. Human dignity

2. Non-discrimination

3. Participation

4. Transparency

5. Accountability

All of the above encompass elements of a human-rights-based relationship between the practitioner and the victim/survivor, and perpetrator. Using Figure 10.2 as a starting point, when thinking about the *principle* of human dignity and personalisation theory (Knowledge), practitioners may re-evaluate their *behaviour*, which may involve an emphasis towards viewing victims/survivors as people with needs to be met, and instead consider people as rights-holders who have self-determination (Daily Professional Practice). The *action* would involve respectful engagement with and discussion of the rights within the relationship between practitioner and victim/survivor, and in their relationship with others, eg confidentiality and freedom from harm (Transformative Social Work Practice). Connecting the stages with one another in Figure 10.2 in an explicit manner will support the development of social workers' confidence in human-rights approaches and expertise.

Expertise also encompasses the importance of 'practice wisdom', that is, knowledge acquired through doing the job of social work, through reflective practice and drawing upon the expertise of victims/survivors. Social workers need to recognise and champion the expertise of the experience of the victim/survivor and consider how these voices inform both day-to-day practice and the overarching social work policies and agendas. This crucial aspect of practice can be developed through practitioners building trusting alliances with victims/survivors as well as victim/survivor-led organisations, which will offer better protection and support more useful interventions (Robbins and Cook, 2018).

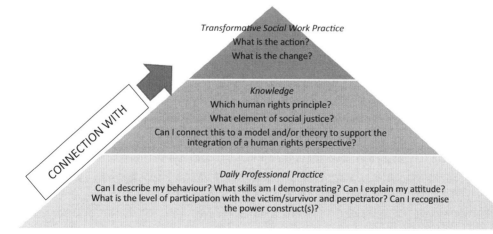

Figure 10.2 Towards a human rights perspective

The restoration of victim/survivor agency can be achieved through access to resources, in part addressing both the 'direct and indirect costs' of domestic abuse (Walby, 2009). For example, the recognition of economic abuse in the context of the new draft Domestic Abuse Bill (Home Office, 2019) highlights the need for practitioners to understand the *'behaviours that interfere with a woman's ability to acquire, use and maintain economic resources'* (Adams et al, 2008, p 564). Economic resources may include finances, housing, food, education, clothes and transportation and is a way of perpetrators limiting a victim/survivor's choice and control. Social workers can support the victim/survivor to address and respond to the impact of economic abuse through encouraging transparency through clear pathways to specialist services and access to complex systems, to maximise their economic resources.

Practitioners need to recognise and work effectively with victims/survivors of domestic abuse and understand that they are anchored and exist within their social context. This means that victims/survivors *'may have made certain decisions but these may be in a context not defined or chosen by themselves, where certain options are or are not available to them'* (Yuill and Gibson, 2011, p 2). For example, practitioners working alongside individuals and communities with a Gypsy, Roma, Traveller (GRT) background need to be mindful that interventions, assessments, communication and resources must recognise the influence and value of GRT culture, attitudes, beliefs and environment. As such, any support must take account of this for meaningful change to take place.

Finally, there is a great need for social workers to build their knowledge about perpetrators as working with the cause of the problem is crucial. Further research and evidence-informed approaches are required to understand perpetrators, how to respond to them and the effectiveness of existing interventions in changing attitudes and behaviour. Currently, perpetrator programmes which are commonplace have high attrition rates, resistance and non-compliance (Lilley-Walker et al, 2018). However, this suggests that further consideration needs to be given towards more evidence-informed and tailored perpetrator programmes, their purpose and function, as it is important that perpetrators are held accountable and are deterred from further abusive behaviours.

Alliance

Research suggests that victims/survivors' experience of working with social workers can be negative, as attitudes can perpetuate victim-blaming with a focus primarily towards child protection risks instead of a more supportive approach towards the adult victim/survivor (Doyle and McWilliams, 2018). Social work values including empathy and understanding vulnerability are fundamental in practice and enmeshed with complex issues of power, trust and inequality (Robbins and Cook, 2018). However, it is important for practitioners to be mindful of their power and not to mirror the type of coercion located in abusive relationships through punitive approaches. As practitioners we need to demonstrate values and qualities such as respect, warmth and integrity as these are the conduits that demonstrate the belief that people have the capacity to change their situation. Being persistent, kind and hopeful can help victims/survivors to develop a belief in a possible and positive future and this can lead to change taking place.

This element refers to the use of the relationship as a mechanism for change with victims/ survivors and perpetrators, as well as in our work other professionals. Effective relationship-based practice is underpinned by a complex process of trust (Smith, 2004). Robbins and Cook (2018) outline that the process of building trust involves being shaped by the knowledge of the practitioner, authentic caring, structural considerations including class, race, gender and age, and whether there is a positive perception of the victim/survivor.

An important message for social workers is that we need to start understanding and responding to the victim/survivor and perpetrator realities differently. There is a slow shift beginning to emerge in moving the question from 'why doesn't she leave?' to 'why doesn't he stop?' which represents the shift towards developing effective relationships and an increased focus towards work with perpetrators to create sustained change (Devaney and Lazenbatt, 2016). It is widely acknowledged that perpetrators need to be held accountable, challenged and take responsibility for their abusive behaviour (LeCouteur and Oxlad, 2010). However, as practitioners it is important to understand why and how perpetrators change their behaviour and use interventions that are evidence-informed and understood to be effective. For example, evidence shows that some services are not doing enough to keep victim/survivors safe and failing in the rehabilitation of perpetrators (HMIP, 2018). One suggestion that may address some of these aspects is to ensure that effective partnership-working is undertaken with perpetrators, which involves an integrated, co-ordinated community approach with a good level of information sharing and excellent communication (Davies and Biddle, 2018). Without practitioners forming such relationships and developing positive localised functions, acts of violence and control perpetrated within intimate relationships are likely to continue undetected by professionals and agencies.

Multi-agency and professional relationships are key, but these collaborations can be difficult due to organisations' different systems, values and beliefs. For example, the distrust of social workers by other agencies, or the unhelpful polarising view of private and voluntary agencies seen as honest and fair (Tonkiss and Passey, 1999) while local government is viewed as punitive. From a psychodynamic perspective, these fraught interprofessional relationships may sometimes mirror intimate partner relationships and the risk is that the victims/survivors may end up losing out as a result of agencies not being unilateral and working together in solidarity (Davies, 2018). This highlights the importance of relationship-based models of practice being embedded within an integrated network of services which can respond to the complexities of domestic abuse and address the needs of the whole person.

Finally, this element involves the importance of recognising how an individual experiences an intervention can be as important as the type of intervention being used. For example, the involvement of victims/survivors in shaping their decisions and plans is crucial both to inform social work practice, as well as to support more effective interventions. The voices of victims/

survivors need to be integral on both a personal and organisational level in the delivery of services and wider policy agendas. For example, McLaughlin et al (2018) suggest that MARACs should be more inclusive and involve victim/survivors in their processes and decision making.

Case Example

Dembe, a 32 year-old Black Ugandan transgender female, struggles to recognise the behaviour from her female partner as abusive sharing that 'I am lucky that I have someone to love me, and the problems within the relationship are my fault'. Dembe's partner controls the couple's finances, Dembe's outfits, phone and social media, isolating Dembe from her friends and family saying, 'No one else will ever accept you and love you' and 'Only I understand what you're going through'.

There is a common misconception that same-sex relationships are not as serious as heterosexual relationships, in terms of commitment, love and other factors. There are many other myths and pressures within the LGBTQIA community which as a practitioner you need to be aware of when working with Dembe, which may support your understanding of the situation. You need to help Dembe understand that anyone can experience domestic abuse and show that you will take it seriously and sensitively work from a strengths-based perspective demonstrating hope and kindness. You may choose to link with specialist agencies, such as Stonewall and SafeLives, to develop your understanding around issues specifically connected to trans people and domestic abuse. This will be alongside building your knowledge around the impact and influence of Dembe's ethnicity upon her experiences, opportunities and life chances, driving you to research the concept of intersectionality. You will need to engage with Dembe's partner and consider the limited resources available to both Dembe, as a transgender female victim/survivor and her partner, as a female perpetrator. You may also consider building Dembe's agency and choice through exploration of her friendships, using an ecomap tool, completing a welfare benefits check, and advocating for Dembe to access community and specialist services and resources.

Support

In working with the messy, sometimes frightening and often distressing experiences of domestic abuse, a range of support is needed within human services to equip the individual practitioner for the demands of the role. This support includes, but is not limited to, individual support, organisational support, wider system support and different approaches.

It is important for social workers to access regular and effective supervision, which is informed by theory and rooted in critically reflective and relationship-based practice (O'Neill and Del Mar Fariña, 2018). The role of the supervisor is key in supporting the practitioner's professional development to deepen their understanding and better navigate the complexities of uncertainty and risk. Increasingly diverse approaches to supervision, such as peer consultation, clinical and group supervision, and different models of support (O'Donoghue et al, 2018), can provide social workers with opportunities to develop and expand their skills. Working alongside survivors and perpetrators of domestic abuse can involve a rollercoaster of emotional demands and as such, there is a need for supervision to be a safe space, one of trust and containment (Egan et al, 2017). This space enables the supervisor to support the supervisee to make sense of the situation, while the supervisee processes and manages their own feelings, and connects with individuals. Arao and Clemens (2013) build on this concept, emphasising the importance of a brave space where courage is needed to encourage genuine dialogue, whereby risks can be both discussed and taken. Brave spaces encourage assumptions and stereotypes to be challenged through a critical lens and are underpinned by diversity issues and inequality. Spaces such as these are necessary to encourage social workers and managers to shift their focus from compliance to processes and risk-management systems towards the social justice roots of the profession, encouraging a transformational social work approach (Thompson, 2017b).

Trauma-informed approaches can help shape the culture of social work practice and service-design in relation to practitioners working alongside domestic abuse. Embedding a multilayered, whole-system trauma-informed approach within an organisation can support practitioners to understand their responses to experiences of domestic abuse through a trauma lens, as well as support the workforce to address the demands and stress that can lead to burnout or vicarious trauma (McCann and Pearlman, 1990). Integrating and connecting practitioners' language, practice and knowledge of trauma throughout the organisational culture can support practitioners to become trauma-informed. Using relational and strengths-based approaches, social workers can begin to understand the nuances of the relationship between a victim/survivor's experiences of trauma, alongside relationship-based social work practice that encompasses kindness, trust, safety, choice and intersectionality (Murshid and Bowen, 2018). To support practitioners to be effective in this area, organisations need to invest in and support their staff to find balance in their practice and make meaning in their work. Organisations have a responsibility to engage their practitioners with valuable physical and psychological self-care approaches and need to address the wider elements of social workers' well-being and working conditions (Ravalier and Boichat, 2018), to encourage a workforce that is healthy, healing and trauma-informed.

However, trauma-informed approaches can be complex, messy, slow to develop and maintain within an organisation, and criticised for pathologising individuals and minimising the reality of the structural inequalities that exist. An integrated trauma-informed approach that takes account of both the individual and wider sociological issues may be helpful for social workers. See examples that follow for the individual practitioner to focus their efforts:

> » Encourage and build existing and new positive relationships between individuals and their wider support network and community.

» Implement a strengths-based partnership approach built on respectful partnerships not demonising, devising, blaming or shaming.

» Encourage and build existing and new positive relationships between individuals and their wider support network and community.

» Acknowledge and understand how to reduce the power dynamics between the social worker and the individual.

» Build consistent, trusting and empowering relationships.

» Understand the different attitudes towards domestic abuse (generational, culture, gendered).

» Trauma-informed principles of transparency, safety and intersectionality.

» Be flexible and creative in your approach and use empathic curiosity.

» Practise in a gender and culturally sensitive manner.

Case Example

Anca, a 19 year-old White Romanian refugee, has recently been diagnosed with personality disorder. Anca's childhood involved significant and long-standing physical, sexual and emotional abuse from a primary care-giver. Anca's early adolescence included physical abuse, control and exploitation perpetrated by an intimate partner. Anca has recently begun a new relationship where there are signs that Anca is being physically abused and may be pregnant. Reports outline that Anca is involved with using illicit drugs and misusing alcohol.

As a trauma-informed practitioner it is important to recognise the impact of enduring complex trauma and how this affects Anca's psycho-social development and communication of her needs. It is important to recognise how Anca is currently presenting and her emotional vulnerability, and how this is understood in the context of past trauma. Principles to underpin your practice with Anca will involve strengths and relationship-based models of practice. For example, building a trusting relationship with Anca, creating a sense of safety and control within Anca's life through collaboration and consistency. You may consider completing practical activities (housing, employment, education, benefits) while providing therapeutic support to address feelings of loss, shame and mistrust. This will take place alongside your reflections about the impact of 'self' within the relationship, with explorations of power differentials and identity. These areas will be explored through supervision, which can provide a brave space for authentic and potentially difficult conversations to be shared while also allowing a safe space to be created, involving organisational containment of your professional vulnerability.

Conclusion

The IDEAS model has demonstrated several key components of relationship-based practice that are crucial in working within the field of domestic abuse: kindness, hope, trust, emotions, safety, empathy and respect. The IDEAS model provides a clear, systematic approach in working with the multi-faceted complexities of domestic abuse. Practitioners can navigate their way through the different sections of the model, using the support of a framework to make sense of the intricacies of domestic abuse in an informed, holistic manner.

References

Adams, A E, Sullivan, C M, Bybee, D and Greeson, M (2008) Development of the Scale of Economic Abuse. *Violence Against Women*, 14: 563–88.

Almond, L, McManus, M, Brian, D and Merrington, D P (2017) Exploration of the Risk Factors Contained within the UK's Existing Domestic Abuse Risk Assessment Tool (DASH): Do These Risk Factors Have Individual Predictive Validity Regarding Recidivism? *Journal of Aggression, Conflict and Peace Research*, 9(1): 58–68.

Androff, D (2015) *Practicing Rights: Human Rights-based Approaches to Social Work Practice*. New York: Routledge.

Arao, B and Clemens, K (2013) From Safe Spaces to Brave Spaces: A New Way to Frame Dialogue around Diversity and Social Justice. In Landreman, L (ed) *The Art of Effective Facilitation: Reflections from Social Justice Educators* (pp 135–50). Sterling, VA: Stylus Publishing.

Beagan, B L (2018) A Critique of Cultural Competence: Assumptions, Limitations, and Alternatives. In Frisby, C and O'Donohue, W (eds) *Cultural Competence in Applied Psychology* (pp 123–38). Cham: Springer.

Danso, R (2018) Cultural Competence and Cultural Humility: A Critical Reflection on Key Cultural Diversity Concepts. *Journal of Social Work*, 18(4): 410–30.

Davies, P (2018) Tackling Domestic Abuse Locally: Paradigms, Ideologies and the Political Tensions of Multi-agency Working. *Journal of Gender-Based Violence*, 2(3): 429–46.

Davies, P A and Biddle, P (2018) Implementing a Perpetrator-focused Partnership Approach to Tackling Domestic Abuse: The Opportunities and Challenges of Criminal Justice Localism. *Criminology & Criminal Justice*, 18(4): 468–87.

Devaney, J and Lazenbatt, A (2016) *Domestic Violence Perpetrators: Evidence-Informed Responses*. London: Routledge.

Domestic Abuse, Stalking and Harassment and Honour Based Violence (2009) *Risk Identification and Assessment and Management Model*. [online] Available at: www.dashriskchecklist.co.uk/wp-content/uploads/2016/09/DASH-2009.pdf (accessed 25 April 2019).

Dominelli, L (1993) *Social Work: Mirror of Society or its Conscience?* Sheffield: University of Sheffield, Department of Sociological Studies.

Dominelli, L (2018) *Anti-racist Social Work* (4th edn). London: Palgrave.

Douglas, H (2018) Legal Systems Abuse and Coercive Control. *Criminology & Criminal Justice*, 18(1): 84–99.

Doyle, J L and McWilliams, M (2018) *Intimate Partner Violence in Conflict and Post-Conflict Societies: Insights and Lessons from Northern Ireland*. Edinburgh: Political Settlements Research Programme (PSRP).

Egan, R, Maidment, J and Connolly, M (2017) Trust, Power and Safety in the Social Work Supervisory Relationship: Results from Australian Research. *Journal of Social Work Practice*, 31(3): 307–21.

Fenton, R A, Mott, H L and Rumney, P N S (2014) *The Intervention Initiative Theoretical Rationale*. [online] Available at: www2.uwe.ac.uk/faculties/BBS/BUS/law/Law%20docs/bystander/toolkit/Theoretical-Rationale/Theoretical-rationale.pdf (accessed 25 April 2019).

Fenton, R A, Mott, H L, McCartan, K and Rumney, P (2016) *A Review of Evidence for Bystander Intervention to Prevent Sexual and Domestic Violence in Universities*, technical report. London: Public Health England.

Ferguson, I and Lavalette, M (2013) Crisis, Austerity and the Future(s) of Social Work in the UK. *Critical and Radical Social Work*, 1(1): 95–110.

French, J R P and Raven, B ([1959] 2001) The Bases of Social Power, reprinted in Asherman, I G and Asherman, S V (eds) *The Negotiation Sourcebook* (2nd edn) (pp 61–73). Amherst, MA: HRD Press.

Grace, J (2015) Better Information Sharing, or 'share or be damned'? *The Journal of Adult Protection*, 17(5): 308.

Healy, L M (2008) Exploring the History of Social Work as a Human Rights Profession. *International Social Work*, 51(6): 735–48.

Her Majesty's Inspectorate of Constabulary (2015) *Increasingly Everyone's Business: A Progress Report on the Police Response to Domestic Abuse*. London: Crown Copyright.

Her Majesty's Inspectorate of Probation (2018) *Domestic Abuse: The Work Undertaken by Community Rehabilitation Companies (CRCs)*. Manchester: Crown Copyright.

Hessle, S (2014) *Human Rights and Social Equality: Challenges for Social Work*. Farnham: Routledge.

Hinson, S and Healey, R (2003) *Building Political Power. Prepared for the State Strategies Fund Convening*. Grassroots Policy Project.

HM Government (2016) *Ending Violence against Women and Girls Strategy 2016–2020*. Violence against Women and Girls Strategy 2016–2020. London: Crown Copyright.

Home Office (2016) *Domestic Violence Disclosure Scheme (DVDS) Guidance*. [online] Available at: https://assets.publishing.service.gov.uk/government/uploads/system/uploads/attachment_data/file/575361/DVDS_guidance_FINAL_v3.pdf (accessed 21 January 2019).

Home Office, Department for Digital, Culture, Media & Sport, Hancock, M and Javid, S (2018) *New Laws to Make Social Media Safer*. [online] Available at: www.gov.uk/government/news/new-laws-to-make-social-media-safer (accessed 25 April 2019).

Home Office (2019) *The Economic and Social Costs of Domestic Abuse*. [online] Available at: www.gov.uk/government/publications/the-economic-and-social-costs-of-domestic-abuse (accessed 21 January 2019).

Home Office (2019b) *Transforming the Response to Domestic Abuse: Consultation Response and Draft Bill*. [online] Available at: www.gov.uk/government/publications/domestic-abuse-consultation-response-and-draft-bill (accessed 21 January 2019).

Kelly, L and Westmarland, N (2016) Naming and Defining 'domestic violence': Lessons from Research with Violent Men. *Feminist Review*, 112(1): 113–27.

Laing, L, Humphreys, C and Kavanagh, K (2013) *Social Work and Domestic Violence: Developing Critical and Reflective Practice*. London: Sage Publications Ltd.

Latané, B and Darley, J M (1970) *The Unresponsive Bystander: Why Doesn't He Help?* New York: Appleton-Century Crofts.

Lazenbatt, A, Devaney, J and Gildea, A (2013) Older Women Living and Coping with Domestic Violence. *Community Practitioner*, 86: 28–35.

LeCouteur, A and Oxlad, M (2010) Managing Accountability for Domestic Violence: Identities, Membership Categories and Morality in Perpetrators' Talk. *Feminism and Psychology*, 21(1): 5–28.

Lilley-Walker, S, Hester, M and Turner, W (2018) Evaluation of European Domestic Violence Perpetrator Programmes: Toward a Model for Designing and Reporting Evaluations Related to Perpetrator Treatment Interventions. *International Journal of Offender Therapy and Comparative Criminology*, 62(4): 868–84.

Lukes, S (2005) *Power: A Radical View* (2nd edn). New York: Palgrave Macmillan.

McCann, I L and Pearlman, L A (1990) Vicarious Traumatization: A Framework for Understanding the Psychological Effects of Working with Victims. *Journal of Traumatic Stress*, 3(1): 131–49.

McLaughlin, H, Robbins, R, Bellamy, C, Banks, C and Thackray, D (2018) Adult Social Work and High-risk Domestic Violence Cases. *Journal of Social Work*, 18(3): 288–306.

Ministry of Housing, Communities & Local Government (2018) *Improving Access to Social Housing for Victims of Domestic Abuse*. [online] Available at: www.gov.uk/government/publications/improving-access-to-social-housing-for-victims-of-domestic-abuse (accessed 21 January 2019).

Ministry of Justice (2015) *Code of Practice for Victims of Crime*. [online] Available at: https://assets.publishing.ser-vice.gov.uk/government/uploads/system/uploads/attachment_data/file/476900/code-of-practice-for-victims-of-crime.PDF (accessed 21 January 2019).

Ministry of Justice, National Offender Management Service and Her Majesty's Prison Service (2012) *MAPPA Guidance 2012, Updated 2017*. [online] Available at: www.justice.gov.uk/peoplepopulationandcommunity/crimeandjustice/compendium/focusonviolentcrimeandsexualoffences/yearendingmarch2016 (accessed 21 June 2019).

Murshid, N S and Bowen, E A (2018) A Trauma-informed Analysis of the Violence against Women Act's Provisions for Undocumented Immigrant Women. *Violence Against Women*, 24(13): 1540–56.

O'Donoghue, K, Wong Yuh Ju, P and Tsui, M (2018) Constructing an Evidence-informed Social Work Supervision Model. *European Journal of Social Work*, 21(3): 348–58.

Office for National Statistics (ONS) (2016) *Focus on Violent Crime and Sexual Offences: Year Ending March 2015*. Crime Survey for England and Wales and crimes recorded by police. [online] Available at: w ww.ons.gov.uk/peoplepopulationandcommunity/crimeandjustice/compendium/focusonviolentcrimeandsexualoffences/yearendingmarch2016 (accessed 21 June 2019).

Office for National Statistics (ONS) (2018) *Domestic Abuse: Findings from the Crime Survey for England and Wales: Year Ending March 2017*. Crime Survey for England and Wales. [online] Available at: www.ons.gov.uk/releases/domesticabusefindingsfromthecrimesurveyforenglandandwalesyearendingmarch2017 (accessed 21 June 2019).

O'Neill, P and Del Mar Fariña, M (2018) Constructing Critical Conversations in Social Work Supervision: Creating Change. *Clinical Social Work Journal*, 46(4): 298–309.

Peckover, S (2014) Domestic Abuse, Safeguarding Children and Public Health: Towards an Analysis of Discursive Forms and Surveillant Techniques in Contemporary UK Policy and Practice. *British Journal of Social Work*, 44(7): 1770–87.

Powell, A (2011) Review of Bystander Approaches in Support of Preventing Violence Against Women. Victoria, New South Wales: Victoria Health Promotion Foundation. Publication P-052-V B. [online] Available at: www.ncdsv.org/images/VicHealth_ReviewBystanderApproachesSupportPreventingVAW_5-2011.pdf (accessed 16 December 2018).

Public Health England (2014) *Evidence into Practice: Tackling Domestic Violence in Universities and the Workplace*. [online] Available at: www.gov.uk/government/news/evidence-into-practice-tackling-domestic-violence-in-universities-and-the-workplace (accessed 25 April 2019).

Ravalier, J M and Boichat, C (2018) *UK Social Workers: Working Conditions and Wellbeing*. Bath Spa University. [online] Available at: www.basw.co.uk/system/files/resources/Working%20Conditions%20%20Stress%20%282018%29%20pdf.pdf (accessed 1 February 2019).

Robbins, R and Cook, K (2018) 'Don't Even Get Us Started on Social Workers': Domestic Violence, Social Work and Trust—An Anecdote from Research. *The British Journal of Social Work*, 48(6): 1664–81.

Robbins, R, Banks, C, McLaughlin, H, Bellamy, C and Thackray, D (2016) Is Domestic Abuse an Adult Social Work Issue? *Social Work Education*, 35(2): 131–43.

SafeLives (2018) *Free to be Safe: LGBT+ People Experiencing Domestic Abuse*. [online] Available at: http://safelives.org.uk/sites/default/files/resources/Free%20to%20be%20safe%20web.pdf (accessed 25 April 2019).

Smith, C (2004) Trust and Confidence: Making the Moral Case for Social Work. *Social Work & Social Sciences Review*, 11(3): 5–15.

Stark, E (2007) *Coercive Control – Men's Entrapment of Women*. Everyday Life. Oxford: Oxford University Press.

Steel, N, Blakeborough, L and Nicholas, S (2011) *Research Report 55 – Supporting High-risk Victims of Domestic Violence: A Review of Multi-agency Risk Assessment Conferences (MARACs)*. London: Home Office.

Steen, J A (2018) Reconceptualizing Social Work Behaviors from a Human Rights Perspective. *Journal of Social Work Education*, 54(2): 212–26.

Thompson, N (2017a) *Theorizing Practice* (2nd edn). London: Palgrave Macmillan.

Thompson, N (2017b) *Social Problems and Social Justice*. London: Palgrave.

Tonkiss, F and Passey, A (1999) Trust, Confidence and Voluntary Organisations: Between Values and Institutions. *Sociology*, 33(2): 257–74.

United Nations (Centre for Human Rights) (1994) *Human Rights and Social Work*. Geneva: UN in collaboration with IFSW and IASSW.

Walby, S (2009) *The Cost of Domestic Violence: Up-date 2009*. Lancaster: Lancaster University.

Watson, D (2017) *Domestic Abuse and Child Protection: Women's Experience of Social Work Intervention*. Glasgow: Iriss.

Wronka, J (2008) *Human Rights and Social Justice: Social Action and Service for the Helping and Health Professions*. Thousand Oaks, CA: Sage.

Yuill, C and Gibson, A (2011) *Sociology for Social Work: An Introduction*. London: Sage.

Chapter 11 | Advocacy not tolerance: relational work with people who identify as LGBTQIA

Heidi Dix with Andy Fell

Introduction

For practitioners working in health and social care settings, having an understanding and appreciation of the life experiences of people who identify as lesbian, gay, bisexual, trans*, queer or questioning, intersex and asexual (LGBTQIA) is important to ensure that the needs of this group are adequately met. However, despite there being in recent years significant developments in culture and legislation, a person's sexuality and gender identity are rarely considered in the creation of social policy initiatives and therefore in the development and provision of health and social care services (Thompson, 2016). A report published by the National Institute of Economic Research (Hudson-Sharp, 2018) suggests that there is also a lack of transgender awareness provided in child and family social work education programmes, and although this has yet to be researched, we suspect that this finding would be the same for a curriculum focused on adults. This means that LGBTQIA people often feel ignored or unable to discuss this aspect of their identity when requiring the services outlined in previous chapters. This can also be an issue for LGBTQIA people who are utilising self-directed support through a Direct Payment or Personal Budget.

Although LGBTQIA people are not a homogenous group and indeed through intersectionality may also identify with the lived experiences of the different groups discussed in the pre-ceding chapters within this book, they are however, likely to have shared experiences of discrimination. This chapter will utilise the IDEAS framework to assist practitioners and personal assistants to consider and reflect on the underlying privileges and subtleties of heterosexism and heteronormativity. Fish (2012, p 166) defines these as follows:

Heterosexism is a system of beliefs which assume that everyone is heterosexual. It assumes the superiority of heterosexuality; for example, it assumes that families comprising an opposite-sex couple are inherently superior to same-sex family relationships and heteronormativity refers to a social and cultural worldview that constructs heterosexuality as the norm.

Definitions

Language is continually changing and adapting to meet the needs of individuals and communities. The LGBTQIA acronym is generally used to cover individuals who are not heterosexual and/or who are not cisgender (a definition of the latter follows).

For the purpose of this chapter, we are using the Stonewall (2018) definitions of the terms described by LGBTQIA people who self-identify as:

Cisgender – a person who was assigned the same gender at birth. Non-trans is used by some people.

Lesbian – a woman who has an emotional, romantic and/or sexual orientation/attraction towards women. Some women define themselves as gay rather than lesbian.

Gay – a man who has an emotional, romantic and/or sexual orientation/attraction towards men; it is also used as a generic term for lesbian and gay sexuality.

Bisexual – an emotional and/or sexual orientation/attraction towards more than one gender.

Trans – is used as an umbrella term to describe people whose gender is not the same as, or does not sit comfortably with, the sex they were assigned at birth. Trans people may describe themselves using one or more of a wide variety of terms, including (but not limited to) transgender, transsexual, gender-queer (GQ), gender-fluid, non-binary, gender-variant, agender, nongender, trans man, trans woman, trans masculine, trans feminine.

In relation to the trans umbrella term used above, Richards et al (2016) suggest that some people have a gender which is neither male nor female and so therefore may identify as both male and female at one time, as different genders at different times, as no gender at all, or dispute the very idea of only two genders. The umbrella terms for such genders are 'genderqueer' or 'non-binary' genders. Such gender identities exist outside of the binary of female and male identities and are increasingly being recognised in legal, medical and psychological systems and diagnostic classifications in line with the emerging presence and advocacy of these groups of people.

For many older lesbian and gay people, the use of the term 'queer' may feel uncomfortable, as in the past this was commonly used as a derogatory label as can be seen through the use of terms such as 'queer-bashing'. Tierney (1997) identifies however, that in recent times the word has been reclaimed by LGBTQIA people as a positive identification, particularly where they do not feel that the other available labels for sexual identity and/or gender identity describe them correctly. There is also a subsequent reduction in the impact of the words and therefore the power of oppression has been reclaimed.

Intersex – is a term used to describe a person who may have the biological attributes of both sexes or whose biological attributes do not fit with societal assumptions about what constitutes male or female. Intersex people may identify as male, female or non-binary.

Asexual – someone who does not experience sexual attraction.

It must be acknowledged that, while LGBTQIA embraces both sexual identifies and gender identities and that individuals within these groups have traditionally come together through a joint understanding and experience of oppression, gender and sexuality are two distinct areas of discourse. Asking people how they self-identify as part of the assessment process demonstrates awareness and can be a helpful step to develop trust and the promotion of a relationship-based approach across difference. For a more comprehensive list of definitions, it is suggested that the reader visits Stonewall's website.

Influence

As discussed throughout this text, a key aspect of this part of the framework is the effective use of the legitimate authority which is inherent within the social work role. Within the context of this chapter, we suggest that the power that professionals hold can be utilised to ensure that the voice of LGBTQIA people does not continue to be hidden in social work services (Fish, 2012). To do this effectively, an awareness of the historic and continued discrimination and oppression experienced by LGBTQIA people is required and utilising Allport's (1954) 'Scale of Prejudice' is helpful to reflect on the challenges faced by LGBTQIA people. Having this insight can also help a practitioner to 'tune-in' (Taylor and Devine, 1993) to some of the life experiences of this group of people and provide support and care that is grounded in empathic understanding, one of the principles of person-centred practice outlined in Chapter 1.

Allport suggests that are several ways that prejudice manifests itself within a society, and this forms a number of levels that increase in seriousness. Allport's scale is often presented in the form of a pyramid (see Figure 11.1).

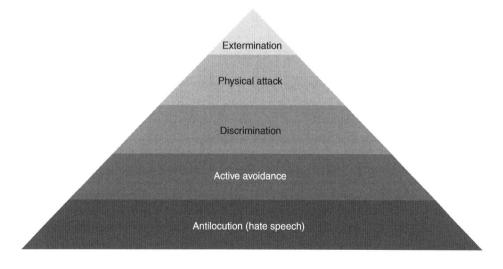

Figure 11.1 Allport's (1954) 'Scale of Prejudice'

Antilocution is the bottom layer and occurs when negative images are portrayed. Prejudice at this level typically manifests itself in verbal abuse, stereotyping, gossiping, negative jokes and myths. An example of this could be where carers are warned to be watchful of somebody due to their sexuality or use discriminatory language when describing them.

The next level, **Active avoidance**, is where individuals are ignored and excluded, causing them to become invisible. For example, older LGBTQIA people living in a residential care home may feel that they need to hide their sexuality and/or gender identity for fear they may be treated less favourably or experience disapproval from both employees and other residents (Willis et al, 2017). Indeed, being explicit about their identity may lead them to experience exclusion from in-house community and social events. People who have disabilities and also identify as LGBTQIA can experience social isolation if access to support is limited, or indeed if they are living in an area where there are not any accessible LGBTQIA venues or activities (Abbott, 2017). A project developed by Norfolk and Suffolk NHS Foundation Trust (NSFT) for people with learning difficulties to explore sexuality issues, found a resident of a care home who was questioning her sexuality did not feel able to discuss this with anyone in her home for fear of their reaction (Devine, 2018).

Moving up the pyramid, the next level is **Discrimination**, where opportunities are restricted, or legislation is in place which results in unequal access to generic and specialist services such as employment, education, housing and healthcare, all of which this group of people have experienced historically. Fish (2007) suggests that during the twentieth century a cultural shift has taken place whereby the formation and refinement of legislation provides LGBTQIA people with greater protection within society. This group now have the opportunity to exercise new rights and responsibilities previously unknown by their predecessors. This includes the right to a Civil Partnership under the Civil Partnership Act 2004, the right to marry following the introduction of the Marriage (Same Sex Couples) Act 2013, and the right to adopt either as a couple or as an individual following the Adoption and Children Act 2002, which came into force in 2005. The introduction of the Equality Act 2010 prohibits discrimination on the grounds of an individual's sexual orientation in the provision of goods and services, which includes health and social care.

As the scale increases, the penultimate level is **Physical attack**, which can include physical assaults, rape, graffiti, physical bullying and criminal damage. Within our society, this can be seen in the raise of hate crime against LGB people in Britain, which has increased by 78 per cent since 2013. In 2017, two in five trans people had experienced a hate crime in the last 12 months because of how they identify (Stonewall, 2017).

The final level is **Extermination**, which includes genocide, murder and suicide. Relating this to people who identify as LGBTQIA, the RaRE report (2015) found that young LGB and trans people under 26 are more likely to attempt suicide and to self-harm than their heterosexual and cisgender peers and 34 per cent of young LGB people made at least one suicide attempt in their lives, compared with 18 per cent of their heterosexual peers. Forty-eight per cent of trans young people reported having made at least one suicide attempt in their lives compared to 26 per cent of their cisgender peers.

Allport's scale demonstrates the need for practitioners and personal assistants to have an awareness of the differing levels and escalation of prejudice that LGBTQIA individuals may have or be currently experiencing. Having this knowledge enables the legitimate authority inherent with the professional role to be utilised to challenge views of heterosexism, heteronormality and homophobia on both a micro and macro level. This may be through questioning and challenging discriminatory language or attitudes that are heard within the workplace and modelling and sharing best practice with colleagues, through to actively championing the rights of LGBTQIA people within society more widely.

Case Example

William is an 84 year-old White British gay man. He recently moved into residential care following a fall in his home where he broke his hip. During the social work assessment, it was clear that William and his partner had been caring and supporting each other and since his partner died, William has been struggling to cope living on his own. Although he was initially reluctant to move into residential care, William has settled in well and is a popular resident. He has developed a bond with Maureen, an 82 year-old White British heterosexual woman who has lived in the home for 18 months, and they often spend time together. On one particularly warm day they were sitting in a secluded part of the garden when Pauline, a White British care worker, walked past and said 'would you two lovebirds like a cup of tea?' William and Maureen both felt uncomfortable about Pauline's comments, particularly as the day before Pauline had assumed that the picture of his partner that William has in his room is his brother (William had told Maureen about this), although neither of them felt able to explain their friendship to Pauline.

The following day William's social worker Andy (White British) chaired a placement review at the home and noticed that William was not his usual cheery self. William said that although he enjoys living in the home, the assumptions that Pauline has made about his sexuality makes him feel that he is not able to be his authentic self. Andy asked William if he wanted to speak with the manager about this and William said he did as long as Andy was present. William, supported by Andy, spoke to the manager and Pauline about how his comments make him feel he is not accepted within the home and that he feels he needed to 'hide' the 40+ years that he had shared with his partner. Pauline listened to William and told him that she hadn't realised that her light-hearted comment made William feel so uncomfortable and apologised. Andy asked the manager about staff training in relation to sexuality and gender and the manager agreed that this was needed and would be included in the training plan for the year.

Although on the surface this appears to be a minor incident, the impact that it had on William was significant. However, through Andy noticing at the review meeting that William did not seem himself and by demonstrating an empathic understanding and an ability to 'tune-in' (Taylor and Devine, 1993) to how William was feeling, Andy was able to use his legitimate authority to support William to meet with the care worker and her manager to challenge the assumptions that had been made about William's sexuality in a way that felt safe for him.

Delivery

This aspect of the framework refers to the professional tools and systems that relate to a particular area of practice and the ability of practitioners to apply these skilfully. The preceding chapters have outlined some of the challenges of utilising a relationship-based approach within organisational constraints and statutory requirements and have made suggestions as to how these difficulties can be overcome. As an individual's sexual orientation and gender identity are just aspects of who people are and *'LGBT people have many other facets to their identity such as disability, faith and age'* (SCIE, 2011), the best practice guidance outlined in the preceding chapters will apply to this group. For the purposes of this chapter, the Delivery aspect of the framework will be discussed through a brief exploration of the key principles of the Equality Act 2010.

While many older LGBTQIA people will have lived through times when there was hate and blatant discrimination aimed at LGBTQIA people, the 2010 Equality Act has made sexual orientation and gender reassignment protected characteristics. This means that everyone, whether they are lesbian, gay, bisexual, trans or heterosexual, are now protected from discrimination because of their sexual orientation and/or gender identity. This includes being free from discrimination while at work and having equal access to goods and services, education, associations and voluntary groups. This is particularly relevant to public service providers – any service for people, whether funded by public money or not, provided free or for a charge, cannot refuse a person a service because they are LGBTQIA as this would be unlawful. This means that care providers cannot refuse to support or offer residential places to LGBTQIA people, and LGBTQIA people with learning difficulties cannot be denied sexual health support.

The Equality Act also provides protection to transsexual people, where the individual's gender identity differs from the gender assigned at birth; within the Act this is known as 'gender reassignment'. There is no requirement for an individual to have undergone any specific treatment or surgery to change from their birth-assigned gender to their preferred gender in order to be protected from gender reassignment discrimination. The Act takes the view that it is an individual's personal process to changing their physiological or other gendered attributes, rather than a medical one. This means that an individual can be at any stage in the transition process, from proposing to reassign their gender or undertaking a process to reassign their gender, through to having completed it fully. While there is no explicit protection from discrimination for Intersex individuals, under the Act individuals cannot be discriminated against because of their gender or perceived gender.

However, discrimination can often be much more subtle than direct discrimination. LGBTQIA people often do not have their needs met as they are not consulted by commissioners of services, either through the process of avoidance described by Allport (1954) outlined earlier or they may feel the need to 'hide' their sexuality or gender identity through fear of rejection and stigmatisation and therefore they are 'invisible'.

When outlining good practice in Personalisation, SCIE (2011, p 1) suggests that as culture progresses, and shifts take place, *'LGBT people are increasingly likely to become more confident and visible as people who use services and carers, so care and support services need to be ready to welcome them. LGBT people need to be able to choose services that are supportive, safe and culturally appropriate for them in both community and residential settings.'*

However, although legislation is important as it protects people and helps to ensure equality at a structural level within society, this alone does not change people's attitudes. Through professional and regulatory bodies, practitioners are likely to be required to promote a fairer and more equal society. For social workers and social work students this is through various domains contained within the Professional Capabilities Framework (BASW, 2018). In 2016, Sheffield University removed a student from their Masters social work programme after he posted on a publicly accessible Facebook page messages of support for an American county clerk who had spoken out against gay rights. In his post the student also referred to a verse in the Bible that called homosexuality an 'abomination' (*The Independent*, 2017). The university believed that the student's behaviour was contrary to the requirements of social workers to keep high standards of personal conduct and ensure their behaviour does not damage public confidence in the profession. The student lost a judicial review against the university's decision (Community Care, 2017).

Combining knowledge of equalities legislation with the influence that practitioners have within their role can help to challenge discrimination, oppressive, and at times unlawful, practice. Thus, in order to undertake holistic assessments and offer effective interventions, practitioners need to combine the specialist knowledge of the Delivery aspect of the IDEAS framework connected to a specialist area of practice, eg working with people who misuse substances, with an awareness of their responsibilities contained within equalities legislation.

Expertise

There is a lack of research into the needs of LGBTQIA to draw upon and inform best practice (Hudson-Sharp and Metcalf, 2016). However, there are some areas where knowledge regarding the needs of LGBTQIA people is increasing. For example, The Alzheimer's Society produced a booklet about dementia for LGBT people (2017) and Abbott and Howarth's book *Secret Loves, Hidden Lives?* (2005) explores issues of sexuality for people with learning difficulties, both of which are helpful guides for practitioners. There is also increasing recognition that domestic abuse can happen to anyone. Research by Stonewall (2012) shows that one in four lesbian and biwomen have experienced domestic abuse in a relationship and almost half of all gay and bimen have experienced at least one incident of domestic abuse from a family member or partner since the age of 16. On Stonewall's website there is information regarding organisations which can support LGBTQIA victims of domestic abuse.

One area that is currently being researched is the use of Chemsex. This is a term used by gay men in areas of the UK which describes the use of psychoactive substances during sex. The term came to prevalence through the use of geo-sexual apps being used by gay men. Stewart (2017) states that Chemsex refers to the use of drugs taken as part of sexual contact and can include any combination of drugs used by men who have sex with men with, before, or during sexual activity. People who use drugs are increasingly at risk of the harm related to illicit substance misuse and associated negative health outcomes (Stewart, 2017). While it must not be assumed the whole population of gay men, bisexual men and men who have sex with men are involved in Chemsex, it is important for practitioners to be aware of developing trends and be alert to any significant risks associated with this practice. Having an awareness of these issues, together with effective communication skills and a supportive approach will enable people to be supported and reduce risk and harm.

The discourse around gender is linked to the field of Queer Theory, which is a critical theory that takes as its premise the idea that identities such as gender are not fixed and therefore do not determine who we are. Queer theory challenges and explores how heterosexuality is constructed as 'normal' and argues that sexuality and gender identity are more fluid and on a continuum. Judith Butler (1990), in *Gender Trouble*, suggests that gender is not a result of nature but is a social construct, and that female and male behavioural roles are not biological, but are constructed and reinforced though society's culture and media. Butler sees gender as a performance and argues that there are a number of embellished representations of femininity and masculinity which create 'gender trouble' through behaviour that disrupts or challenges the culturally accepted notions of that specific gender.

Understanding differing aspects of a person's sexual and gender identity can assist the appropriate and relevant provision of support and services. Through using a respectful questioning approach, it is possible to identify unique aspects of an individual's identity and subsequently enables practitioners to develop effective relationships. Considering the following five specific areas can enable a better understanding of the individual and help practitioners to build trust and undertake a strengths-based approach.

1. How does an individual identify in relation to their gender? Do they describe themselves using traditional binary roles, ie as female/woman/male/man, or do they identify as another gender altogether?

2. What is their gender expression? This may be feminine, masculine, or less rigid and more fluid.

3. How do they describe their sexuality? People experience attraction in many different ways. Commonly, people describe the attraction they may or may not be experiencing as 'sexual' and 'romantic'. Sexual attraction is the drive to engage in physically intimate behaviours and romantic attraction is the drive to engage in socially intimate behaviours (Ferguson, 2016). Individuals may experience both, only one, and some people experience neither

4. What pronouns do they use? For trans and non-binary individuals the correct use of pronouns is crucial, as it shows respect for the person and an understanding of trans lived life experiences. There are an infinite number of pronouns, and as suggested in the introduction to this chapter, language is constantly evolving and therefore new pronouns emerge over time. By a professional simply asking which pronoun a person prefers to use, this indicates a recognition of the diversity of genders and will indicate a level of awareness and respect. The most commonly used pronouns are the use of 'she' and 'her' for people who identify as female, 'he' and 'him' for people who identify as male and gender-neutral pronouns such as 'they', 'them', 'their', which are used for people who are more fluid in their gender identity.

It is again worth considering the underlying privileges and subtleties of discrimination and oppression in relation to LGBTQIA people, as this contributes to the understanding of the Queer Theory discourse. All LGBTQIA people grow up, work and live within a society that is heteronormative and this normalisation is so pervasive that most heterosexuals are not even aware that it exists – it has been likened to the 'air that we breathe'. Heteronormativity is the normalising process which supports heterosexuality as the means of reproduction without which human beings and society would not exist and strongly determines cultural norms and lifestyle arrangements. This in turn leads to 'Heterosexism', with the belief that being heterosexual is natural, normal, moral and better, and is the only option for intimate human relationships. This is so pervasive that it promotes the belief that everyone is heterosexual, which feeds the belief that if someone does not identify with this they are seen as abnormal, and immoral. Therefore, it is important for practitioners to pro-actively seek information and training in relation to LGBTQIA matters. Through being culturally competent in such issues, practitioners can effectively support and advocate if necessary on behalf of LGBTQIA individuals they are working with, their colleagues and potential individuals they come into contact with.

Case Example

Patrice is a 26 year-old mixed-heritage (Black African and White Polish) trans woman who has learning difficulties. She has a personal budget which supports her to live independently. Recently, a new support worker, Evelina, has joined the care agency that supports Patrice. Patrice wants to re-join a support group for trans people that she previously accessed and has informed Evelina that she needs her to accompany her to the next session. Evelina has not provided support to a trans person before, so did some web-based research before first meeting Patrice. She also spoke to her manager to see whether there were any training courses available to support her knowledge and understanding of providing support to a trans person. When she first met Patrice, she asked her which pronoun she uses and Patrice took this opportunity to talk to Evelina about her gender identity and some of the challenges that she has faced. Evelina listened to Patrice's experiences and thanked her for sharing her knowledge with her as it has helped her to gain a better understanding of the life experiences of trans people.

Alliance

'Coming out' is a vital part of developing a positive LGBTQIA identity and for many people a great deal of thought is given to how and when to do this. While young people are coming out at an earlier age (Shilo and Savaya, 2011), some older LGBTQIA people may not feel able to do this due to the legal status of homosexuality when they were younger. Stereotypes and prejudice against LGBTQIA people remain within some families, peers and communities, and these prejudices send a strong message to individuals thinking about coming out, particularly in relation to the fear of rejection.

As a practitioner, it is important to be aware of the courage it takes, and the trust invested in you if an LGBTQIA person comes out to you while working with them. It is likely that this decision would not have been taken lightly and the person would have spent a great deal of time thinking about whether they can trust you with the hope that it will be a supportive experience. Utilising strengths-based approaches and drawing on aspects of person-centred theory such as unconditional positive regard and offering an empathic understanding can help to develop a relationship based on trust and understanding. Hafford-Letchfield (2017) suggests that there are ways of offering support and understanding in subtle ways, such as asking same-sex couples who are not married 'Have you lived together a long time?', and 'You obviously mean a lot to each other'.

The process of coming out to family, friends, peers, work colleagues and organisations is a lifelong process and in 1979 Vivienne Cass produced what was originally known as the 'Cass Model for Homosexual Identity Development'. Cass made the assumption that an individual's identity develops through a process and that process includes change due to their contact and interactions with other individuals, organisations and the environment in which they live. The theory suggests there are usually six stages of identity development that occur in a specific sequence: **'Identity Confusion'**, **'Identity Comparison'**, **'Identity Tolerance'**, **'Identity Acceptance'**, **'Identity Pride'** and **'Identity Synthesis'** (Cass, 1979, pp 219–35).

In order to be able to develop relational work with individuals, it is helpful for social workers to understand these stages and the feelings and emotions connected to each juncture. It is also important to understand what support and action can be taken to support and empower individuals to develop a positive sense of their own LGBTQIA identity. While Cass identified this theory as being related to homosexual development, it is also relevant for individuals who identify as trans and their transition journey.

Identity Confusion stage – is where an individual first becomes aware that their thoughts, feelings and behaviour are in conflict with their assumed heterosexual identity. This leads to the creation of internal confusion and turmoil and in response, individuals may experience denial of their feelings at this stage. Alternatively, they may be beginning to explore their feelings. Here practitioners can best support this exploration by offering kindness and acceptance, being sensitive about the use of labels and terminology to describe identity and sexuality and providing basic value-free, non-discriminatory information.

The next stage in the sequence is **Identity Comparison** where the individual is beginning to consider they may identify as LGBTQIA. As the process of reflection begins, the difference between their self and others begins to magnify, and people can begin to feel isolated and aware that their sexual identity may conflict with family and friends' beliefs. At this stage, making contact with other LGBTQIA people formally or informally may be considered. Building on the support offered at the previous stage, practitioners can best support individuals at this stage by again offering acceptance, unconditional positive regard and empathic understanding. On a practical level, offering information about specific support groups within the community or online can reduce isolation, and counter myths with factual information. Issues of risk and of safety also need to be discussed at this time when working with people who may be vulnerable to exploitation to prepare people to make contact with other LGBTQIA individuals.

The third stage of Cass's Identity Model, **Identity Tolerance**, suggests that people move into a more active state where their confusion is lessened, which allows them to acknowledge their individual emotional, social and sexual needs. Here they may search out other LGBTQIA people to further reduce their sense of isolation and as their perception of themselves grows, they may 'come out' to other LGBTQIA people. At this stage the individual may be more open to engage in conversations about their sexual identity and/or gender identity, and practitioners can support this by using strengths-based approaches such as solution-focused brief therapy to support the development of self-esteem and self-advocacy.

Next comes **Identity Acceptance** which has two main aspects: acceptance by the individual of their LGBTQ identity in a positive way rather than just tolerating it and the individual may share their sexual and/or gender identity more widely. A network of family, close friends and other LGBTQIA people may have been established and many people remain at this point, sharing their identity with people within their support network. At this stage practitioners need to respect the right and need of the individual to be part of the LGBTQIA community, to assist in the exploration for new friends and partners and explore with them the interpersonal skills required to enter into new spaces and to meet new people. Working in partnership to discuss and plan who may be safe and who may be unsafe to come out to at this stage in their lives can also be helpful.

The penultimate stage is **Identity Pride** where individuals have a strong affiliation with LGBTQIA pride and may have a strong focus on LGBTQIA issues, activities and campaigning. This emerges from the conflict between their new open identity and society's assumption to be heterosexual or stay hidden and may show itself in anger towards the heterosexual community and the testing of different environments they begin to access in relation to their sexual and/or gender identity. While practitioners at this stage need to continue to be supportive, there may also be the need to help the individual work through the feelings they have to move into acceptance. As the socialisation process develops, discussions around safety and risk are increasingly important as is the need to inform individuals around issues of hate crime and subsequent reporting.

The final stage in Cass's theory is **Identity Synthesis** where people are likely to socialise with both LGBTQIA friends and accepting heterosexuals and there will be some congruence between a person's private and public identity. An individual may still not have come out to everyone and where full integration may not be possible if their family, friends or community are not accepting, they may have to be 'straight acting'. Even though LGBTQIA individuals may appear confident in their LGBTQIA identity, there is still a role for practitioners at this stage. 'Coming Out' is a lifelong process: many people experience homophobia, biphobia and transphobia at many different levels, and offers of support can be made in response to experiences shared with workers. Practitioners are able to strengthen the relationship by offering empathy and affirming with the individual that their journey to this stage has been a long one and has required courage, strength and determination to overcome the challenges presented to them by society.

Cass's model has been criticised for a number of reasons, including the absence of considering the social and cultural context that people live within and the idea that people have to go through a linear process in order to develop and form their identify (Kaufman and Johnson, 2004). Nevertheless, this is a helpful model for practitioners to think about in the development of their relationships with LGBTQIA people.

Support

Organisations must ensure that their employees and volunteers, at all levels, have access to high-quality professional development on an ongoing basis that equips them to be knowledgeable about contemporary legislation and trends in relation to LGBTQIA people. A 2008 survey found that 45 per cent of LGBT respondents had experienced discrimination when using social care services (CSCI, 2008) and Ross and Carr (2010) highlight the importance of education and training for practitioners so that they are themselves empowered to challenge discriminatory practice and oppressive behaviour by other colleagues and people who use services. A commitment to critically reflective supervision where values, assumptions and stereotypes can be explored in a safe way can help to develop inclusive practice. Thompson (2018, p 229) suggests that professional practice is *'premised on the notion of reflective practice, in so far as it is expected that staff should avoid unthinking, uncritical routines'*. He goes on to suggest that reflective, accountable practice can promote equality and can be used to:

- » challenge routinised, uncritical forms of practice and policies, procedures or managerial/supervisory practices that encourage them;

- » promote an ethos in which equality issues are openly and explicitly on the agenda;

- » give a clear message to anybody in the organisation who would wish to condone inequality and discrimination that they are likely to face conflict and resistance.

(Thompson, 2018, p 229)

There also needs to be a formal mechanism for organisations to consider if there is a culture of heteronormativity in the provision of services, ie are there in-built assumptions and practices that are discriminatory and oppressive? An initial step is to ensure that the workplace or setting is LGBTQIA inclusive; first impressions count and evident cues that the individual worker and organisation is LGBTQIA supportive will reassure and enable the process of relationship development to be easier. An organisational commitment to support and advocate for LGBTQIA people (including employees and users of services) enables the creation of settings, policies and practice that develop and add to culturally competent knowledge and understanding.

From a business perspective, an LGBTQ-supportive organisation can help to assist the constancy and productiveness of employees (Barclays, 2015), both important in this time of austerity, when budgets are being significantly reduced. Guasp and Balfour (2008) found that where there was a perception that employees perceived their workplace climate to be LGBTQIA supportive, this helped to engender a sense of loyalty to their employers. Guasp and Balfour (2008) also suggest a range of initiatives that demonstrate an organisation's commitment to a safe, supportive workplace environment. These include the formulation of an equality and diversity strategy, with the implementation team reporting directly to senior managers and leaders, establishing an Employee Network Group which provides support and career development for LGBTQIA people, an overt public statement about the inclusion and importance of LGBTQIA people working within the organisation, alongside the monitoring of staff based on sexual orientation and/or gender identity. These ideas link with Kittay's notion of 'nested dependencies' (1999) outlined in Chapter 6, which suggests that organisations need to care in specific and practical ways to enable their employees to carry out their 'caring' role with people and provide practical ways for this to occur.

Conclusion

Many LGBTQIA people will have personal experience of being oppressed as a direct result of their sexual identity and/or gender identity. Although there has been legislative change over recent years, many will have experienced overt discrimination and hate crime. However, the majority of LGBTQIA people will have felt more subtle, unintentional, institutionalised oppression. Rapport and trust building and the development of genuine and honest relationships that are grounded in principles of person-centred practice will enhance the support that practitioners are able to give LGBTQIA people. Taking an informed, strengths-based approach to both assessment and intervention, particularly regarding establishing identity expression, can help LGBTQIA individuals to feel there have been no assumptions made about them because of the way they may look or act. SCIE's guide to personalisation (2011) says that LGBTQIA people need to have accessible, sensitive mainstream services as well as the opportunity to receive support from specialist services, and the challenge for social workers and the organisations in which they work is to consider how they are best able to offer services and interventions that are inclusive to all.

References

Abbott, D (2017) *LGBTQI+* Disabled People and Self-directed Social Care Support*. Bristol: The National Institute for Health Research (NIHR). The School for Social Care Research.

Abbott, D W F and Howarth, J (2005) *Secret Loves, Hidden Lives? Exploring Issues for People with Learning Difficulties Who Are Gay, Lesbian or Bisexual*. Bristol: Policy Press.

Adoption and Children Act (2002) [online] Available at: www.legislation.gov.uk/ukpga/2002/38/contents (accessed 4 January 2019).

Allport, G W (1954) *The Nature of Prejudice*. Reading, MA: Addison-Wesley.

Bachmann, C L and Gooch, B (2017) *LGBT in Britain Hate Crime and Discrimination*. Stonewall/You Gov. [online] Available at: www.stonewall.org.uk/sites/default/files/lgbt_in_britain_hate_crime.pdf (accessed 4 January 2019).

Barclays (2015) *Diversity and Inclusion in the Workplace*. [online] Available at: www.barclayscorporate.com/content/dam/corppublic/corporate/Documents/insight/diversity-and-inclusion-in-the-workplace.pdf (accessed 4 January 2019).

British Association of Social Work (BASW) (2018) *Professional Capabilities Framework*. British Association of Social Work. [online] Available at: www.basw.co.uk/system/files/resources/Detailed%20level%20descriptors%20for%20all%20domains%20wi%20digital%20aug8.pdf (accessed 21 June 2019).

Butler, J (1990) *Gender Trouble: Feminism and the Subversion of Identity*. New York: Routledge.

Cass, V C (1979) Homosexuality Identify Formation: A Theoretical Model. *Journal of Homosexuality*, 4(3): 219–35.

Carr, S (2010) Seldom Heard or Frequently Ignored? Lesbian, Gay and Bisexual (LGB) Perspectives on Mental Health Services. *Ethnicity and Inequalities in Health and Social Care*, 3(3):14–25.

Civil Partnership Act (2004) [online] Available at: www.legislation.gov.uk/ukpga/2004/33/contents (accessed 4 January 2019).

Clements, P and Spinks, T (2006) *The Equal Opportunities Handbook: How to Recognise Diversity, Encourage Fairness and Promote Anti-discriminatory Practice* (4th edn). London: Kogan Page.

Commission for Social Care Inspection (CSCI) (2008) *Putting People First: Equality and Diversity Matters. 1. Providing Appropriate Services for Lesbian, Gay, Bisexual and Transgender People.* London: CSCI.

Devine, D (2018) *Sexuality and Learning Disability.* [online] Available at: www.learningdisabilitytoday.co.uk/lgbt-support (accessed 4 January 2019).

Equality Act (2010) [online] Available at: www.legislation.gov.uk/ukpga/2010/15/contents (accessed 4 January 2019).

Farmer, B (2017) Christian Student Loses Appeal against University Expulsion for 'anti-gay' Views as Campaigners Warn of 'chilling effect'. *The Independent.* [online] Available at: www.independent.co.uk/news/uk/home-news/felix-ngole-high-court-appeal-homophobic-comments-bible-facebook-sheffield-university-christian-a8023186.html (accessed 4 January 2019).

Ferguson, S (2016) *Here's What It Means When Your Romantic and Sexual Orientations Are Different.* [online] Available at: https://everydayfeminism.com/2016/07/cross-orientation-101 (accessed 4 January 2019).

Fish, J (2007) Getting Equal: The Implications of New Regulations to Prohibit Sexual Orientation Discrimination for Health and Social Care. *Diversity in Health and Social Care*, 4(3): 221–8.

Fish, J (2012) *Social Work and Lesbian, Gay, Bisexual and Trans People Making a Difference.* Bristol: Policy Press.

Guasp, A and Taylor, J (2012) *Stonewall Health Briefing.* London: Stonewall.

Guasp, A and Balfour, J (2008) *Peak Performance: Gay People and Productivity.* London: Stonewall.

Hafford-Letchfield, T (2018) *Working with Lesbian, Gay, Bisexual and Transgender Older People. Practice Guide.* Community Care Inform Adults. [online] Available at: https://adults.ccinform.co.uk/practice-guidance/social-work-lesbian-gay-bisexual-transgendered-older-people (accessed 23 February 2019).

Hudson-Sharp, N (2018) *Transgender Awareness in Child and Family Social Work Education. Research Report.* National Institute of Economic and Social Research, Department for Education. [online] Available at: www.niesr.ac.uk/sites/default/files/publications/Transgender_awareness_in_child_and_family_social_work_education.pdf (accessed 21 June 2019).

Hudson-Sharp, N and Metcalf, H (2016) *Inequality among Lesbian, Gay, Bisexual and Transgender Groups in the UK: A Review of Evidence.* National Institute of Economic and Social Research. [online] Available at: www.niesr.ac.uk/sites/default/files/publications/160719_REPORT_LGBT_evidence_review_NIESR_FINALPDF.pdf (accessed 21 June 2019).

Kaufman, J and Johnson, C (2004) Stigmatized Individuals and the Process of Identity. *The Sociological Quarterly*, 45(4): 807–33.

Nodin, N, Peel, E, Tyler, A and Rivers, I (2015) *The RaRE Research Report: LGB&T Mental Health – Risk and Resilience Explored.* Project Report. PACE (Project for Advocacy Counselling and Education). London.

Richards, C, Bouman, W P, Seal, L, Barker, M J, Nieder, T and T'Sjoen, G (2016) Non-binary or Genderqueer Genders. *International Review of Psychiatry*, 28(1).

Rogers, M (2016) *Trans and Gender Diversity: Messages for Policy and Practice.* In Ahmed, A and Rogers, M (eds) *Working with Marginalised Groups from Policy to Practice* (pp 86–104). London: Palgrave.

Ross, P and Carr, S (2010) It Shouldn't Be Down to Luck: Training for Good Practice with LGBT People – Social Care TV. *Diversity in Health and Care*, 7: 211–16.

Samuel, M and Stevenson, L (2017) *Social Work Student Expelled after Calling Homosexuality 'a sin' on Facebook Loses Court Appeal.* Community Care. [online] Available at: www.communitycare.co.uk/2017/11/01/social-work-student-expelled-calling-homosexuality-sin-facebook-posts-loses-court-appeal (accessed 4 January 2019).

Shilo, G and Savaya, R (2011) Effects of Family and Friend Support on LGB Youths' Mental Health and Sexual Orientation Milestones. *Family Relations*, 60(3).

Social Care Institute for Excellence (SCIE) (2011) *At a Glance 42: Personalisation Briefing Implications for Lesbian, Gay, Bisexual and Transgender (LGBT) People.* [online] Available at: www.scie.org.uk/personalisation/specific-groups/lgbt (accessed 4 January 2019).

Stonewall (2018) *Glossary of Terms.* [online] Available at: www.stonewall.org.uk/help-advice/glossary-terms (accessed 4 January 2019).

Stuart, D (2016) A Chemsex Crucible: The Context and Controversy. *Journal of Family Planning & Reproductive Health Care*, 42(4): 295–6. doi: 10.1136/jfprhc-2016-101603.

Taylor, B and Devine, T (1993) *Assessing Needs and Planning Care in Social Work.* London: Routledge.

Tierney, W G (1997) *Academic Outlaws: Queer Theory and Cultural Studies in the Academy.* Thousand Oaks, CA: Sage.

The Alzheimer's Society (2017) *LGBT: Living with Dementia.* The Alzheimer's Society. [online] Available at: www.alzheimers.org.uk/download/downloads/id/3629/lgbt_living_with_dementia.pdf (accessed 15 April 2018).

The Marriage (Same Sex Couples) Act (2013) [online] Available at: www.legislation.gov.uk/ukpga/2013/30/contents/enacted/data.htm (accessed 4 January 2019).

Thompson, N (2018) *Promoting Equality Working with Diversity and Difference* (4th edn). London: Palgrave Macmillan.

Willis, P, Raithby, M, Maegusuku-Hewett, T and Miles, P (2017) 'Everyday Advocates' for Inclusive Care? Perspective on Enhancing the Provision of Long-term Care Services for Older Lesbian, Gay and Bisexual Adults in Wales. *British Journal of Social Work*, 47: 409–26.

Conclusion

Sue Hollinrake and Heidi Dix

Relationship-based practice is essentially about how to be, as social work practitioners, with people who receive or may require social care services and what supports and guides that relationship to achieve the best results for them in addressing needs in times of difficulty. As discussed in the first chapter of this book, social work writers have continued to argue for the centrality of relationships, putting them 'at the heart of social work', despite the prevailing policy trend in recent decades to overlook the significance of the working relationship between social workers and people who use services, through the culture of managerialism and the instilling of market principles as a result of the dominance of neo-liberal political ideology. The concept of the rational autonomous individual that has permeated Western philosophy since the Enlightenment, and which neo-liberal thinking has embraced and translated into social care policy and legislation, is being countered in social work academic literature with a growing acknowledgement (eg Becket et al, 2017; Dickens, 2012; Meagher and Parton, 2004; Thomas and Hollinrake, 2019) which expands and embraces a more caring approach based on an exploration of the relevance of an ethic of care in policy and practice. The significance of this is discussed in Chapter 1 and in some of the chapters in Part 2.

The linked policies of personalisation and co-production, while emerging from a neo-liberal policy trajectory, nonetheless offer social work an opportunity to re-engage more explicitly and more fully with relationship-based practice through incorporating the knowledge, skills and values as presented in this book. However, the current pre-occupation with the embedding of strengths-based practice both at community and at an individual level is welcome, but it needs to be thought about carefully. The strengths perspective has its philosophical roots in the Greek philosophy of Aristotle whose theory of human flourishing (eudaimonia) stresses that an individual has to take charge of her or his own life and exercise choice and control to take action to flourish and achieve their innate potential. This approach to self-actualisation underpins the humanistic, person-centred approaches to psychology of Maslow and Rogers, which again have a very individual, self-help focus and the lineage then of the strengths perspective is clear. These approaches stress that each individual adult has an internal motivating force that seeks more than just survival. There is a drive to be the best that he or she can be and this is expressed through a variety of related approaches such as solution-focused, narrative and motivational interviewing approaches. The tendency with all these approaches is for a rational, inductive process to explore and develop the individual's capacity to recognise and utilise their own strengths. However, the emphasis on individual autonomy and responsibility fits very well with the neo-liberal project, just as it does at a community level, where a strengths-based approach is also championed in current policy literature as seen in Chapter 2. The language of current government documents which support the application of the Care Act 2014 in practice (Department of Health, 2017, 2019) make use of the language of social justice but place the emphasis for change on the individual and fail to acknowledge in any depth the lower levels of the triangle of Maslow's hierarchy of needs (Maslow, 1943), where self-help just does not have any strength to work against the power of structural forces that determine the use eg of food banks rather than a fair living wage for everyone. Social workers must be wary of an uncritical perspective on a strengths-based approach and also acknowledge and work in whatever way they can to address the damage caused by structural inequalities that affect the everyday lives of those they work with and which no amount of attention paid to inner strengths can significantly ameliorate, as these arise from political decisions and ideological choices. Viewed in this light, the rhetoric of empowerment and inclusion appears to have been hijacked from the self-help movements which have fought for the liberation of marginalised people from a collective social justice position, and been used to advocate for a process that operates only at an individual level. Social work has been grappling for a long time with its position as largely an individually focused and state-led endeavour and through the current pre-occupation with strengths-based models, it continues to do so.

In practice, practitioners cannot avoid encountering the damage done to individuals and families through economic policies and approaches to welfare that have moved from a more compassionate, universalist and collectivist approach to a much more residual and individual approach in the past four decades. They will encounter hopelessness and associated feelings in practice and they will need to engage with these within the context of the relationships in which they take part. We know from research mentioned in Chapter 1 (eg Beresford et al, 2008) that people using services value being recognised as whole people who think and feel, not just consumers of commodified services making choices, so it is very important to recognise the significance of the role of emotions in practice – both in the social work practitioner and in the adult using services who they are working with. This requires organisational recognition as well as professional recognition, to acknowledge the frustration that can arise in the practitioner from an awareness of structural factors such as poverty and social exclusion, which are common experiences of many adults using social care services, and which can produce emotional reactions in practitioners as well as the individuals they are working with.

The IDEAS model, which is introduced in Part 1 and applied to practice with different groups of adults using services, offers a framework to manage the tensions and conflicts as well as hopes and gains that can be achieved in practice and we hope that as a reader, whether a social work student, newly qualified or experienced practitioner, you find this approach useful to maintaining a critical, compassionate and human approach to the complexities of a relationship-based approach to social work practice with adults.

References

Beckett, C, Maynard, A and Jordan, P (2017) *Values and Ethics in Social Work* (3rd edn). London: Sage.

Beresford, P, Croft, S and Adshead, L (2008) 'We don't see her as a social worker': A Service User Case Study of the Importance of the Social Worker's Relationship and Humanity. *British Journal of Social Work*, 38 (7):1388–407.

Department of Health (2017) *Strengths-based Social Work Practice with Adults. Roundtable Report.* London: Department of Health. [online] Available at: https://assets.publishing.service.gov.uk/government/uploads/system/uploads/attachment_data/file/652773/Strengths-based_social_work_practice_with_adults.pdf (accessed 25 April 2019).

Department of Health and Social Care (2019) *Strengths-based Approach. Practice Framework and Practice Handbook.* London: Department of Health and Social Care. [online] Available at: https://assets.publishing.service.gov.uk/government/uploads/system/uploads/attachment_data/file/778134/stengths-based-approach-practice-framework-and-handbook.pdf (accessed 6 March 2019).

Dickens, J (2012) *Social Work Law and Ethics.* New York: Routledge.

Maslow, A H (1943) A Theory of Human Motivation. *Psychological Review*, 50(4): 370–96.

Meagher, G and Parton, N (2004) Modernising Social Work and the Ethics of Care. *Social Work & Society*, 2(1): 10–27.

Thomas, W and Hollinrake, S (2019) The Politics of Care: Wicked Concerns Constituent in Care Reforms. In Thomas, W, Hujala, A, Laulainen, S and McMurray, R (eds) *The Management of Wicked Problems in Health and Social Care* (pp 21–33). New York: Routledge.

Index

Gower College Swansea
Library
Coleg Gŵyr Abertawe
Llyrfgell